MIND, LANGUAGE AND INTENTIONALITY

MIND, LANGUAGE AND INTENTIONALITY

BY

RANJAN K. PANDA

Department of Humanities and Social Sciences
Indian Institute of Technology Bombay,
Powai, Mumbai - 400 076

BKP

BHARATIYA KALA PRAKASHAN

DELHI (INDIA)

First Published : 2008

Published by **C.P. Gautam**
BHARATIYA KALA PRAKASHAN
3421-A, IInd Floor, Narang Colony,
Tri Nagar, Delhi-110035.
Phone : 32967505, Telefax : 011-27393083
E-mail : bkp3421@yahoo.co.in

ISBN : 978-81-8090-213-0

Laser Type Setting by
A-ONE GRAPHICS
JD-18C, IInd Floor, Pitampura, Delhi-110053
Phone : 55640278, Mob. : 9811167357

Printed By :
BDH Printer at Salasar Imaging Systems
Delhi, Ph. 9312245804

DEDICATED
TO
MAA

PREFACE

It is more than a few decades now John R. Searle has drawn the attention of many philosophers and the thinkers of other disciplines. Searle's philosophical engagement with the problems related to language, mind and society is quite deep. The depth of his philosophical theses is reflected in his lucid writings - the analysis of philosophical issues and problems. Many of us would agree that he has succeeded in giving a turn to the naturalistic understanding of the mind. The two basic issues that the Searlean philosophy addresses are the problem of substance dualism and materialistic reductionism. The substance dualism advocated by Rene Descartes has been interpreted quite differently. Some of the philosophers of the mind of the recent time discuss the problem of the Cartesianism and have made serious attempt in explaining the mind away from the discourse. Such an attempt certainly nullifies the theoretical significance of the mind. The Searlean philosophy makes a serious intervention challenging his contemporaries and throwing light in a new direction. The path shown in this direction is philosophically interesting. It is especially more for those who still cherish the little of dualism in their cup. This dualism may not be of Searlean kind but can be any form - as dualism is experienced in daily life. How do we reject our won subjectivity? How do we reject that world in which we live? The critics may have their significant answers to these questions. But this is indeed the hard reality that we are engaged with. In his philosophical endeavor, Searle retains naturalism and the human subjectivity. The mind has no theoretical significance without making an intentional engagement with the world and keeping also its own subjectivity away from the other. In this regard, the Searlean analysis of the substance dualism does alter the Cartesian thesis, not by eliminating the mind but by reasserting the mind in a unique way. This aspect of the Searlean philosophy is discussed in this book.

This debate is not new to those who have been reading Searle's philosophy vis-à-vis his contemporaries like Daniel Dennett, Jerry Fodor, Ruth Millikan, Collin McGinn, Grant Gillett and many others whom I have discussed here. But I am sure this book will be still a help to those who are making their early reading and trying to get into the contemporary philosophical discourse of the mind. Moreover, my reading in philosophy of mind began with John Searle's Minds, Brains and Science, is a collection of his famous Reith lectures given in BBC. It immensely helped me to get into the other problems of philosophy of mind such as intentionality, meaning, free will, etc. Eventually, I wrote two of my dissertations on Searle's philosophy at the Department of Philosophy, University of Hyderabad for my M. Phil. and Ph.D. degrees. The present work is my Ph.D. research work. I am indebted to many who have helped me in shaping this work and encouraged me in pursuing my career in philosophy. First of all, I express my gratitude to my teacher and supervisor Professor R. C. Pradhan for his care and guidance. It is his systematic training and keen interest in my work that has helped me in present exploration into this difficult subject. I am grateful to Professor John R. Searle for sending some of his published and unpublished writings and encouraging me to publish the work. I am grateful Prof. A. Ramamurthy, Prof. Amitabha Dasgupta, Prof. S. G. Kulkarni, late Prof. Chinmoy Goswami, Dr. K. S. Prasad, Mr. Anand Azelwar, my teachers, at Department of Philosophy, University of Hyderabad for teaching me philosophy. I am thankful to Professor Suresh Chandra, Hyderabad, Professor Ashok Vora, Delhi, Professor Daya Krishna, Jaipur, Professor P. C. Kar, Baroda, and Professor A. K. Pujari, Hyderabad for their encouragement. I am also benefited from the discussion with my friends who are now at different institutes and universities in India and abroad, they are Hara Prasad Padhy, Koshy Tharakan, C. A. Tommy, N. Shreekumar, Anand Mahanand, Ramakanta Bal, Deabasis Pattnaik and Manas Ranjan Patra. I thank my philosophy colleagues, Professor N. J. Vyas, Anupam Yadav, Yogini Nighoskar, at M. S. University Baroda and Professor P. R. Bhat, Vikram Singh Sirola, C. D. Sebastian, Ratikanta Panda, Siby George, and Rajakishore Nath at IIT Bombay.

My sincere gratitude to ICPR, New Delhi for providing me J.R. F and allowing me to consult the books of its library at Lucknow. I am also indebted to the IGM Library University of Hyderabad and Central Library at IIT Bombay.

I am grateful to all my family members. I am also grateful to Puspanjali and Abhipsa. Without their love and care this work would not have been possible. I express my deep gratitude to my mother Santilata Panda for her encouragement. This book is dedicated to her.

Lastly, I am thankful Dr. Rabindra Panda, M. S. Unviersity, Baroda and to Shree C. P. Gautam Bharatiya Kala Prakashan, New Delhi for undertaking the publication of this book.

September 10, 2007 **Ranjan K. Panda**
Bombay

CONTENTS

Chapters *Page Nos.*

Preface *(vii-viii)*

Introduction *(xv-xviii)*

I. BIOLOGICAL NATURALISM : Towards an Alternative Metaphysics of Mind **1-53**

i. What is Biological Naturalism?

ii. Descartes' Philosophy of Mind

iii. The Materialist's conception of Mind

iv. The Functionalist Theory of Mind

v. The Methodological Unity and Explanation in Naturalism

vi. Searle's Rejection of Materialism

II. REDISCOVERING CONSCIOUSNESS **54-108**

i. Searle on the Structure of Consciousness

ii. Dennett's Sub-personal view of Consciousness

iii. What is it like to be Consciousness?

iv. Shoemaker's Description of Quasi Qualia

v. Dennett on Quaining Qualia

vi. Searle Against the Cartesian and the Dennetian view of Consciousness

vii. The Searlean Subjectivity

III. NATURALIZING INTENTIONALITY **109-169**

i. Searle's theory of Intentionality

ii. Functionalistic Plea for Intentionality

iii. Dennett : Looking beyond the realm of Fodorian Qua Language

iv. Neo-Phenomenological Interpretation of Searle's Intentionality

v. Intentionality Naturalizd

IV. LANGUAGE, REPRESENTATION AND MEANING **170-235**

i. Searle's concept of Language and Meaning

ii. Langauge of the Mind

iii. Gillett's Semantic Representation

iv. Intention Based Semantics

v. Searle's conception of Literal Meaning

vi. Structure of Consciousness and Isomorphism

(a) Structure of Consciousness and Language.

(b) Consciousness and Language.

V. SEARLE'S BIOLOGICAL NATURALISM : A CRITIQUE **236-299**

i. Searle's Cartesian Legacy

ii. Searle's Functionalism and Description of Consciousness

iii. Does the Background Condition meet Hardware Explanation?

iv. Why Cognitivism is not a theory of Mind?

v. Mind-Body problem: Naturalism and Beyond

vi When the Searlean Subjectivity meets Transcendental Subjectivity

BIBLIOGRAPHY **300-311**

PHILOSOPHERS INDEX **312-313**

SUBJECT INDEX **314-322**

examines how does Searle's theory of mind strongly opposes metaphysical *dualism* and responds sharply to the scientific attitude of *reductionism* in the contemporary philosophy of mind. These are the two basic issues which dominate my study of Searle's philosophy of mind.

Searle's response to these above problem started more than three decades ago when he tried to respond to an important question, i.e., "How do the words relate to the world?", which appeared in his book *Speech Acts* (1969) Searle's main thrust was to find out a stable answer to the question: What is the underlying principle that works *behind* language use in establishing relationship with reality? The question opened up a passage from the philosophy of language to philosophy of mind. In his investigation, he did not make any paradigm shift from the linguistic and to the mental. Rather, his endeavour was to point out the necessary connection between the mind and the world. Language and mind do not stand as separate phenomena, according to him. In this regard his primary attempt has been to show the relationship between language and mind. For him, the *language use* or *speech act* is special sort of action, which could be characterized as purely intentional. The meaning of the speech is derived from the intentional utterances of the speaker. Meaning is ultimately derived from speaker's intentional interpretation of the non-intentional entities. Intentionality is the unique feature of language and mind. Therefore, the very conception of language as related to the reality is due to the intentional property of the subject who uses language. Intentionality as a basic property means *directedness* or *aboutness*. It shows how language use is always directed towards the world. Searle's investigation is thus an investigation into the intentionality of mind and language. So the basic question Searle faces is: where does the notion of intentionality flow from?

Consciouly Searle' consciously ignores the classical phenomenological tradition which attempts to understand intentionality of transcendental philosophy. He gives through the method of naturalistic foundation to his theory of intentionality. Intentionality, however, for him, is an independent phenomenon in the sense that the ontology of intentionality underlies the ontology of the mental. The intentionality manifested in the language use is *derived* from the intentionality of the mental states. In this regard, there is an intentional relationship between the mental states or mental representations and the linguistic representations or the linguistic expressions of mental states. Mental states are both intentional and unintentional in the sense there are conscious and unconscious mental states. Then the question arises: What is the root of intentionality? Consciousness is the ground of intentionality. Intentionality is the intrinsic feature of consciousness. Consciousness *emerges* in the structural form of intentional states or representational states. So the emergence of conscious intentional states shows the emergence of intentionality. Searle argues that consciousness is an emergent property of the neurophysiological processes of the brain. Neurophysiological function that *causes* consciousness is a product of the evolutionary process of the biology. So the ontology of language, intentionality and consciousness is ultimately founded on biology. That explains the evolution or the emergence of life in the physical world. Thus, consciousness is a part of the ontology of the physical reality.

The ontology of consciousness has no doubt a root in the neurophysiological processes of the brain. The Searlean biological naturalism does not deny the independent function of consciousness. Consciousness as a constitutive property of the mind has composite features. It possesses *intentionality, subjectivity, phenomenality, mental causation, etc.* for its own function and explanation. That is to say, the explanation of the mental phenomena does not depend on the neurobiological properties of the brain. The function of the conscious mental process is determined by the irreducible properties of the consciousness itself. So the ontology of consciousness cannot be reduced to the causal function of the neural states and processes of the brain. Thus, both consciousness and the neural functions of the brain are real. They affect each other in the sense that "consciousness is *caused by* the brain processes and *realized in* the brain processes." Searle introduces *micro* and *macro* levels of reality to explain the interrelationship of the mental phenomena and the physical phenomena. Each phenomenon has its micro level constituents and the macro level manifestation. For example, liquidity is a macro level feature of any liquid object. But the basic form of the micro properties is not liquidity. Liquidity constituted of certain type of micro elements make an object liquid, such as water, blood, etc. The micro constituents of water are certainly different from their macro level manifestation as the form water. Similarly, the sub-micro level function of the neurons *causes* consciousness and consciousness constitutes the mind. Consciousness is the macro level manifestation of the potential capacity of the human neural systems at the micro level. In Searle's worldview of biological naturalism, we cannot deny either the reality of the brain function not that the *first-person conscious experiences*. Both are really real. So dualism is inevitable, in the sense, we have to accept the naïve form of the physical and the naïve form of the mental. Accepting the naïve form of dualism, Searlean biological naturalism provides an ***alternative metaphysics*** for the explanation of the reality as whole. According to him reality is not just the physical but also it embodies the mental. The goal of philosophical inquiry is to see how the physical is related with the mental and yet have their distinct function and explanation. Advocating an alternative worldview, Searle rejects thoroughly the substantial dualism, which is the result of the seventeenth century Cartesian scientific explanation of reality. According to him, the Cartesian worldview still persists in some form or other in the 21st century philosophical discourse. This sort of pursuit of science or scientific methods in the philosophical discourse to resolve the philosophical problems limits the very explanation of reality and thereby the limits the very form of human thinking. Searle's metaphysics questions the very foundation of the worldview that advocates dualism between mind and matter. It characterizes such metaphysics as dogmatic in the sense that it goes against the spirit of science. Scientific attitude must help in redefining and resolving the perennial problems that exist in the very common understanding of reality. This problem is discussed the first chapter of the book with reference to naturalism. Naturalism in its explanation to the reality is scientific. Now the question arises, i.e., can we have a causal explanation of the reality of consciousness? Or, Is it possible to have complete causal explanation of consciousness? Furthermore, will such explanation reduce to the mental phenomena or consciousness as whole to the physical or neurophysiological processes of the brain? These are the serious questions to be discussed in the chapter. The Searlean naturalism is critical of the reductionists' approach of behaviourism and functiona-lism as they strictly follow the causal explanation of mental phenomena. As a better version of the scientific explanation, Searle's biological naturalism provides a sound alternative metaphysics to the explanation of mind. It advocates that mental along with its basic properties cannot be reduced the brain processes.

In the second chapter, we discuss the nature of consciousness as the underlying principle of the mental. The discussion is specifically about Searle's notion of *structure of consciousness*. The basic mental properties like *phenomenality* or *qualia*, *subjectivity* or *first-person accessibility*, and *intentionality* remain intrinsic to consciousness so far as the structure of mental states are concerned. Furthermore, these properties help in explaining the mental phenomena. For Searle, consciousness is to be explained from *first-person* perspective, as a subjective phenomenon. It is ontologically a real stuff. However, for Dennett, consciousness can be explained away with the help of the brain processes. Dennett's *sub-personal level* of explanation and *multiple draft model* bring out the micro level explanation of the brain process and emphasize how the brain functions as a system explains consciousness. If the micro level function of the brain constitutes the mental then brain process as whole explains away the very notion of consciousness. Moreover, once consciousness is explained away, it will then lose its intrinsic features like qualia and intentionality. For him, qualia or the subjective first person experience can be quantified. The chapter also discusses the views of Nagel and Shoemaker with reference to the problem of qualia in consciousness. We finally conclude with the view that qualia and subjectivity are necessarily related to consciousness. They can neither be reduced to any brain processes nor can be quantified by any automata. Rather they are intrinsic to consciousness and pertain to the human mind. So, in this sense the Searlean naturalism 'reestablishes the conscious-ness', by bringing subjectivity in to the discourse of consciousness.

It is the intentionality that characterizes consciousness and the mental states in general. Mental states as representational states have directedness. They are conscious states and are therefore in principle intentional in character. Intentionality is one of the intrinsic features of consciousness. It shows how mind is related to the world. So the question arises; can there be self-referentiality embedded in the very nature of intentionality *per se*. It is important to discuss, 'can the intentionality be naturalized?' Since consciousness is a natural emerging property of the brain processes, Searle claims that intentionality also shares the biological basis of consciousness. On the other hand, consciousness remains an independent phenomenon in its relationship with the brain processes. It implies that intentionality is not only intrinsic to consciousness but also not related with brain processes as such. The third chapter opens up with different interpretations of Searle's conception of intentionality. Searle brings out the network of intentional states. It is the network that determines its own realization. The realization involves the property of intentionality in the sense that it shows how the mental states are constituted and represented. That is to say how intentionality determines the *content* of mental states. The Searlean conception of content is intentional. The intentional character of content determines the semantic exercise of it. So the realization condition of content is necessarily a conscious activity and therefore it cannot be *evaluated* within the neurosyntactical process of the brain function. In this regard Jerry Fodor's conception of *language of thought* for the evaluation of content in the process of mental representation has been discussed. Fodor stands opposed to Searle on explaining the nature of content. Now the question explaining arises can there be a language of thought being not accessible to our consciousness? If at all it is the case then how could it resolve the mental and the linguistic dichotomy? Rather, such a thesis eliminates the basic fact that there is a *conscious thought process*.

In Searle's theory of mind, language processing is an intentional activity. There is no structural difference between the mental representation and the linguistic representation. In other words, the intentional states are linguistically structured. So, there is no independent language existing in the mind apart from the conscious thought process. In the fourth chapter we mainly discuss the relationship between language and mind. For Searle, there is an isomorphism between the basic functions of thought and their expression in language. Here we focus on Searle's intention based semantics. It illustrates the view that linguistic activity or language use is intentional. The conventional force or the intentional force of language is derived from the intrinsic intentionality of mental states. Meaning is part of the mental processes. That is to say, content of meaning that is embedded in the linguistic representation is derived from the mental content. Since language use is an intentional activity the content is not reduced when it is expressed in language. Rather it is the same content. In this regard, meaning is not a cognitive and physical activity as the other exponents of intention based semantics like Schiffer and Loar advocate. For them, intention based semantics is purely rational and cognitive based on the propositional attitudes of neurological states of the brain. They accept the *mentalese* conception of *language of thought* and give a physicalistic interpretation to meaning or the *content* of meaning denying the fact that content is not associated with consciousness but is a product of neural-syntactic function of the brain.

In the fifth chapter, we discuss how far Searle's position is tenable in the over all naturalistic framework. We thus attempt at a critique of biological naturalism. The central focus of this chapter is restricted to his three main rejections; first, his rejection of Cartesian dualism, second, the rejection of reductionism and third is naturalistic interpretation of intentionality. Though Searle accepts naïve dualism by rejecting substantial dualism still he shares some sort of Cartesianism. The mind is not only irreducible but also functional independently of the brain processes. That is precisely because consciousness is not only independent of the brain processes but also determines its own function for the realization of mental states. As a result it leads his naive form of dualism to a stronger version of dualism. On the other hand, he is very much emphatic about consciousness and so the basic or real intentionality that is intrinsic to consciousness opens a space for the transcendental interpretation of intentionality. Transcendental consciousness and intentionality are not causally bound up in the physicalistic sense. Intentionality is a free and physically unconstrained feature of consciousness. It signifies the fact that mind has an edge over the material world.

Chapter - I

BIOLOGICAL NATURALISM :
Towards an Alternative Metaphysics of Mind

In this chapter, I intend to illustrate Searle's theory of biological naturalism. The chapter is divided into five sections. The first section gives an expository account of the biological naturalism. Since Searle strongly opposes the Cartesian and materialistic conceptions of the mind, I discuss the nonreductionistic approach of the Cartesian framework in the second section, and the identity theories of the mind in the third section. The fourth section gives an overview of the methodological unity and the explanation of the naturalistic, especially the materialistic conception of the mind. The fifth and the concluding sections focus on the methodology of biological naturalism as an alternative worldview to the materialistic theorization of the mind.

I. What is Biological Naturalism?

Biological naturalism as a theory of mind puts the problem of mind-body dualism and the related context of consciousness in a new perspective. It provides a broad naturalistic framework for the explanation of consciousness and other mental phenomena. The theory is based on the hypothesis that *mental phenomena are* **caused by** *and* **realized in** *the brain processes*. Moreover, as Searle defines his theory, "Mental phenomena are caused by the neurophysiological processes in the brain and are themselves features of the brain. To distinguish the view from many others in the field, I call it "biological naturalism". Mental events and processes are as much a part of the biological natural history as digestion, mitosis, or enzyme secretion."[1] Let's try to explicate the theory with its etymological meaning. The theory is called *biological* because it deals with the neurophysiology of the brain as the central part of the human organism. This theory is a part of a biological worldview which is based on the theory of evolution. The human life is manifested in the evolutionary process of the universe. On the other hand, the *natural* aspect of the theory shows that the brain, as the central part of the human organism *causes* mental life. The mental life is comprised of both conscious and unconscious activities of the brain. The conscious aspects include conscious and unconscious mental states along with their basic features, like intentionality, subjectivity, free will, etc. whereas the unconscious aspects of brain signify its neurophysiological functions. That is to say, the brain embodies a certain causal capacity to produce *consciousness*. And it is a part of the natural process of the brain causing consciousness and other conscious features. For instance, mitosis as a natural process in the living organism manifests the causal efficacy of a cell. That is, the continuous division of a cell helps in the very growth of a living body. And this precisely shows that there is life in the body. Similarly, the brain causing consciousness is as natural as the principle of mitosis explaining the multiple growth of cells. The growth of cells in an organism, thus bears an independent function, like the brain causing consciousness.

Searle's hypothesis precisely establishes this principle, i.e., *the principle of neurophysiological sufficiency*. As he writes, "Whenever a mental phenomena is presented in the mind of an agent—for example, his feeling pain, thinking about philosophy or wishing he had a cold beer—causally sufficient conditions for these phenomenon are entirely in the brain.

And indeed the thesis that mental phenomena are caused by and realized in the brain has the consequence that, for any mental phenomena whatever, causally sufficient conditions are in the brain. Let us call this the principle of neurophysiological sufficiency."[2] The neurophysiological sufficiency of the brain can be understood by taking not only one part of the brain processes into account, but also the various subsystems of the brain, that are working together to produce consciousness or any other mental phenomena. The subsystems in this regard are causally interconnected. The causal interrelationship shows only the causal sufficiency of the brain as a whole, causing and realizing mental phenomena. This is quite typical of the function of the brain insofar as other biological systems are concerned. Searle remarks, "I see the human brain as an organ like any other organ, as a biological system. Its special features, as far as the mind is concerned, the feature in which it differs remarkably from other biological organs, is its capacity to produce and sustain all of the enormous variety of our consciousness life."[3] The emergence of consciousness is a unique feature of the brain function. This feature of the brain has double functions, i.e. it both produces the mental states or conscious mental life, and at the same time it has the capacity to regenerate the conscious states. This regenerating process in the brain reveals the realization of the mental states in the brain processes. For instance, when someone is feeling hungry, he searches for food where it would be possible for him to get it. The person is not only experiencing hunger, but also believes that he can get relief from hunger only by eating the food he somehow manages to get. Here experiencing hunger is a neurophysiological process that causes the mind to get to form the belief about food. And the satisfaction that he gets after eating the food, will show the realization of his belief state. Moreover, the entire process of securing food by adopting alternative means shows the sustainable capacity of the brain. The whole, process commencing from the emergence of the mental states to its culmination in the realization states, shows that there is interdependency in the relationship between the brain and the mind.

It is not just the mental and the physiological processes of the brain that are interdependent; rather the relationship is intrinsic to the very nature of the brain. The double order function of the brain has this intrinsic relationship with the mental phenomena. How does one describe this intrinsic relationship? Searle says, "The brain has an intrinsically mental level of description because in any of the given point, it is causing actual conscious events and is capable of causing further conscious events. Because the brain has both conscious and unconscious mental states we are also inclined to suppose that they are intrinsically inaccessible to consciousness."[4] This intrinsic relationship between the neurophysiological processes of the brain as a continuous source of causation of the mental states avoids mind-brain dualism. The mental and the physical do not belong to two separate realms of descriptions. Rather the neurophyisological process having the capacity to generate conscious events must be understood as the higher level physical feature of the brain. There is a hierarchy in the levels of the brain function. This higher level function is accessible to the realm of mental description. In that sense, the mental is a part of the physical reality. The mental as the part of the physical is defined as having higher order relationship with each other. That is to say, the mind is emerging out of the higher neurological processes of the brain organism. Searle says, "On these definitions, consciousness is a causally emergent property of the systems. It is an emergent feature of the certain systems of the neurons in the same way as solidity and liquidity are the emergent features of system of molecules. The existence of consciousness can be explained by the causal interaction of the elements of the brain at the micro level, but consciousness cannot itself be deduced or calculated from the sheer physical structure of neurons without some additional account of causal relations between them."[5] The emergence of the conscious mental states is a causal emergence. Searle has two levels of causal explanation; they are, micro level and macro level. At the micro level we have only neurons, synapses and axons carrying some physico-chemical processes. At the macro-level we have conscious mental states. This shows the embodiment of the causal properties in the neural structure of the brain. Hence the mental phenomena at the macro level are explicated by the causal function of the brain processes at the micro level. The macro level only shows the overall system functions of the neutral system. That is, in the case of human beings, we can only know what the beliefs, desires and intentional states are at the macro level. They are all called conscious states. Consciousness arises because of the causal properties of the neural configuration of the brain.

The human being as an organism has a systemic structure. The causal properties of the sub-structural parts together get manifested in a certain order. Thus consciousness as a systemic feature is manifested in the conscious behaviour of the human beings. So causality is involved in both the macro and micro levels of function. To give an analogy, the solidity of the table at the macro level can be defined through the causal structure of the molecules at the level of lattice structure. In the micro level we have only molecules, not the solidity. Solidity of an object is totally a systemic feature, which emerges out of the configuration of different molecules. Thus solidity of a table has a macro level description. To quote Searle, "In fact, such a combination of relation is very common in nature: so solidity of the table I am working on and the elasticity and puncture resistance of my car are both examples of causal properties that are themselves caused by and realized in the underlying microstructure. To generalize this point we might say that two phenomena can be related by both causation and realization provided that they are so at different levels of description."[6] Similarly, there is a cause and effect relationship between the micro level brain processes and macro level conscious mental life. This conscious mental life as an effect of the neural processes of the brain is understood as a macro level or a higher level feature.

The emergentism needs to be further explained in Searle's biological naturalism. The Searlean interpretation of the notion of emergence has a different meaning. Though consciousness, including all the mental life, emerges from the micro order function of the brain processes, it is not defined by the causal powers of the neurophysiological structure of the brain. This is because the causal property of the brain is different from the causal feature of the consciousness. As he says, "If consciousness is emergent$_{2,}$ then consciousness could cause things that would not be explained by the causal behaviour of the neurons. The naïve idea here is that consciousness gets squirted out by the behaviour of the neurons of the brain, but once it has been squirted out, it then has a life of its own."[7] Searle makes the distinction between emergent$_1$ and emergent$_2$. In the case of emergent$_1$, if *C* is caused by the causal properties of *B* then *C* can be further reduced, to or can be explained by the properties of *B*. On the other hand, emergent$_2$ signifies that C may be caused by the properties of *B* but *C* cannot then be reduced to *B* again. It is because the properties of *C* logically differ from the properties of *B*. Thus consciousness being an emergent feature of the brain's neurological processes falls in the category of the emergent$_2$ and not in the emergent$_1$. And to say that consciousness has its own life, is to say that it has its own functional capacities. That is different from the functional capacity of the neurons firing in the different circuits of the brains, or their chemical processes within the neural structure itself. The basic functional features that consciousness embodies are subjectivity, intentionality, free will, mental causation, etc. These features are caused by neurophysiological process of the brain whereas they don't carry any physical or chemical properties in them. Moreover, they all constitute the basic feature of the mental life. So the mental states and processes are not identical with the physical states and processes. As the neurophysiological properties of the brain are intrinsic to the brain organism, similarly, the mental features are intrinsic to consciousness.

Biological naturalism does not allow any sort of reduction from mind to brain. According to this theory the mental states are not the same as the brain states. Of course, there is a duality involved in the understanding of reality. It is because the physical is causing the mental reality. The ontological problem must be resolved by the micro level and macro level descriptions. What is specific about the irreducibility of consciousness? For Searle, "the point of argument is ontological not epistemic."[8] Philosophers who have tried to reduce the mental to the physical have emphasized the epistemic aspects of the reality. For them, it is the epistemic aspect that can explain the objectivity of the mental states. The objectivity of knowledge must be grounded in the third-person point of view. In this connection, the objectivity of various features of conscious mental states can be determined by studying the neurophysiological processes of the brain. And this is possible only through scientific observation. On the other hand, the person's feeling and sensations cannot be determined by the third persons' point of view. That is because when a person is having a good feeling he is experiencing joy at that moment. The objectivity of that person's joy can only be felt by the person himself who is experiencing it. No doubt it embodies certain neurological process but what is important to note for defining the person's conscious *feeling* is his subjective experience. This is purely a macro level description of the mental life. The moment we try to reduce the subjective conscious experience of sensation or feeling to the neurological processes of the brain, we will fall into the trap of ontological reductionism.

Thus he says, "The first person feeling is important. This fact has obvious epistemic consequence: My knowledge that I am in pain has a different sort of basis than my knowledge that you are in pain. But the antireductionistic point of the argument is ontological and not epistemic."[9] Searle's antirductionism tries to establish the notion of that subjectivity or first person experience of the mental phenomena is grounded in the ontology of brain processes. The ontology must be correlated with consciousness, because subjectivity of mental states is basically related with the conscious states and feelings.

The above notion of Searle's antireductionism entails a dualism. Dualism is about consciousness along with other co-features and the neurophysiological processes of the brain. However, Searle strongly opposes the Cartesian conception of dualism as well as the reductionism advocated by the materialistic philosophers. According to Searle, dualism and materialism provide an incoherent theory of mind. Dualism of the Cartesian variety divides the reality into two substantial categories, that is, the mind and the matter are considered as independent substances. On the other hand, materialism tries to reduce the whole of the mental life into the physical processes of the brain. Searle believes that "if you take those categories seriously—the categories of mental and physical, mind and body—as a consistent dualist, you will eventually be forced to materialism. Materialism is thus in a sense the finest flower of dualism."[10] Cartesianism no doubt takes the categories seriously, i.e., the explanation of the mental and the physical belong to two separate categories. However, materialism claims that the reality of the mental lies in the physical states of the brain organism. Then the question arises: what sort of dualism is entailed by Searle's theory of biological naturalism? The antireductionis-tic approach of biological naturalism advocates the notion of *conceptual dualism*. As Searle proposes, "It is customary to think of dualism coming in two flavours, substantial dualism and property dualism; but to those I want to add a third, which I call "conceptual dualism". This view consists in taking the dualistic concepts very seriously, that is, it consists in the view that in some important sense "physical" implies "nonmental" and "mental" implies "nonphysical". Both traditional dualism and materialism presupposes conceptualism, so defend."[11]

Conceptual dualism does not reject the ontology of the mental and the physical. Rather it tries to understand the reality of both the phenomena by giving a naïve explanation of the mental and the physical. The mental is the product of the higher order physical processes of the brain organism. The higher order neurophyisioloigcal processes of the brain are not completely characterized as mere physical body. The hierarchy of different levels has to be understood through their subtle functions. These subtle functions of the brain causing consciousness and other mental phenomena shows the relationship between the mental and the physical. That is, at a particular state of neurophysiological processes of the brain it is difficult to determine the very nature of the mental and the physical. Therefore, conceptual dualism can only talk about interrelationship between the mind and the brain not by separating them but by relating them together. Before going to Searle's rejection of the Cartesian dualism and materialism, I would like to discuss some of the philosophical questions related to dualism and materialism.

II. Descartes Philosophy of Mind: Rejection of Reductionism

Descartes formulated the mechanistic explanation of the phenomena of nature by introducing the *hypothetical* model. For him, hypothesis needs to be formulated to explain the imperceptible causal properties of the perceptible body. The causal properties of the matter include both the material and the sufficient causes. And the combination of the imperceptible particles together would be able to constitute the perceptible body. The imperceptible particles are the micro states of matter and the perceptible particles are the macro states of matter, which could be explained through the basic properties called shape, size, and motion. And the formulation of mechanistic hypothesis for the explanation of natural phenomena is to bridge the gap between our sensory experiences of matter and their causal capacity. As Clarke mentions, "The distinction between our subjective experiences or sensations and their objective causes, between primary and secondary qualities, opens up an epistemic gap that can only be bridged by some other strategy apart from the assumption of resemblance. This strategy is hypothesis, or guesswork. Our guesswork may turn out to be secure and there may eventually be many reasons for thinking that they are as certain as one can hope for u."[12] Secondary qualities are mostly subjective in their appearances whereas primary qualities are objective. Here the primary qualities of the matter are the basic properties of it, such as its shape, size and motion through which matter can be explained.

Now one may ask, how do we have the ideas of these imperceptible properties of matter? Descartes elaborates it in his famous example of *wax*. Wax in its original state (fresh from the hive) possesses qualities such as sweetness, fragrance of honey, colour, size, etc. If the same piece of wax is heated, then its size expands, its sweetness disappears, and the colour changes. That is, a certain transformation takes place between the time period before heating and after heating. However, we still have the common notion of wax. And during the course of transformation, we know that heat operates in the composite structure of the wax. We don't perceive the movement of the minute parts of the wax during the period of transformation. Still the conception of wax remains because some essential qualities persist and they help us in identifying the wax as wax after its transformation. For Descartes, this notion of wax could be comprehended neither by perception nor by imagination that physics deals with. Rather, the comprehension of this idea is possible by *understanding*. Understanding deals with "pure intellect". As Wood describes, "After the exclusion of sensation and imagination there remains one possibility, namely, that understanding, exercising its powers of conception and judgement for the synthesizing and unifying function which constitutes the self identity of the piece of wax."[13] Understanding is a special mode of formulating such ideas as ascribed to the function of the intellect. The intellect has a unique way of judging the observable facts. It is through its intellect alone that material bodies are comprehended.

Descartes' philosophy of mind emerges from his reflections on nature as a mechanistic system. He locates the beginning of this philosophy in our subjective experiences. As Clarke cites, "where the metaphysics is concerned, we begin with such everyday experiences as the experience of thinking, feeling, moving, etc. Among these experiences, Descartes favors the most accessible and widely available experiences because he hopes thereby to find indubitable foundation."[14] Among these experiences thinking is considered as the most indubitable and simply accessible feature of our knowledge. Thinking or *cogito* is easily comprehensible. Consciousness includes all mental activities, like thoughts, sensations, imaginations, experiences, etc. The Cartesian metaphysics is based on the principle of *cogito* which is most indubitable and certain. As Descartes claims, "I am nothing so long as I think that I am something. So after considering everything very thoroughly, I must finally conclude that proposition, I am, I exist, is necessarily true whenever it is put forward by me and conceived in my mind."[15] Thus thinking or *cogito* lays down the foundation for any sort of knowledge claims, including the mechanistic explanation of the universe. Consciousness is the basic metaphysical reality in Descartes' philosophy. For him, the very nature of understanding consciousness is different from the understanding of the nature of the body. The body or matter is usually defined as something extended in space, that can be perceived, and also has movement in connection with other bodies. It is different from the mind which is neither perceived no is extended in space. Descartes says, "For according to my judgement, power of self-movement, like the power of sensation or of thought was quite foreign to the nature of the body; indeed it was a source of wonder to me that certain bodies were found to contain faculties of these nature."[16] The self-movement describes the independent function of consciousness. It is not dependent upon the other mechanical functions of the body. Thereby consciousness is characterized as a unique feature of human organism. The human organism is not just sensitive to the external world nature but also intelligent enough to think and describe it.

Descartes' metaphysics of mind goes beyond the boundaries of physics and physiology. It situates the mind beyond the finites of mechanism. The physiological structures of a living body, especially of human beings are organized in a certain way so that they bear certain mechanical functions. These functions include digestion, blood circulation and palpitation of the heart, various movements of limbs, etc. Beyond the functions the conscious behaviour of the body is described by the presence of the soul in the living organism. The soul is placed in the *small gland* in the middle of the brain. The brain is taken as the vital part of the body connected with all other parts of the body through the nerve fibres to carry out the sensations. It is the pineal gland that converts the blood into *animal sprits*. The sprits are kept in the cavities and further they enter into the muscles through the nerve fibres. The flow of spirits vary depending upon the impressions that are carried to the soul. Descartes also says, "And conversely, the mechanism of the body is so constructed that simply by this gland's being moved in any way by the soul or by any other cause, it drives the surrounding spirits towards the pores of the brain, which direct them through the nerves of the muscles; and in this way the gland makes the spirit move the limbs."[17] This mechanical composition of the body no doubt has a certain biological capacity to generate the movement. All these movements of the body are not derived from the soul and do not have any necessary relationship with consciousness. The heat generated by the natural composition of the body, for instance, is unique to the function of the body. Descartes says, "it has been believed, without justification, that our natural heat and all the movements of our bodies depend on the soul; whereas we ought to hold, on the contrary, that the soul takes its leave when we die only because the heat ceases and the organs which bring about bodily movement decay."[18] The decomposition of the physiological feature of the body is a natural phenomenon in biology. The body is unable to generate heat or other physiological functions like digestion, palpitation, etc. because it loses certain biological capacities. Now the question arises regarding the interaction of the consciousness with the body or of the soul with the body. Soul has two parts; the rational and the sensitive. The rational part of the soul includes thought processing. It is the higher level having other features like, willing, imagining, having sensory perception. The sensitive level is only related to the bodily function. It is a lower level function because there is no willingness or volition present in this level of consciousness. The body being sensitive to nature is related to this lower level function. Thus, it is the soul or consciousness which acts on the body.

However, the existence of a person is defined by his being conscious. Consciousness signifies the higher order function of thinking, not just being sensitive. The higher order function of consciousness designates self-movement of the soul. This higher order function is not dependent on the function of the bodily movement whereas "thinking is inseparable from me." Descartes points out, "I am, then, in a strict sense only a thing that thinks, that is, I am a mind or intelligence, or intellect, or reason—words whose meaning I have been ignorant of until now."[19] Thinking entails the *real* existence.

Thus, in Descartes, consciousness or thinking is not associated with the physical or the biological function of the body. Therefore it cannot be reduced to the physical properties of the body. The biological function of the body remains different from the function of consciousness. On the other hand, the outer behaviour or movement of the body is manifested due to the active participation of the soul. The active participation reveals the basic features of the soul. Moreover the interaction remains a mystery. The mystery of the body being conscious, or the body as having a conscious mind is not explicable by the mechanistic model. Conscious-ness is objectively 'real'. It is autonomous. This is asserted from the first person point of view. I am only aware of my being conscious. I can only realize my acting consciously or thinking consciously. The moment I cease to think, I am unable to comprehend my existence any more. Hence consciousness plays a necessary role for my understanding the world and representing it. Consciousness has to be understood as an irreducible and independent principle of knowledge. It is because neither can it be reduced to a bodily function nor can it be explained sufficiently by bodily function. Consciousness, thus, is metaphysically distinct from the material body. This is the source of the Cartesian mind-body dualism.

III. Materialists' Conception of Mind

Materialism argues against the Cartesian conception of mind. Cartesianism divides mind and body into two different realms of existence. And insofar as consciousness is concerned, it is the metaphysical foundation for the scientific as well as commonsensical explanation of the mental phenomena. Materialism as an alternative conception of mind explains the reality of the mental through the reality of the physical phenomena. That is to say, mind is not just a part of the physical organism but itself is characterized as the physical organism called brain. The mind can be known through the various activities of the brain, i.e., it involves the physical behaviour of the brain comprising of the different states and events that are occurring in the brain. Hence there is no dualism between the mental and the physical. Materialism includes various theories of the mind like behaviourism, physicalism and functionalism. All these theories talk about some sort of identity relationship between the mental phenomena and the neurophysiological states and processes of the brain.

Behaviourism, as a theory of mind, advocates the empirical study of the mind through behaviour. As Churchland puts it, "By 'behaviour' behaviourists' mean the publicly observable, measureable, recordable activity of the subjects at issue: bodily movements, noises emitted, temperature changes, chemical released, interaction with environment, and so forth."[20] It is the behaviour which is the source of our knowledge of the mind. Rather mind, as such, is nothing but the behaviour itself. We do not, therefore, observe the mental phenomena. It is basically the behaviour which is observed. And this observable behaviour is to be taken into account in order to explain the mental phenomena.

In this sense, the definition of the behaviour of human beings includes both voluntary or conscious actions as well as involuntary or unconscious actions. Voluntary action includes the person's intention and will, whereas the involuntary actions excludes the persons' intention and desires. It includes the biological actions of the body. The behaviour is studied by undertaking both the outer environmental conditions as well as the inner potential capacities of human beings. As Churchland puts it, "Instead of appealing to mental states, behaviourists proposed to explain any organism's behaviour in terms of its peculiar environmental circumstance. Or, in terms of environment plus certain observable features of the organism. Or, in terms of certain *un*observable features of the organism—

dispositions, and innate and conditioned features meet a very strict condition: they must be such that their presence or absence could always be decisively determined by behavioural test, as solubility of sugar is revealed by its actually dissolving (the behaviour) when placed in water (the environmental circumstances)."[21] Insofar as the mental state is concerned, there are two aspects which count mostly for explaining the mind: they are the dispositional capacity as an intrinsic feature of the human beings' organic structure and the environmental condition as an outer condition in which a person is being situated. Environment is an external condition which has a direct impact on human behaviour.

The inner feature of behavioural capacity is known as the dispositional property of behaviour. The *disposition* is an unobservable factor which gets manifested in the behaviour itself. For example, brittleness is the dispositional property of glassware. Glass, being a physical phenomenon, contains brittleness as its physical dispositional property. Similarly, human beings' behaviour is determined basically by the dispositional feature of the brain or brain states. That is, for all of our outer physical behaviour there must be a causal dispositional state in the brain. Dispositions are thus built into the structure of an object. For example, whenever any glassware falls from my hand or is hit heavily, it lies broken on the ground. The brittleness is a part of the atomic structure of each piece of the broken glass. It is also true that there is some external factor operating for causing the glass to slip from my grip. The disposition of the glass is simply that if breaks whenever it falls to the ground. Similarly, in certain environmental and physical conditions human beings behave in a particular order. Hence, in order to determine the human dispositions we must observe or measure the particular order of the external behaviour of the human beings. Besides in the case of human behaviour, we must observe the dispositional features of the brain states. Brain states, for the behaviourists, are the physical states. Behaviour is identified with the brain states, i.e. corresponding to a particular behaviour there must be a dispositional state in the brain organism. We generalize about dispositions by seeing the constant occurrence of the same type of behaviour in typical external condition. Thus we arrive at general causal laws regarding behaviour.

The mental phenomena like desire, belief, sensation, feelings, imagination, etc. are a part of the dispositional features of the brain. The brain being a physical organism is directly causing behaviour. There is no further necessity for admitting the mental states and features as the cause of the behaviour. The reality of the mental is basically a physical dispositional feature of the brain. Thus behaviourism in a way rules out the reality of the mental as a necessary condition for explaining behaviour. Moreover, it only looks for the behaviour as such, as real, along with the physical conditions that are causing the behaviour.

Behaviourism as a theory of mind is strongly criticized by another group of materialist philosophers like J.C.C. Smart, D.M. Armstrong and U.T. Place. They reformulated the behaviourists' conception of identity between the dispositional states of the brain and the behaviour by introducing the hypothesis of *causal brain process* for the explanation of behaviour. The causal process of behaviour must have a scientific explanation. Scientific explanation deals with the law of causality. Since mental process is understood as a physical processes of the brain, the mental life needs a causal explanation. In that sense, the brain process can be taken as the cause of the mental phenomena.

D. M. Armstrong defends the central-state identity theory[23] according to which the brain states are the same as the mental states. Each state of the mind is causally responsible for a piece of behaviour. Hence, there is a causal relationship between the states of mind and the expressions of behaviour. The behaviour is not simply an automatic process caused by the dispositional character of the mind. Rather the brain process is identical with the mental sate.

Armstrong strives for a synthesis of two conflicting theories of mind, namely, the Cartesian theory of soul-substance which considers the autonomy of the mental as real and the behaviourists' theory which considers behaviour as the only reality. As he describes the synthesis, "My proposed synthesis is that the mind is properly conceived as an inner principle, but a principle that is identified in terms of the outward behaviour it is apt for bringing about. This way of looking at the mind and mental states does not itself entail a Materialist or Physicalist view of man, for nothing is said in this analysis about the intrinsic nature of these mental states. But if we have, as I have asserted that we do have, general scientific grounds for thinking that man is nothing but a physical mechanism, we can go on to argue that the mental states are in fact nothing but physical states of the central nervous system."[22] The synthesis emphasizes the scientific study of the mental phenomena. The reality of the mental phenomena is established by identifying them with the central states of the nervous system. The central nervous system brings out the physical processes involved in the organism for causing several behaviour. And behaviour is causally explainable through the identification of the underlying physical processes of the brain. So neither behaviour nor the reality of the mental is ruled out. What the identity theory of the mind tries to look at is the inner principle which is the essential link between mind and behaviour.

This above conception known as the "Central-state Theory" involves two doctrines: the *psycho-chemical materialism* and the *attributive theory of mind*. Psycho-chemical materialism takes into account the processes of the nervous system of the brain and tries to formulate the physical and chemical laws for explaining the processes themselves. Armstrong writes, "[it] is to identify these inner states with physical chemical states of the brain. This is a contingent and scientific identification, and it yields Central-state Materialism."[23] Since the psycho-chemical materialism of Armstrong emphasizes the scientific study of the mental, it holds the contingent identity relationship between the mental states and the brain processes. This contingency is an observable fact about their identity relationship. And from the observable facts of the physico-chemical processes of the brain, psycho-chemical laws are formulated.

The attributive theory holds that mind is a causal attribution to the so called process of stimulus and responses. As Armstrong points out, "Man as an object is continually acted upon by certain physical stimuli. These stimuli elicit from him certain behaviour, that is to say, a certain physical responses. In the causal chain between the stimulus and response, falls the mind. The mind is that which causally mediates our response to stimuli. Now central state theory wants to say that between the stimulus and response fall physical processes in the central nerves system, nothing else at all, not even something 'epiphenomenal' ."[24] The reality of the mental is not ruled out. The functions of the mental states are identified with the functions of the brain processes. Brain as the central part of the whole organism, involves inner processes. That holds a causal link between outer behaviour and the inner brain process. "Central-state Materialism holds that, when we are *aware* of our mental states, what we are aware of are mere physical states of the brain. But we are not certainly aware of mental state *as* states of the brain."[25] We are not aware of these mental states as identical with the brain processes. But our awareness of something happening in the mind is always about the physical processes that are going on in the brain. The identity principle holds good because only the physical processes of the brain are going on. Armstrong further puts it, "the Materialists theory allows a peculiarly simple theory of the nature of unconscious mental states. The materialist will say that, as a matter of empirical fact, they are simply a physical state of the brain. Now most modern philosophers would admit that in such a case as the patient struggling under nitrous oxide, or the chicken sexer sexing a chick, there are brain processes going on which are responsible for, or at any rate closely connected with this behaviour. And if we are forced to admit the possibility of unconscious mental states any way, it will be an aggregate economy to say that they are nothing but brain processes."[26] Thus for any sort of action there is a corresponding process in the neurophysiological structure of the brain. Actions are identified with those physical processes of the brain which are causing such behaviour.

U. T. Place finds Armstrong's identity theis is inadequate. It does not resolve the gap between the brain processes and the mental states. He extends the identity hypothesis further by advocating a strong identity between consciousness and the brain processes. He offers the hypothesis that consciousness is an outcome of the brain processes. According to Place, this hypothesis remains powerful till today because of its consistency with the empirical evidences. And thereby it has become an established thesis.[27] However, Place's formulation of the *hypothesis* is such that the brain-mind identity is not a logical identity; it is an empirical theory based on scientific evidences. Therefore, for him, the statement , 'Consciousness is a brain process' is a reasonable scientific hypothesis. The hypothesis says that conscious states and events can be identified with certain pattern of brain activity. As he says "What do I want to assert, however, is that the statement 'consciousness is a process in the brain', although not necessarily true is not necessarily false. 'Consciousness is a process in the brain' in my view, is neither self-contradictory nor self-evident; it is a reasonable scientific, hypothesis, in the way, 'lightening is a motion of electric charges' is a reasonable scientific hypothesis."[28] 'Consciousness *is* identical with brain processes'. Here, 'is' has two functions; one is of *composition,* and other is of *definition*. Consciousness or conscious mental states are composed of certain physicochemical processes of the brain. And when we are consciously behaving, we can identify consciousness with behaviour, but always a physicochemical process does take place in the brain. Empirically, the conscious states are the physico chemical processes in the brain. For instance, the cloud that we observe in the sky is nothing but a mass of rain-bearing particles. But, scientifically speaking, "A cloud is large semi-transparent mass with fleecy texture suspended in the atmosphere, whose subject is continual and kaleicdospic change". This is, however, not a logical definition of 'cloud'. So it is not a contradiction to say that cloud is a mass of rain-bearing particles.

According to Place, the identity relationship between consciousness and the brain processes consists in that of the occurrences of the conscious mental states, and the change corresponding in micro structure of brain processes are simultaneous events. These are in fact no two events occurring; there is only one event, though it is described in two ways. For instance, as Place says, one and the same phenomenon can be simultaneously observed from two points of view—one from the scientific point of view and other from the common man's point of view, as we have seen in the example of the cloud. Both stand points are systematically and causally related with each other. One goes parallel with the other. Similarly, whenever we talk about consciousness we talk usually about the various conscious experiences, not about the micro physicochemical events and processes that go on in the brain. Thus our description of the mental phenomena is given through the secondary qualities that are attributed to the phenomenal field. This sort of description results in *phenomenological fallacy,* according to Place; because it ignores the fact that underlying our so called phenomenological experience, there is a physical process going on. Place writes, "We describe our conscious experience not in terms of the mythological "phenomenal properties" which are supposed to be inhere in the mythological 'objects' in the mythological phenomenal 'field', but reference to the actual properties of the concrete physical objects, events and processes which normally, though not perhaps in present instance, gives rise to the sort of conscious experience which we are trying to describe."[29] So, for Place, the real description of our conscious experience must include the physical properties of the brain states and process. This is because, the brain process is the only reality that exists. And brain process is considered real, because it is the cause of our phenomenal experiences.

J.C.C. Smart advocates *strict* identity between the mental states and the brain processes. He supports Place's notion of identity, because it emphasizes only scientific aspects of notion of identity. It is not necessary to talk about the logical aspects of the identity. For example, lightening is scientifically described as electrical discharge. Scientific explanation itself is based on the contingent description of lightening because it is also a logical possibility that this description of lightning may change after some other new scientific discovery about lightning. Smart says, "On the brain processes thesis, the identity between the brain process and the experience is a contingent one. So it is logically possible that there should be no brain process, and so processes of any other sort either (no heart process, no kidney process, no liver process) There would be the experience but no physiological process with which we might be able to identify it empirically."[30] Smart argues that though this is a possibility, empirically it is not the case. He asserts the relation of identity stating that all experiences are composed of the physical properties of the brain processes. This could be treated as an *a priori* notion because "what could be composed of nothing cannot be composed of anything"[31]. In this regard the brain possesses physicochemical properties which causes sensation, feelings and other mental states. A conscious experience is a very complex process involving a vast number of neurons. It is a process, not a stuff. Brain process is an inner phenomenon which needs to be identified by the advanced science of neurophysiology.[32] He describes the complexity involved in the human mental life by saying: "for a full description of what is going on in man you would have to mention not only the physical processes in the tissue, glands, and nervous system, and so forth, but also his states of consciousness: his visual, auditory, and tactual sensations, his aches and pains, etc. That these should be correlated with brain processes does not help, for to say that they are correlated is to say that they are something 'over and above'."[33] Brain processes are not 'over and above' of all our conscious experiences including our linguistic behaviour. For example, when someone says he is experiencing pain in his right toe, he is experiencing the pain because there is stimulation of the C-fiber of the neurological structure of the brain processes. He says, "All it claims is, that in so far as a sensation statement is a report of something, that something is in fact a brain process, sensations are nothing over and above brain processes."[34] Though the brain process is not publicly observable, it is an underlying factor responsible for all our mental activities. Moreover, Smart claims that "All that I am saying is that 'experience' and 'brain processes' may in fact refer to the same thing, and if so we may easily adopt a covention (which is not to change our present rules for the use of experience words but an addition to them) where it would make sense to talk of an experience in terms appropriate to physical processes."[35]

IV. The Functionalist Theory of Mind

Functional identity theory advocated by Hilary Putnam and other functionalists philosophers like Dennett and Fodor reject the brain state identity theory advocated by Armstrong, Place and Smart. Putnam finds the brain-state identity *unintelligible*. Functional identity theory rejects the two important theses of behavioural state-identity theory.

One is their 'empirical reduction' and another the direct dispositional states (brain states). Empirical reduction emphasizes only the state and its observational synonymity. For example, water *is* H_2O or temperature *is* the 'mean molecular kainetic energy'. Here we talk only about the property or the properties of water and temperature. As Putnam uses the notion of property "I shall use the term 'property' as a blanket term for such things as being in pain, being in a particular brain state, having a particular behaviour disposition and also for magnitudes such as temperture, etc., i. e., for things which can naturally be represented by one, or more - are place predicates or function"[36] The functionalists adopt the empiricist method for explaining the mental functions. Moreover, the functionalist theory explains the constitutive and the functional character of the mental states. It rules out the type-type identity of the mental states and the brain processes. On the other hand, the functional identity principle projects the notion of "functional economy". It demands reasonable identity between the input and output of the human behaviour. It leads to the economy of the mind by eliminating reference to a variety of mental states which are causally connected to the brain states.[37] Functionalism argues in support of a common mental structure, irrespective of the fact that the same mental structure is manifestated in different behavioural systems. That is, the same mental states can be realized in different organic systems differently. The most typical features of this structure is its functional organization. This functional organization is necessary and sufficient for a given psychological state.[38] According to the functionalists, the brain-state identity theory failed to provide a complete view of the structure of mental states and processes. It either derived the mental states from the brain states or completely reduced the former to the latter. That, consequently, results in the disappearance of the mental states, consciousness, propositional attitudes, etc. Thus the problem of mind remains unsolved. Functionalism therefore offers a theory of token-identity to solve the problem.

Functional identity theory holds that "The mental states" are abstract, *functional* states, characterized solely in terms of their causal relationships to each other, to input, and to output. Human purposive behaviour is then explained in terms of how this hypothesized system of states, takes the organism from sensory input to behaviour. Because functionalism insists upon a *network* of mental states, it insists upon 'the holism of the mental' upon the way in which mental states operate together to explain behaviour."[39] It accepts that mental states constitute a structure. In that structure of mental states each is causally connected with the other. The mental states do not function in isolation, rather they function within the causal correlationship with other mental states. The function of mental states also takes into account the effect of the environment in which the subject or agent is placed. The organism or the system must be well equipped to receive the input from the environment and to produce the output.

Functional identity, however, postulates a parallelism between the structure of the mental states and the brain processes. This parallelism persists, because both the structures are functionally isomorphic. As Putnam defines, "Two systems are functionally isomorphic if there is a correspondence between states of one and the states of other that preserves the functional relations."[40]

This functional isomorphism holds due to the causal capacity of the functional states. For example, when I have a pain, there is a neurophysiological process corresponding to the mental state because of the fining of the C-fiber. Here there is not only a neurophysiological process for the pain in the brain, but also there is the simultaneous occurrence of different mental states. Thus identity between the mental states and physical process of the brain is established from the *functional point of view*.[41] That is, in functional terms, the brain state is isomorphic with the mental state. The mental state is so to say realized in the brain state.

Functional identity theory, however, is supported by various scientific theories like artificial intelligence, cognitive science, and neurobiology etc. Artificial Intelligence advocates computational theory of mind which argues in favour of the functional similarly between computational states of the artificial system and the neurophysiological states of the brain. In the mid 19th century, the hypothesis of AI that "machine can think" became very popular after Alan Turing's article on "Computing Machinery and Intelligence,".[42] This hypothesis states that machines are the *probablistic automata,* and the functions of the automata is analogous to the functions of human brain. And thereby it claims the hypothesis that machines think intelligently like human beings. Putnam writes, "Probabilistic Automatom has been generalized to allow for 'sensory inputs', and 'motor outputs'—that is, the Machine Table specifies, for every possible combination of 'state' and a complete set of 'sensory inputs' an instruction which determines the probability of 'next state' and also the probabilities of motor outputs."[43] Like the neurological states and processes of the human brain the machine also undergoes certain processes in determining the output. The machine goes through the following steps in reaching its outputs: (i) the *description* of the sequence of states (procedure), (ii) description of *rules,* and (iii) the explanation of the *rationale* of the entire procedure.[44] The comparing machine is a system constructed of different subsystems that are functioning inside to process the inputs and to produce the output. Once the input is simulated in the machine, it tries to match the simulating state with the states that are already computed and mapped in the system. This mapping order follows certain syntax or rules. The syntax is responsible for the correlation of *total cognitive states.* The entire process of simulation, thus, can be called rational process. This rational process not only justifies the strong notion of identity, but also helps in explaining the process involved in the machine itself. However, the simulation takes place between the functions of the two functionally isomorphic systems, that is, between software that constitutes the programme, and the hardware or the machine which helps the software to run the electromagnetic process. The function of the two isomorphic structures can thus be explained in terms of the machine table.

Dennett, emphasizing the cognitive psychology and computational functionalism writes, "This story is fine in principle, I think, and the day may come when this imagined isomorphism down to the neuronal level (but not back stage) is proclaimed, but in fact we see nothing remotely like this in current AI work. We see instead models that diverge in nature very early on the downward path. AI programs typically model relatively high level cognitive features, such as the concept of learning or revision of goals or beliefs, and it does indeed often take millions of basic computer events to simulate just a handful of *intended model features*—but no one really knows or cares what these basic events are, for no one supposes that any of the saliencies in the mass of activitiy that surserves the intended features, are to be taken seriously as psychology or physiology."[45] Human beings perform various activities: thy learn language, acquire various knowledge states or belief states, and there are changes in their belief states, and so on. All these activities are independent biological activities of human life. Dennett anticipates that there would be a system whose progrmme will be such that it would be self-dependent in all its functions. That would be able to replace or stand parallel to the human intelligence. And, further, the function of the artificial system will help us in explaining the various mysterious features that are ascribed to the human life. Thus the strong notion of functionalism not only advocates the identity between the mental states and the brain processes, but also explains the different basic features of human beings such as consciousness, intentionality and subjectivity, etc. by bringing the feature of functional isomorphism into account.

Eliminative Materialism (*EM*) advocates a strong identity thesis by strictly denying the functional autonomy of mental states. As Churchland describes, "Eliminative materialism is the thesis that our commonsense conception of psychological phenomena constitutes a radically false theory, a theory so fundamentally defective that both the principles and the ontology of the theory will eventually be displaced, rather smoothly reduced, by completed neuroscience."[46] EM tries to explain the whole nature of mental life within the conceptual framework of neuroscience. By eliminating the ontology of mental life it tries to displace folk psychology by neuroscience. Neuroscience directly focuses on the nature and function of the neurological structure and processes of the brain that cause behaviour. Folk psychology deals with the generalisation of mental states and processes. In its generalisation it tries to formulate the laws of mind by observing the typical behaviour and relating them with their causal mental states like belief, desire, fear, intention, hope, etc. Therefore, in the case of folk psychology, the explanation of behaviour is through the mental states and then to the neural networks. EM only questions the ontological status of the metal states advocated by folk psychology. According to Churchland, "Identity theory optimistically expects that folk psychology will be slowly reduced by completed neuroscience, and its ontology is preserved by the dint of transtheoretic identities."[47] The transtheoretic identity establishes the ontology of neuroscience which defines the neural processes in the causal vocabulary of the physical theory. Eliminative materialism rejects the following features of the mental states. One is the normative character of folk psychology which takes into account mental states like belief, desire and intention. And the second is the abstract nature of folk psychology with reference to the network of causal relation and the functional character of their internal mental states. The normative features of representation of metal states would show the *regularity* involved in the function of mental states and their representations. And with the help of the notion of regularity, the laws are drawn which are seen as parallel to the classical gas laws. Churchland writes, "To draw a relevant parallel, the fact that the regularities ascribed by classical gas law are predicated on arithmetical relations between numbers does not imply anything essentially normative about the classical gas law. And the logical relation between propositions are as much as an objective matter of abstract fact as are arithmatical relations between numbers."[48] By observing the regularity of mechanical processes of the neural structure of the brain it tries to formulate the laws of neuroscience. The laws of neuroscience are equally objective. Thus, neuro-science reflects on the reality of the neurological structure and processes of the brain, and not on the mental states and phenomena. Thereby it eliminates the notion of the mental from its discourse.

V. The Methodological Unity and Explanation in Naturalism

In our above discussions on functional identity theory, central state identity theory and eliminative materialism, we find a common naturalistic methodology in explaining the nature of the mental in general and the mind-brain identity theory in particular. We call these theories naturalistic because they adopt a naturalistic methodology. That is, they approach the study of the mental through the collection of scientific data in the brain sciences. The scientific explanation of the mental phenomena is based on the law of causality. The causality that is involved operates within the neurophysiological structure of the brain states. The function of brain states has the power to explain behaviour causally. As Michel Tye observes, "Mental states are simply having enough of the relevant causal features. Such an approach is tantamount to the thesis that mental state terms express prototype concepts, whereas prototype draws on certain sorts of commonsense causal features and no others."[49] Since the mental attributes are causally defined, they are subsequently taken into the domain of causal laws which prevail in the domain of physical sciences. This is one way of treating the mental as a part of the physical phenomena, and consequently as a part of natural phenomena.

Naturalism as a philosophical theory deals with the systematic analysis of the natural phenomena. Rudlof Carnap, who advocates the unity of science, rightly points out, "we use the word science here in its widest sense, including all theoretical knowledge, no matter whether in the field of social sciences ... what usually called science is merely a systematic continuation of those activities which we carry out in our every day life."[50] Carnap's intention was to develop a unified science. And the naturalists in general follow Carnap's approach to the unity of all science. The naturalists' conception of the mental falls under the Carnapian programme of unifying all sciences under the physical sciences.

The very talk of unity in science logically presupposes divergent practices in different sciences. Sciences like biology and physics seem to be different sciences, so far as their study of phenomena is concerned. Biology, as a science of organism, deals primarily with the study of the organism and its processes, whereas physics is concerned with the study of matter. Thus, in sort, they generally deal with two different domains of science. The function of the brain in particular, as an organism, is more closely connected with biology than with physics. Furthermore, biology is divided into two levels, (i) the psychological and social and (ii) the general biological sciences.[51] The 'psychological field is concerned with the dispositional aspects of the behaviour of the human beings including these other features which are relevant to the behaviour of the human beings. Thus, the study of the behaviour of the human beings comes under the scope of biology. However, the notion of *unity* is taken seriously by the naturalists. That is, they tend to explain in a natural manner the phenomena within one `language of science', called physical sciences in general or physics in particular. Smart, who shares the same thought with Carnap, points out "[a]ll the objects in the universe are suitably structured in order to be expressed in the language of physics ... Now the brains are the part of the physical universe and so would not be psyche or vital force ... Psychology is a part of biology. In the really scientific core of psychology, there is a core tie up with neuro-physiology and hence with bio-physics and bio-chemistry."[52] But what is the logical relation between two different sciences? The relationship is logical in the sense that they share a common methodology. And the relationship is further explicated through the method of *reduction*. Reductions result in the equivalence between the two phenomena. That is, they are equivalent in terms of properties that occur both in the physical processes of the brain and the mental states. And those properties are identical with each other.[53]

Jerry Fodor argues in favour of property reductionism. The property that occurs in the phenomena of a particular domain of any special sciences can be, reduced to the domain of physics through the help of *bridge laws*. Bridge laws, in the case of psychology, establish the identity relationship by taking into account the properties of the mental states and the properties of neurophhysiological the states. As Fodor symbolizes :

"(1) $S_1x \rightarrow S_2Y$ [Law of special science S]

(2a) $S_1x \rightarrow P_1x$

(2b) $S_2y \rightarrow P_2y$ [2a and 2b represent bridge law]

(3) $P_1x \rightarrow P_2y$"[54] [Physical law]

Birdge law is the connecting principle between the laws

of the special sciences and the laws of the physical sciences. The bridge law shows that the transitive relationship between the properties predicated in S_1 and S_2 are also predicated in the physical law. Fodor says, "The upshot of the remarks so far is that the reduction of science requires that any formula which appears as the antecedent or consequent of one of its proper laws must appear as the reduced formula in some bridge law or other."[55] Reduction of one special science to physics is possible, if we can observe that the properties of one special science are reduced to those of physical science. Bridge law plays an intermediary role for reducing one special science to physics. For Fodor, "psychology is presumed to reduce to physics via, say, neurology, biochemistry and other local stops. The present point is that it makes no difference to the logic of the situation so long as the transitivity of '→' is assumed."[56] The implication or '→' in the case of bridge law must be read not just as connectives but something that is *causing*. This causal relationship holds as a symmetric relationship. The symmetric relationship will justify the proper identity relationship between the laws of special sciences and the laws of physics. However, as Fodor summarizing his notion of reduction, writes, "To summarize: I shall be reading reductionism as entailing token physicalism, since, if bridge laws state nomologically necessary contingent event identities, a reduction of psychology to neurology would require that any event which consists of the instantiation of a psychological property is identical with some event which consists of the instantiation of neurological property. Both reductionism and token physicalism entail the generality of physics, since both hold that any event which falls within the universe of discourse of a special science will also fall within the universe of discourse of physics."[57]

Hence, the notion of reduction is central to the naturalistic explanation of the mental. The unity of sciences is brought about only by the method of reduction. The reduction does not depend on the commonsensical knowledge of the world. Rather it is based on the natural laws. Carnap says, "there is a unity of language in science; it is a common reduction basis for the terms of all branches of science, the basis consisting of a very narrow and homogeneous class of terms of the physical thing-language. This unity of terms indeed is less far-reaching and effective than the unity of laws would be, but it is a necessary preliminary condition for the unity of laws."[58] The laws in the case of physical sciences are formulated in terms of the observable phenomena. Thus, for both Carnap and Fodor the unity of science can be achieved through the help of the unity of the laws. And the unity of the laws makes the reduction simple. In the case of biology and other special sciences like psychology or economics, too, the terms are determined finally by physics. Physics is considered as the proper science and it deals with the most fundamental natural laws. In this regard, the terms in the various branches of sciences must have logical connection for predication as well as reduction. The logical connection is possible through language. Hence, for Carnap the unity of language of science is the basis for the practical application of theoretical knowledge.

In this connection, the materialistic or the naturalistic theory of the mind in its study of the mental, holds not only a *proscientific* worldview, but also a strong version of reductionism. Since the mental states are caused by the physical brain processes, they can obviously be characterized as physical. The causal law that operates among the physical phenomena is applicable to the brain states and the mental states. The mental states, being the part of the physical, are spatio-temporally limited. And causal law functions within the spatio-temporal limitation. Thus, with this methodology, the materialists argued their theses and opted for the identity relation between the mental and the physical, without explaining the various features of the mental fully. At the same time, this sort of positivistic attitude towards the domain of the mental resulted in the physical theory of mind or physicalism. The goal of physicalism is the 'growth of knowledge'.[59] The growth of knowledge is concerned with the scientific development, related especially to the epistemological and methodological issues. The physicalistic methodology is not only reductive in its approach, but also its strong version is eliminative in character. The eliminative materialism exclusively emphasizes the neurobiology or neurophilosophy, which categorically eliminates the role of the mental.[60]

Naturalism as a theory of the mental is grounded in certain principles of the physicalist theory. It accepts the psysicalist model of explanation for all kinds of natural phnomena. The very goal of scientific explanation of the natural phenomena, as Clark quotes Hampel: "What scientific explanation, especially theoritical explanation, aims at is not [an] intuitive and highly subjective kind of understanding, but an objective kind of insight that is achieved by systematic unification, by exhibiting the phenomenon as manifestation of the common, underlying structures and processes that conform to specific, testable basic principles."[61] However, Clark is of the opinion that *determinism* in physical theory, especially in classical physics follows reduction. It is deterministic in the sense that observing the occurrence of a typical behaviour and simultaneously relating it with neural functions, as well as identifying the same behaviour with the neural states, consequently, results in construing the laws of the brain processes as physical laws. Besides, it is mostly statistical in nature. Clark points out that the statistical law explanation, is deductive as well as probabilistic. It is deductive because the law is deduced from a set of observable events occurring in a certain pattern. The probabilistic features of the laws follow from the fact that they comprehend and explain the probable occurrence of new phenomena falling within the theory. It is precisely because the "consequence of statistical laws is a statement of probability of a given event."[62]

Insofar as the mental states are concerned, physicalism either reduces the mental states to the micro level physical structure of the neural processes, or adopts some sort of an eliminative method. The reduction of the mental phenomena to the micro-level neural structure is eliminative in character. In the case of *emergent properties,* which result from a certain level of complex functions, such properties can be reduced to the micro-level functions of the neural states. However, the physical laws are successful only in explaining the function of non-living matter, whereas the mental states and their correlations are properties not of mere physical non-living matter, but of living organism.[63] Therefore, the latter cannot strictly be explained by the deterministic statistical laws.

In order to explain the function of the living organism it is necessary for us to take biology as our model rather than physics, because biological categories are different from physical categories. According to Millikan, biological categories are not just concerned with the structural and dispositional properties of the organism, rather they are concerned with the history of the organism, i.e., how the organism has evolved. She further states, "Biological categories, are carved not by looking at the actual structure, actual dispositions or actual functions of the organ or system that fall within the category but by looking at (or speculating about) its history."[64] To talk about the history of the organism is to know how the organism has developed in relation to the environment. Human beings are the products of the evolutionary process of history. The *proper function* of human beings' development, whether it is linguistic or physiological or cultural, must need to be looked at from the biological states and processes through which it has biologically evolved. All linguistic and physiological aspects of human life are a part of the biology of life.

The proper function of the species includes a *fixed mechanism* or a pattern of behaviour, that can be studied from the standpoint of the designed stance of the organism. Millikan writes, "My claim will be that it is the "proper function" of a thing that puts it in a biological category, and this has to do not with its powers but with its history. Having proper function is a matter of having 'designed to" or being 'supposed to' (impersonal) perform certain function. The task of the theory of the proper function is to define this sense of 'designed to' or 'supposed to' in a naturalist, non normative, and non mysterious terms."[65] The species' behaviour is always with reference to its designed stance, i.e., as regards its structure in its relationship and interaction with the environment. Furthermore, the value of proper function is ascribed to this interrelationship between the environment and the species. The interrelationship shows that a normal or average function exists in biology.

However, this proper function is sustained in the process of evolution because biological organism has a certain capacity of sustainability not only to survive, but also to reproduce. Millikan says, "If a man is a natural creature and product of evolution, it is reasonable to suppose that man's capacity as knower is also a product of evolution. If we are capable of believing and knowing things, it must be because these capacities, and the organs in us that are responsible for these capacities, historically performed a service that helped to proliferate."[66] As we have said, the capacity of the organism not just shows basic or average function but it also explicates that there are different evolving properties of the organism. These evolving properties have determinate function. It is determinate in the sense that it is a *standard* or a *normal function* within its environment. This determinacy is relatively defined with reference to the environmental conditions. It can, therefore, be called *relational proper function*. For instance, amoeba has a relational proper function to flow in a direction determined by a relation, or as a function (in a mathematical sense) of the chemical variations in the water around it. This function of ameba is relative to the environmental condition of water. Thus proper function is a relational proper function.[67] Therefore, a species' existence in its environment and functioning in that environment will have a normal explanation. "Normal explanation is an explanation of how a particular reproductively established family has historically performed particular proper functions."[68] Normal explanation propounds what basic features and properties are involved in the proper function of the organism. Once we are able to make out the actual conditions of their functioning and the other possible properties involved in the function, then it would be easy to determine their behaviour. And consequently we can formulate laws about the behaviour which could be added, to the natural laws. Thus, the biological explanation of Millikan adheres to the naturalistic causal explanation, because biological function of an organism is part of the causal order of the universe. Referring to the physiological function of the organism, Millikan suggests, "Once the physiologist has in his hand a hypothesis about what a proper functions of a body part or system is, he can tackle the task of finding out how it performs these functions. Her eventual aim is to describe the Normal constitution of the simplest component parts of the system in terms of such that how the system functions can be understood by principles of physics and organic chemistry etc."[69] Laws in physical sciences are taken as standard and stable laws, and the same value can be attached to the physiological function of the body if the properties of the organism could be determined. It is the determinate function of the properties which help in either formulating or deriving the laws. These laws too can be associated with the natural law or the laws of causality in particular. The law of causality is taken as one of the fundamental laws of physical science. Thus, the physiology as biological science can be reduced to physical sciences. And the naturalistic scheme of Millikan's will not have any objection to this. The hypothesis of normal explanation is that it basically tries to capture the stabilizing order of the proper function of the organism. Thus ultimately the biological explanation constitutes a part of the naturalist and physicalist explanation of the universe.

IV. Searle's Rejection of Materialistim: Towards an Alternative Methodology

The materialistic conception of mind, as we have discussed above, holds that the mental phenomena are either identical with, or reducible to the physical states and processes of the brain. The materialists deny the reality of mind. And, for them, the physical alone is real. Thus materialism, in short, rejects the mind-body dualism. Searle pointed out general as well as specific defects in the materialistic conception of the mind. Insofar as the general defects are concerned, Searle seriously objects to the very conception of the brain-mind identity as well as the reduction of the mind to the brains. The mental, according to him, cannot be reduced because the essential features of the mind are as real as those of the physical reality. Hence to reduce the mental to the realm of the physical is to reduce the constituting features of the mental, which is an impossible task. That is why the materialist try to exclude the mental phenomena like subjective consciousness and intentionality from their discourse. As Searle remarks, "The deepest reason for consciousness is that consciousness has the essentially terrifying feature of subjectivity. Materialists are reluctant to accept that feature because they believe that to accept the existence of subjective consciousness would be inconsistent with their conception of what the world must be like."[70] Materialism does not accept the reality of consciousness in general and conscious subjectivity, intentionality, freedom of will, etc. in particular. However, it is these particular features which constitute the reality of the consciousness and the mind. Biological naturalism of Searle's finds the materialist worldview inconsistent and incomplete for not accommodating consciousness within its world-picture. Searle's naturalism, on the contrary, admits the reality of consciousness.

Searle's criticism of materialism can be enumerated as follows:

1. Behaviourism has two difficulties. It does not clarify the notion of disposition as the cause of behaviour. And secondly, there is a circularity involved in explaining the mental phenomena. If we are not clear about which dispositional states are causing what sort of behaviour, it is difficult to formulate the hypothesis that behaviour is caused by dispositions. This dispositional account of explain-ing behaviour, entails circularity, that is, "to give analysis of belief in terms of behaviour, it means that one has to make reference to desire, to give analysis of desire, it seems that one has to make reference to belief."[71] In this way the explanation of behaviour moves in a circular order without reaching the real cause of it.
2. Identity theory, advocated by Armstrong, Smart and Place is mostly an identity between the physical types of events with the mental types of events. That is, the mental states and process are identical with the physical states and processes. For example, the neurological properties of pain must be identical with the mental properties of the pain. Neurological properties refer to the C-fiber simulation and some of the physicochemical processes of the brain whereas the mental property signifies the subjective feeling or one's awareness of his pain. In this context, Searle says, identity theory talks about property dualism though not substantial dualism. Then, in that case, we have not really gotten rid of the mind. We are still left with a form of dualism, *albeit* property dualism rather than

substantial dualism. We are still left with sets of mental properties, even though we have gotten rid of mental substance. If on the other hand, we try to treat "pain" as not naming a subjective mental feature of certain neurophysiological events, then meaning is left totally mysterious and unexplained."[72] Identity theory, though aware of the mental properties does not specify the mental properties and only talks about the neurophysiological properties. Since they are never able to specify the mental properties, they never assert the existence of these properties. Moreover, this does not deny the essential feature of my being aware of my pain which is different from your feeling of pain. Type-identity entails property dualism because all mental properties are not identical with the physical properties of the brain processes. The type identity theory always talks about the same type of neurological states and processes. For Searle, it only gives a one-side view of the mental by overemphasizing the reality of neurophysiological process. Searle calls this 'neural chauvinism.' (op. cit.)

3. Though functionalism advocates that mental states are causally related and that they help determine the qualia, it leaves out certain specific *qualitative subjective feelings.*[73] Because the causal structure of the mental states and their function does not specify the subjective feeling, rather it is part of the consciousness involved in the very nature of experiencing. Functionalism eliminates consciousness from their discourse in mind. My experience of seeing the Taj Mahal is certainly different from that of Sahajahan's, the Moghul emperor who built the Taj Mahal. It is difficult to specify the qualitative feature of mental states. Hence functionalism fails to explain our subjective experiences.

4. Functionalism, especially the theory of Strong Artificial Intelligence or the computational model of the mind argues that information processing is similar to the thought processing. But the programme or the software which plays a vital role in information processing is only a syntactical configuration of the input cognitive states, and it does not have semantical content, whereas the thought process itself contains both syntax as well as semantics. Searle remarks, "Because the programme is purely formal or syntactical; and because minds have semantic contents, any attempt to produce mind purely with computer programs leaves out the essential features of the mind."[74] The syntax alone does not help to understand language. Rather its semantics is essential for understanding language. Semantical content is specific to the human mental life.
5. Eliminative materialism takes an extreme position by denying the ordinary mental entities, like our belief, desires, etc. Does it really leave out the mind? We do feel pain, thirst, etc. And if we believe that there is water in the pot; we believe that drinking a glass of water may quench our thirst immediately, and so on. It is commonsense knowledge that we do talk about beliefs, desire and intention, etc. as the part of the mental. As Searle writes, referring to Churchland, "Unlike the earlier materialist theories, eliminative materialism doesn't so much leave out the mind, it denies the existence of anything to leave out in the first place. When confronted with the challenge that eliminative materialism seem too insane to merit serious consideration, its defenders almost invariably invoke the heroic age-of-science maneuver."[75] The merit of neuroscience lies in explaining better the very function of brain

> processes. That will help us in understanding the cognitive process. But thereby it would not be logical to state that it does not have the mental features.

It is true that both identity theory and eliminative materialism are strongly influenced by the scientific discoveries in neurophyiology. Identity theory advocates that there is nothing 'over and above' physical states: physical type states are identical with mental type states. On the other hand, eliminative materialism denies the importance of the mental states and eliminates them altogather. Hence, there is no notion of identity maintained here. This Searle calls a "paradoxical asymmetry" in the history of the materialistic theory of mind. The asymmetry shows that one theory of materialism feels that the mental is not a separate phenomenon from the physical, but there could be an identity relationship, whereas another theory holds that there is no separation, hence no identity. As Searle briefly remarks, "I find this pattern very revealing, what it reveals is an urge to get rid of mental phenomena at any cost."[76]

Biological naturalism of Searle rejects the materialistic or physicalistic methodology for the explanation of the mental phenomena. Physicalistic methodology in the name of unity of science pursues reductionism. Mental phenomena which are studied by the some of the special sciences like biology, psychology , neuroscience, etc. are ultimately reduced to the laws of physical phenomena. It is precisely because the mental is not only treated as the physical, but that the laws of the special sciences are analogous to the laws of physical sciences. How do the specific properties of the mental phenomena like consciousness, subjectivity, intentionality get reduced to certain physical properties? This question is never answered satisfactorily by the mentalists. Biological naturalism, on the other hand, propounds an integral view of the phenomena of mental life. This approach has been holistic in explaining the mental life of human beings. The scientific explanation of the mental and physical phenomena, particularly in the dualistic as well as the naturalistic and materialistic frameworks has been a difficult task. Searle tries to resolve this in the context of the twentieth century scientific worldview, which has witnessed the rise not only of physical sciences but also of biological sciences including neurobiology. He accepts radical differences between the physical sciences and the sciences which explain human behaviour. For him, a discipline should be considered scientific if and only if it is systematically arranged and it explains every piece of knowledge in that domain. Searle notices a radical difference between physical and behavioural sciences. He writes, "The radical disunity between social and natural sciences doesn't come from the fact that there is only disjunctive connection of social and physical phenomena. It doesn't even come from the fact that social disciplines have constitutive concepts which have no echo in physics nor even from the great complexity of social life. Many disciplines such as geology, biology and meteorology have these features but that does not prevent them from being systematic natural sciences."[77] An adequate emphasis is given to the special sciences. For instance, meteorology must itself be treated as an independent science, and it should be sufficient enough to explain all the complexity involved in the phenomenon of weather. And similar is the case with the other sciences too. In this regard Searle's naturalism does not remain confined only to physical sciences. Rather, naturalism has a broader perspective, when it is extended to include the realm of the mental. Biology has better success with the mental than the physical sciences. As he describes, 'Biology, for example, requires the concept of organism, and organism has no echo in physics, but biology does not thereby cease to be a hard science.' Searle's naturalistic method of analysis takes biology as a standard science, precisely in the sense that mental phenomena and biological phenomena, for Searle, are equally real, and the former is caused by the latter.

Searle's biological worldview is the combination of the two fundamental conceptions of science, namely the *atomic theory of the universe* and *evolutionary biology*. Searle summarizes, "Our world picture, though extremely complicated in detail, provides a rather simple account of the mode of existence of consciousness. According to the atomic theory, the world is made up of particles. These particles are organised into subsystems. Some of these systems are living, and these types of living system have evolved over long periods of time. Among these, some have evolved brains that are capable of causing and sustaining consciousness. Consciousness, thus, is a 'biological' in which feature of certain organisms, in exactly the same sense of "biological" in which photosynthesis; mitosis, digestion, and reproduction are biological feature of the organisms."[78] The atomic theory advocates the systemic organic features of both living and nonliving bodies of the world. Everything has a structure and can also be divided into substructures. The substructures are constituted of molecules and particles. Their structural configuration has a causal explanation because each particle is causally related with other particles in order to constitute the whole system. Brain as a system of living organism has not only a causal structure of subsystems but also has evolved in the process of evolution. Consciousness is therefore, an evolved phenomenon because the brain causes consciousness. Brain is not like any other ordinary physical organism. It is a highly complex organism. Thus consciousness, as a part of the human mental life, has to be placed within the domain of atomic theory of matter and evolutionary biology. Referring to the specific feature of human mental life, Searle writes, "Basic to our world view is the idea that human beings and other higher animals are part of the biological order like any other organism. Humans are continuous with the rest of nature. But if so, the biologically specific characteristics of these animals—such as their possession of a rich system of consciousness, as well as their greater intelligence, their capacity for language, their capacity for extremely fine perceptual discriminations, their capacity for rational thought, etc. are biological phenomena like any other biological phenomena."[79] Moreover, the significant fact is that consciousness is a species-specific feature. Consciousness as a specific-specific feature of human beings signifies its various functional characteristics such as intelligence, language use, etc. Consciousness has survived because the species itself is surviving in the process of evolution. So the conscious life of human beings in the environment has a survival value. Survival value shows the surviving capacity of an organism. Hence, consciousness has a functional description or macro level description. However, Searle writes, "In evolutionary biology, there are characteris-tically two levels of explanation, a 'functional' level where we can explain survival of the species in terms of the 'inclusive fitness' which depends on phenotypical traits possessed by members of the species and 'causal' where we explain causal mechanism by which the traits in question actually relate the organism to the environment."[80] The functional description of the organism is mainly about the species' capacity for survival in the environmental changes. On the other hand, the causal description is about the species' internal mechanism, i.e. the neuro-physiological processes that take place in the case of the human beings. In this regard, the fact that the human beings act in the world in order to survive, has an intentional description because his act of surviving is with reference to his mental states which are in principle intentional. Whereas the causal explanation shows how the neurophysiological processes of the organism give rise to the mental states. Thus there are two levels of description possible to explain the conscious mental life of human beings.

Now we need to understand the basic co-features that our mental life comprises. There are four essential features of the mental life that biological naturalism is concerned with. They are, consciousness, intentionality, subjectivity, and mental causation. All these features are intrinsically correlated with each other, insofar as the mental life is concerned. For Searle, "By 'mind' I just mean the sequences of thoughts, feelings and experiences, whether conscious or unconscious, that make up our mental life."[81] It true that mind is constituted of both conscious and unconscious mental states. It is important to note that these mental states constitute our life of experiences and feelings. All this is revealed by the analysis of the basic features of consciousness. And by explicating these features we could understand the very nature of mind itself. Since consciousness as a prime feature of the mind has direct emergence from the neural processes of the brain, the other features of consciousness are also causally related to the brain processes.

Consciousness according to Searle, is the central feature of the human mind. To quote, "Consciousness is the central fact of specifically human existence because all our other aspects of our existence—language, love, humour, and so on would be impossible without consciousness".[82] Human beings are not just conscious beings living in the world. Rather human beings are consciously engaged in the various activities of the world around. The conscious engagement shows his relationship with the world. And this relationship is disclosed in a human being's use of language for communicating ideas, describing the world, etc. This linguistic relationship is also attached with emotional and psychological aspects of life. Human beings not only live but also imagine, expect, hope, etc. All these are related to the social surroundings. In brief, a person social life is necessarily related with his personal life and thereby with his conscious life. Human beings besides, are capable of choosing and acting according to their will. All these are part of their rational life. The conscious activities of man are intrinsically endowed with the biological structure of the being.

According to Searle, "Intentionality, the feature by which our mental states are directed *at*, or *about*, or *refer to*, or are objects or states of affairs in the world other than themselves. Intentionality is much like the question about consciousness."[83] The act of consciousness reveals the directedness or aboutness of being conscious of something. That is, whenever someone is thinking about something or saying something he must be consciously representing his or her mental states. For instance, I believe someone is standing there at the main entrance of my house who looks like my friend. This composite expression includes a belief state that someone is already there; someone looks like my bosom friend; and furthermore I feel suddenly happy to see such a person being there, and I too intend to go near him to recognize the person, and so on. So the state includes states of belief, happiness, intention, etc. Moreover, belief, desire, and intention are core mental states which describe the function of intentionality. Intentionality is the basic feature of the mental states. That is to say, all conscious mental states are intentional states. Therefore, in short, consciousness and intentionality are intrinsically related with each other. And like consciousness, intentionality is also an emergent property of neurophysiological processes of brain. As Searle puts it, "Both consciousness and intentionality are biological processes caused by lower level of neural processes in the brain, and neither is reducible to something else. Furthermore, consciousness and intentionality are essentially connected in that we understand the notion of an unconscious intentional state only in terms of its accessibility to consciousness."[84] The biological basis of intentionality reveals that there cannot be an explication of consciousness without referring to intentionality and vice versa. Since consciousness has the biological origin, it is obvious that intentionality as an intrinsic part of consciousness will also have neurophysiological embodiment. Moreover, intentionality is not only there with the conscious mental states, but also there in other unconscious mental states. Unconscious mental states are logically related to consciousness. It is obvious that one is not conscious of everything at a moment. Thus intentionality includes both conscious and unconscious mental states.

Whenever, we are claiming that we are conscious of so many things of the world and we know so many things about the world, we usually refer to our own mental states. We all have our own way of looking and describing the world. In brief, our awareness of the mental phenomena and our own representation of the world reveal that the mental phenomena are subjective. They are subjective because they always represent a *first person point of view*. My mental states and my attitude will differ from my friend's mental states and attitude. Searle remarks, "This subjectivity is marked by such a fact that, I can feel my pain, and you cannot, I see the world from my point of view; you see it from your point of view. I am aware of myself and my internal mental states as quite distinct from the selves and mental states of other people."[85] To illustrate it, a meteorologists observation of clouds and the direction of wind blowing from north to south will create a different mental state than a poet's looking at the same clouds floating in the sky and the cool wind touching his body. Though the same world is represented to both meteorologist and poet, the difference arises because of their mode of perceiving to the phenomena. Similarly my feeling of pain will certainly vary from your realization of the same pain that I am experiencing. Thus, precisely, subjectivity is a part of the world order. This order establishes the first person ontology, namely of the 'self' or 'I' of being conscious of something specific or uniquely different from what others believe and feel. However, this subjectivity as a feature of my consciousness is also a feature of the neurophysiological process of the brain. Searle says, "My state of consciousness is a feature of my brain, but its conscious aspects are accessible to me in a way they are not accessible to you. And your present state of consciousness is a feature of your brain and your conscious aspects are accessible to you in a way that they are not accessible to me. Thus, existence of subjectivity is an objective fact in biology."[86]

According to Searle, the mind-body problem arises because we have not yet understood the features of the mental properly. Philosophers while trying to solve the problem of dualism either have eliminated consciousness or have tried to reduce the mental phenomena to the physical phenomena. As he writes, "It seems to many people whose opinion I respect, that the irreducibility of consciousness is the primary reason why the mind-body problem continues to seem so intractable. Dualists treat the irreducibility of consciousness as incontrovertible proof of the truth of dualism. Materialits insist that consciousness must be reducible to material reality, and that the price of denying the reducibility of consciousness would be the abandonment of our over all scientific world view."[87] Searle tries to put consciousness back along with its other intrinsic co-features as central to the study of the mind.

Notes and References

1. John R. Searle, *The Rediscovery of the Mind,* The MIT Press, Massachusetts, The Bradford Book, 1993, p. 1 (Henceforth will be shortly used as *RDM*).
2. John Searle, "Minds, Brains without Programs," *Mindwaves: Thoughts on Intelligence, Identity and Consciousness,* ed. Colin Blackmore, and Susan Greenfield, Basil Blackwell, Oxford, 1987, p. 229.
3. Searle, *RDM,* p. 227.
4. *Ibid.,* p. 233.
5. *Ibid.,* p. 112.
6. Searle, *Intentionality: An Essay in the Philosophy of Mind,* Cambridge University Press, Cambridge, 1983, p. 266. (Henceforth, *Intentionality*) Searle further clarifies the macro and

micro relationship with reference to the hypothesis that mental is caused by the brain process and realized in the brain processes in his *Minds, Brains and Science*, The Harvard University Press, Cambridge, 1984, 21. (Henceforth, *MBS*)

7. Searle, *RDM.*, p. 112.
8. *Ibid.*, p. 117.
9. *Ibid.*, p. 118.
10. *Ibid.*, p. 26.
11. *Ibid.*
12. Desmond M. Clarke, "Descartes Philosophy of Science and the Scientific Revolution," *Cambridge Companion to Descartes*, Cambridge University Press, Cambridge, p. 261. (Henceforth, CCD)
13. Ledger Wood, "Descartes Philosophy of Mind", *Philosophical Review*, Vol. XLI, (41) No. 5, 1932 p475
14. Clarke, op. cit., p. 272.
15. Rene Descartes, *Second Meditation*, "The Nature of Human Mind is better known than the Body", *Meditations on First Philosophy*, *trans.* John Cottingham, CUP, Cambridge, 1986 pp. 17-18.
16. *Ibid.*, p. 18
17. *The Philosopjical Writtings of Descartes, Vol. 1*, Trans. J. Cottingham, Robert Stoothoff, Dugald Murdch, CUP, Cambridge, 1955, The Passion of the Soul, p. 341.
18. *Ibid.*, p. 329.
19. Descartes, *Second Meditation*, p. 18.
20. Paul Churchland, *Matter and Consciousness*, The MIT Press, Massachusetts, 1989, p. 88. (Henceforth *MC*)
21. *Ibid.*, pp. 88-89.
22. *Ibid.*, p. 75.
23. D.M. Armstrong, *A Materialist Theory of the Mind*, Routledge and Kegan Paul, London, 1968, p. 91. (Henceforth, AMTM)
24. *Ibid.*, p. 78
25. *Ibid.*
26. *Ibid.*, p. 115.
27. See, U.T. Place, "Thirty Years on—Is Consciousness Still a Brain Process?" *Austalisian Journal of Philosophy*, Vol. 66, No. 2, June 1988.
28. Place, "Is Consciousness a Brain Process?" *M-BIT*, pp. 43-44.
29. *Ibid.*, p. 50.

30. J.C.C. Smart, "Sensations and Brain Process", *M-BIT*, p. 58.
31. *Ibid.*, p. 64.
32. By citing *stuff*, Smart refers to the Cartesian notion of mental as ghostly stuff which cannot be explained. *Ibid.*, p 165
33. Smart, "Consciousness and Brain Process" reprinted in his book *Essays on Metaphysical and Moral*, Basil Blackwell, Oxford, 1987, p. 190.
34. *Ibid.*, p. 192.
35. *Ibid.*, p. 62.
36. Putnam, "The Nature of Mental States,"p. 51.
37. See, Churchland, *MC*, p. 36.
38. See, Putnam, "The Nature of Mental States," p.56.
39. "Mind and Body: Some forms of Reductionism", *An Encyclopedia of Philosophy*, ed. GHR Parkinson, Routledge, London, 1988, p. 409.
40. Putnam, "Philosophy and Our Mental Life", in *Philosophy of mind: Classical Problems/ Contemporary Issues*,ed. Brain Beakley and Peter Ludlow, The MIT Press, Massachusetts, 1992, p. 91.
41. *Ibid.*, pp. 37-38.
42. Alan Turing "Computational Machinery and Intelligence," *Mind*, p. Vol. LIX, No. 236, Oct., 1950.
43. Putnam, "The Nature of Mental States," p. 54.
44. Putnam, "Mind and Machine", in *Mind and Machine*; ed. Allan Ross Anderson, Printice Hall New Jersy, 1958, p. 78.
45. Daniel C. Dennett, "Artificial Intelligence as Philosophy and as Psychology", *Brainstorms*, The MIT Press, A Bradford Book, Massachusetts, 1981, pp. 114-115.
46. Paul M. Churchland, "Eliminative Materialism and Propositinoal Attitude", *The Journal of Philosophy*, Vol. 78, No. 2, p. 1981, p. 67.
47. *Ibid.*, p. 72.
48. *Ibid.*, p. 82.
49. Michael Tye, "Naturalism and the Mental", *Mind*, Vol. 101, No. 403, July 1992. P.425.
50. Rudlof Carnap, "The Logical Foundations of the Unity of Science", *Essential Readings in Logical Positivism* , ed. Oswald Hanfling, Basil Blackwell, 1981, pp. 114-15.
51. Carnap makes the distinction between "psychological field" and "the field of general biology", p .116.

52. JCC Smart, "The Revival of Materialism", *The Essays on Metaphysical and Moral* , p p. 240-241. In this regard Carnap remarks, " Biologists have to know the laws of physics in studying the process or organisms. He needs them for the explanation of these processes." , Carnap, op. . cit., pp. 114-15. Smart also says that "Biologists ... apply the law of physics and chemistry in order to understand certain structure and processes which occur in certain sort of terrestrial organism." Smart, "Under the form of Eternity", op. cit., p. 121.
53. See Carnap, *Ibid.*, p. 120.
54. Jerry Fodor, "Special Sciences", *Representations: A Philosophical Essays on Foundation of Cognitive Science*, Harvester Press, London, 198, p. 128.
55. *Ibid.*, p. 129.
56. *Ibid.*, Moreover, Implication or '→' represents as "causes". Insofar as the bridge law is concerned it holds a symmetric replationship not an asymmetric relationship.
57. *Ibid.*, p. 131.
58. *Ibid.*, p. 128.
59. Both Rudlof Caranp [op. cit, pp128-29]and Jeffrey Poland discuss about the conception of 'unity of science' which refers to the growth of knowledge. Poland further makes the distinction between growth of knowledge and structure of knowledge. Structure of knowledge refers to the knowledge in relation to reality. J Poland, *Physicalism: The Philosophical Foundations*, Clarendon Press, Oxford, 1994, p. 12. (Henceforth Physicalism).
60. For a detailed discussion of eliminative materialism, see P.M. & P.S. Churchlands'.
61. Cf. "Explanation in Physical Theory", *Philosophy*, Supplement, Vol. 27, 1990, p. 157.
62. *Ibid.*, p. 161.
63. Clark further cites the words of William Thompson, First Bron Kelvin, in his popular scientific lectures, "allued to what he looks to be an absolute portion between living and dead matter and he claimed that laws of living matter quite independent of the laws of dead matter." Ibid., p. 167.
64. Ruth G. Millikan, "Thought without Laws and Cognitive Science with Content", *The Philosophical Review*, Vol XCV., No. 1, January 1986. She further says that though organic chemistry and physiological explanation deal with the function of the micro-level organisms, "but the fundamental difference is that the

organic chemistry and the physiologiologist wish to understand how the system they study work in rather different sense of 'work', *Ibid.*, pp. 50-51.

65. Ruth Garrett Millikan, *Language, Thought and Other Biological Categories*, The MIT Press, Massachusetts, 1984, p. 17. (Henceforth, *LTOBC*
66. *Ibid.*, p. 7.
67. *Ibid.*, p.
68. Normal explanations are of two types: one is, most approximate normal explanation and other is less approximate normal functions. See, Millikan's *LTOBC*, p.
69. Millikan, "Thought without Laws and Cognitive Science without Content", p. 57.
70. Searle, *RDM*, p. 55.
71. *Ibid.*, p. 34.
72. *Ibid.*, p. 37.
73. *Ibid.*, p. 42.
74. *Ibid.*, p. 45.
75. *Ibid.*, p. 48.
76. *Ibid.*, p. 49.
77. Searle, *MBS*, p. 84
78. Searle, *RDM*, pp. 92-93.
79. *Ibid.*, p. 90
80. *Ibid.*, pp. 89-90.
81. Searle, *MBS*, pp. 10-11.
82. *Ibid.*, pp. 15-16.
83. *Ibid.*,p16.
84. Searle, *RDM*, p. xii
85. Sealre, *MBS*, p. 16.
86. *Ibid.*, p. 25.
87. *Ibid.*, p. 116.

Chapter - II

REDISCOVERING CONSCIOUSNESS

According to Searle, the four features of the mental, namely, consciousness, intentionality, subjectivity and mental causation have to be understood clearly in order to resolve the problem of dualism. In this chapter, we shall explain the reality of consciousness. The importance of the reality of consciousness is due to its being intrinsic to human mental life. Consciousness constitutes the basic feature of mental life. Its constitution has a structure and the explanation of the structure reveals its constituting features.

The chapter contains seven sections. The first section gives a complete picture of the structure of consciousness as provided by biological naturalism. Biological naturalism says that the notion of consciousness stands for a composite phenomenon involving various intrinsic features which not only define consciousness, but also constitute the human mental life. In order to grasp the objective aspects of the structure of consciousness, the functionalist conception of consciousness with special reference to Dennett's theory is discussed in second section. The third section tries to explain consciousness by taking into the account of the subjectivity of consciousness or *qualia*. In the fourth section we discuss the functionalists' notion of qualia by focusing on Shoemaker's interpretation to qualia. The fifth section is about Dennett's notion of *quining* qalia. The sixth section focuses on the rejection of both the Cartesian and the Dennetian theory of consciousness. In the concluding section we talk about the subjectivity of consciousness which cannot be ruled out insofar as the conscious experiences are concerned. The Searlean study of the subjectivity of conscious-experience establishes the ontology of consciousness. The ontology of consciousness plays a vital role in explaining the structure of consciousness. Besides, it also explains how intentionality and language are the intrinsic features of mental life.

I. Searle on the Structure of Consciousness

Searle's endeavour in his theory of biological naturalism is to put back the notion of consciousness in the study of the mental phenomena. Consciousness, according to him, occupies the central position in the discourse of the mental. The centrality of consciousness as a constituting factor of mental life not only defines other co-features but also establishes consciousness itself as an intrinsic life property. The logic of consciousness as an intrinsic feature of life reveals its autonomy. As Wittgenstein rightly remarked, "Consciousness is life itself."[1] That is, it has its own independent function. Consciousness as an autonomous principle defines the mental life of human beings. Consciousness as a principle of life can be explained by itself without considering any physicalist explanation of its origin. Thus, in this sense, consciousness is the metaphysical reality that precedes all modes of our understanding. Therefore, we must focus on the genuine understanding of this phenomenon. As Johnston points out, "To understand the concept of consciousness we do not need to define or to describe it, but to recognize what is involved in saying that someone is conscious; what is important is not a description, but an understanding of the significance of the concept."[2] A concept is understood by seeing the function of the concept in various occasions of its use. So, understanding the notion of consciousness needs to be seen or experienced from various points of view, i.e. both from the *first person point of view* as well as from the *third person point of view*. The first person point of view gives an account of the subjective experience of the phenomena, whereas the third person point of view brings forth the intersubjective realisability of the phenomena. That will perhaps result in establishing the objectivity or the reality of consciousness. Searle's biological naturalism brings out the objectivity of consciousness by relating both the points of view. Before going to discuss the objectivity of consciousness we need to see what are the constituting features involved in the structure of consciousness.

The *structure of consciousness* is basically understood in terms of the three main feature of consciousness: intentionality, phenomenality or qualia , and reflexivity, but the Searlean perspective provides a wider view of the structure. According to Searle, there are a dozen structural properties which constitute the structure of consciousness. They are, finite modalities, unity, intentionality, (aboutness), subjective feelings or *qualia*, connection between consciousness and intentionality, (the Background conditions) The Figure-Ground, Gestalt structure of conscious experience, aspect of familiarity, overflow (imagination), the center and periphery of consciousness, boundary conditions, mood, (conditions of satisfaction) the pleasure/ unpleasure dimension. All these features are correlated with each other and together constitute the structure of consciousness.

Finite modalities of consciousness show human beings' awareness of sense experiences and thought processes. Searle says, "Human consciousness is manifested in strictly limited number of modalities. In addition to the five senses of sight, touch, smell, taste, and hearing and the sixth the 'sense of balance', there are also bodily sensations and the stream of thought."[3] Sense experiences or bodily sensations play a vital role insofar as one's knowledge of feeling pain, listening to music, smelling beautiful fragrance, etc., are concerned. The thought process includes all these and also aspects of imagination, emotions, etc. There is an emotional state when someone is listening to music or creating a new lyric and giving music to it. It results in creating different images in one's mind.

Secondly, consciousness or conscious experiences are always figured in a **unity**. When someone is listening to music, he is aware of all its bits, the pitches on which rhythm is based, the frequencies of the volume, etc. And all these appear to him in an interrelated piece of conscious events. Unity is defined through one's awareness of many things in one's visual or auditory experiences. The unity of consciousness is mainly comprised of two sub units: *horizontal* and *vertical*. Horizontal unity is the organization of conscious experiences through stretches of time. For example, when I am speaking about something or thinking something, in due course I am aware of what I have been stating throughout or what I had started with at the beginning. On the other hand, the conscious experience has a vertical unity when someone is simultaneously aware of the diverse features of conscious states. For example, one can be simultaneously aware of his watching the programme on television and taste of the food, and feeling pain in his leg, etc.[4]

Thirdly, most of our conscious experiences are **intentional**: "For large number of cases, the consciousness is indeed a consciousness of something, and the 'of' in 'consciousness of' is the 'of' of intentionality." [5] Our conscious experiences are always *about* something, i.e. whenever we are conscious we are conscious *of* something. So there is an *aboutness* or *directedness* involved in the form of conscious experiences. And the representation of these conscious experiences reveal the *intentional* feature of the states. For Searle, all our conscious experiences are not intentional in the sense that there may be conscious experiences which are not about anything particular. For instance, one's feeling of sudden joy may not have any cause and thereby the person may not be able to cite the intentional referent of his happiness.

These conscious experiences vary from person to person. There is a **subjective feeling** attached to one's conscious experience. We see varieties of things in the world, but whenever we see them we see them from our *point of view*. That is, each one of us sees the things from a different perspective. Searle writes, "My experiences, unlike the objects of the experiences, are always perspectival. They are always from a point of view. But objects themselves have no point of view. Perspective and point of view are most obvious for vision, but of course they are features of our other sensory experiences as well."[6] Moreover, seeing the things *as something* and associating a subjective feeling with conscious experiences is unique to conscious beings. For example, a gardener, a poet and a botanist may have different perspectives and feelings when they watch the roses in a garden.

There is a **conceptual connection** between consciousness and intentionality. We are not always conscious of all our mental states. Some are therefore called unconscious mental states and some are called conscious mental states. The person's present awareness of his mental states and the other experiences seem to have intentionality. It is also true in the case of unconscious mental states. Searle says, "The claim is this: only a being that could have conscious intentional states could have intentional states at all, and every unconscious intentional state is at least potentially conscious."[7] In other words, both conscious mental states and unconscious mental states are in principle conscious and thereby can be called intentional, because they are potentially conscious. Hence, there is a temporal gap between potency and manifestation. One is aware of some mental states at present. That is the mental states get manifested in conscious-ness whereas the unconscious states only carry the potency to get manifested.

Our conscious experiences always figure against a

background. This is more evident in visual experiences. For example, whenever I see my books, I see them lying on the table. Here table is the background of my seeing books. The same table I find in the background of the wall and the floor on which it is resting. On the other hand, when I see my study room, I find it as a part of our house. Then the house becomes the background for everything there is in the house.

In most of our conscious experiences **familiarity** plays a specific role especially in the case of recognition. Moreover, we are all familiar with our own environmental situations; if not already familiar, we try to become more and more familiar as we get more and more acquainted with it. Familiarity as a feature of consciousness grows or develops by constantly living in same environment. It establishes a close link between a person and his environment or the world. Searle says, "The aspects of familiarity comes in varying degrees; it is a scalar phenomenon. At the top of the familiarity scale are the objects, scenes, people and sights of my ordinary, everyday life. Lower down are strange scenes in which the objects and people are nonetheless easily recognizable and categorizable by me."[8] Familiarity not only helps in recognizing things but it develops a sort of likingness towards the things as well. The likingness is part of constant seeing of things from a particular perspective or point of view. And that comes on the higher or top order categorization of the familiarity conditions. Whereas in the lower down categorization of familiarity the person does not want that things should happen in diverse perspectives.

However, there is an **overflow** of consciousness over certain of our conscious experiences. It signifies a person's emotional bond with the environment and particularly it refers to the imaginary aspects of thoughts. The content of a piece of conscious experience can be extended in the imagination in various ways. For instance, when a poet is writing a poem he is so much impressed by the beauty of the scene that there is an overflow of thoughts which enriches the poem. It shows the emotional linkage or that is, how the person is being affected by seeing the sight or how the person *experiences* the sight.

Sometimes we are conscious of everything that we see in a particular sight. A sight as a *field* of conscious experience has many things in it. Searle says, "Within the field of consciousness, we need to distinguish between those things that are at the center of our attention and those that are at the periphery. We are conscious of a very large number of things that we are not attending to or focusing our attention upon."[9] Our awareness or consciousness of certain things in the field of consciousness is called the **center** of our cons-cious experience. It is because attention is focused on those things. Others things though existing in the same field of experience are not consciously attended to. They can be called the **periphery** of one's experiences.

Human conscious life is bound by a *spatio-temporal-socio-biological location*. Searle calls it the **boundary condition,** which a person unconsciously takes for granted. He remarks, "In the course of reflecting about the present, I have at no point had any thoughts concerning where I am located, what day of the month it is, what time of year it is, how long it is since I had breakfast, what my name and past history are, which country I am a citizen of, and so on. Yet it seems to me, all of these are part of the situatedness, part of the spatio-temporal-socio-biological location of my present conscious states. Any state of consciousness is in that way characteristically located. But the location may itself not be at all the object of consciousness, not even at the periphery."[10] A being consciously participates in various activities. But the location in which he is *participating* and in which his conscious life is situated is obviously taken for granted. He never doubts his biological or social situatedness, and he need not have to assert consciously his *existence*. Existence is a part of *spatio-temporal-socio-biological* history. Rather, he is conscious about what he *does* in the society as a conscious or intelligent being.

We have said that some conscious states are not intentional. Their nonintentionality is not because they don't possess directedness but because they do not have a proper *direction of fit* or any object of directedness. Thus, there is no condition of satisfaction. Direction of fit results in bringing my intention into realization of representation. When someone is making a request or passing an order, if his request or order is effectively carried out then it results in a condition of satisfaction. Thus the content of representation is determined partially by the intentional **mood** of the person. Searle says, "I mentioned earlier that often we have moods that are not themselves intentional, though they are conscious. I can be in an elated mood or a depressed mood, a cheerful mood or a downcast mood, these need not be consciously directed at any intentional condition of satisfaction. A mood, by itself, never constitutes the whole content of a conscious state. Rather the mood provides the tone or colour that characterizes the whole of conscious states or sequence of conscious states."[11] Human beings are always in some mood or other and all need not be intentional because they do not necessarily determine the direction of fit. However, since human conscious life is always found in some mood. Moods are part of our conscious experience.

The intention of human beings' conscious activities has two different dimensions known as **pleasure** and **unpleasure dimension**. Searle states, "Remember that we are considering the whole of conscious states, a slice out of the stream of consciousness big enough to have the unity and coherence I am trying to describe. For such a chunk, it seems to me there is always a dimension of pleasure and unpleasure."[12] Pleasure and unpleasure are the consequential contents of my representational states. These dimensions are the effect of the representation of our conscious activities. Furthermore, there are subdivisions of these two dimensions, which are irritation, happiness, disgust, pain, etc. We often get irritated when our intention is not fulfilled, but if it is effective and fulfilled, we feel happy. Thus the condition of satisfaction is the basic feature of representation of mental states, precisely because it determines the representational intention of the person.

These constitutive features of consciousness not only explain the structure of consciousness but also explain the very function of consciousness. The significance of the function is revealed through two levels of its operation. I would call it internal level and external level. The internal level function of consciousness reveals how there is a conceptual link between conscious and unconscious mental states and their function in the whole network of mental states. This is otherwise known as *conscious thought processing* or thinking. Moreover, the determination of the intentional content of representation shows that there is *unity* of conscious thought processing. These are fully part of the conscious activities of the internal aspects of the mental life. On the other hand, the external aspect shows the conscious activities of being in the world, that is, how a person behaves intelligently in the social framework. Thus, consciousness as *a system feature* gets manifested in conscious activities. Consciousness, however, does not separate these two aspects logically. Rather it establishes the strong link between them. Every conscious activity presupposes thinking. And thoughts are represented in actions.

Consciousness is thus treated as the foundation of the structure of mental life. The notion of consciousness is foundational to the Cartesian philosophy of mind. It is the metaphysical presupposition of the distinction between mind and matter. For Descartes, consciousness is the deep reality and there is nothing beyond. Now the question arises: Does Searle hold the Cartesian notion of consciousness as valid or not? For Searle, consciousness is real and is to be treated as the most fundamental reality. It is presupposed by all dispositions of our mental life. In this sense he is close to Descartes. As Rosenthal points out, "Any attempt to explain consciousness by formulating a necessary and sufficient condition for a mental state to be conscious will thus automatically fail. If consciousness is already built into mentality, any such explanation will be uninformative. If not, then, on the present view, the concept of mind on which our explanation of consciousness is based will unaviodably be radically defective."[13] We are thus aware of the reality of consciousness from the ontological point of view. This is, the awareness is confirmed by reflexivity, or introspection, which is very much a feature of consciousness. Introspection is taken as the means of knowing mental states. In this regard it does not really explain consciousness.

II. Dennett's Sub-personal view of Consciousness : Consciousness Deconstructed

Dennett attempts a conceptual revision in his theory of consciousness. The conceptual revision is needed because the Cartesian or the dualist's notion of consciousness advocates an ontology of 'self', the concept of 'inner life', qualia, etc., which are ultimately part of the ontology of consciousness. This is a purely traditional way of looking at the notion of consciousness which results in 'cognitive illusions' which results from the Cartesian and phenomeno-loigcal description of consciousness. That does not really explain the *mystery* of consciousness. In explaining consciousness, as Dennett says, "we need to answer now not only 'strictly philosophical' conceptual questions of mind, but also still quite abstract questions *that* bridge the gap between the physiological theory and philosophical understanding of the mental concepts."[14] The advancements in the sciences like biology in general and physiology and psychology in particular are directly related to the problems of mental life. And a lot of problems in the philosophical analysis of the mental phenomena can be solved if we can extend our scientific understanding to the philosophical problems of mental life. Otherwise there would be cognitive illusions about consciousness. This is exactly what happens because the Cartesian and phenomenological analyses give less importance to the functional aspects of consciousness. It does not go to the root of the problem but rather revolves round a circular description of consciousness. That is, consciousness has been explained by certain conscious features or properties which are themselves conscious in principle. Hence, the explanation remains incomplete.

Dennett's functional explanation of consciousness includes two approaches; I) the sub-personal view of consciousness (SPL), and, ii) the mutiple-draft-model of consciousness (MDM). Both the approaches are analogous to each other because they adopt the physicalist's methodology and give a functional analysis of consciousness. The *SPL* model explains consciousness and other mental activities through the help of neurological states and processes of the organism whereas the *MDM* advocates how an artificial system behaves intelligently. Moreover, these two models focus on analyzing consciousness from the aspects of perception, problem solving and language use. It is because these are the key features of conscious human beings. A human being not only has the perceptual experiences but also think in terms of language. He is a linguistic being. Language use is a part of human consciousness and is a deep underlying feature of the thought process.

Dennett gives the functional explanation of consciousness, in his *SPL* model as follows: "Functionalist theories are theories of what I have called the sub-personal level. Sub-personal theories proceed by analyzing a person into an organization of subsystems (organs, routines, nerves, faculties, components, even atoms) and attempting to explain the behaviour of the whole person as the outcome of the interaction of these systems. Thus, in the present instance, the shortcoming emerged because the two access notions introduced, computational access simpliciter and computational access of a printout faculty, were defined at the sub-personal level; if introduced in the psychological theory they would characterize relations not between a person and a body, or a person and a state of affairs or a person and anything at all, but rather, at best, relations between parts of person (or other bodies) and other things. So far as I can see, however, every cognitive theory currently defended or envisaged, functionalist or not, is a theory of the sub-personal level."[15] The sub-personal level of explanation of consciousness tries to show not just how the human beings are system of organism but how the system is being constituted and how the various functions involved in different physiological parts of the organism function together. And that functional structure would help us in defining the *capacity* involved in causing consciousness or what we call conscious behaviour. So the *SPL* analysis is more fundamental than analyzing persons as conscious beings. *SPL*, thus, brings out the significance of the neurophysiological functions of the brain. Brain as an organism plays a vital role not only in controlling behaviour but also in experiencing it. Moreover, an explanation of consciousness through the *personal level* of description, i.e., by ascribing consciousness to a person, is Cartesian in its approach. Differentiating the personal level (*PL*) from the sub-personal level (*SPL*) of conscious mental states, Dennett says, the *PL* analysis involves introspection as a method of accessibility to *conscious thought experiences*.

Introspection of one's own experience has only a personal accessibility. One can only talk about what he experiences or what he thinks. In this regard a person's awareness of his thought processes, feelings, experiences etc., has first person objectivity. And the objectivity is a consequence of *introspective certainty*. A description of this sort of conscious experience or consciousness Dennett calls *intentional*. It is because *personal level* description of consciousness does not go beyond the realm of consciousness. Since intentionality is a part of the conscious-thought-experience, such an experience is called intentional. On the other hand, the *SPL* gives an *extensional* description of conscious behaviour. The extensional description in the case of *SPL* would directly refer to the brain processes. As Dennett writes, "on the sub-personal level, it will be the expression of the input into human speeh centre (which receives its inputs from more sources than just perceptual analyzers) and *as such* it is immune from error relative to the outside scene. In fact, of course when we intend our utterances to be immune in this way, when we intend, that is, the others judge them in the light, we frame our expression in the 'I seem' to see 'idiom.' In using this idiom a person is not intentionally expressing the input of his speech centre, for he has no notion of speech centre input at all, most likely; what accounts for the immunity to error is nothing the *person* doesno personal *action*, intentional or otherwise– but what is going on the brain."[16] For example, the expression of pain will have both an intentional and an extensional explanation. The intentional explanation will give the *first person account* of pain and that is the expression of pain behaviour. That is to say, it only reveals the person's own feeling of pain which may qualitatively differ from an other's feeling of pain. The extensional description, on the other hand, shows the neural transmission of pain stimuli, i.e. the function of the c-fibre being activated. It gives an internal description of the functions of *neural networks*.

In this connection, for Dennett, the fundamental aspect of feeling pain is caused by the cerebral structure of the organism. As Dennett observes, "When a person or animal is said to experience pain there is an afferent input which produces an efferent output resulting in certain characteristic modes of behaviour centering on avoidance or withdrawal, a genuine pain behaviour is distinguished from feigned pain behaviour by virtue of the strength of afferent-efferent connections – their capacity to overrule or blockout other brain processes which would produce other motions. That is, the compulsion of genuine pain behaviour has cerebral foundation."[17] The brain has the discriminating capacity to receive the input or afferent stimulus and then process it accordingly for an appropriate efferent. If we emphasize only on a person's personal expression of the pain description we will miss the *real* aspect of feeling pain. Dennett writes, "The lesson has occasionally been misconstrued, however, as the lesson that the personal level of explanation is the only level when the subject matter is human minds and actions. In an important but narrow sense this is true, for as we see in the case of pain, to abandon the personal level is to stop talking about pain. In another important sense it is false, and it is this that which is often missed. The recognition that there are two levels of explanation gives birth to the burden of relating them and this is a task that is not outside the philosophers' province."[18] Dennett does not reject totally the personal level description. But he considers that it would be false if one emphasizes only the intentional description and not the extensional one, as has been done by the Cartesians. Rather, for him, it is the extensional explanation is more fundamental to the explanation of behaviour than the intentional or personal explanation.

The extensional explanation of our behaviour, however, excludes the notion of *conscious-thought-experiences*. This is precisely because there is no consciousness involved in the brain process. We are not *aware of* what really goes on in the neural structure of the brain; whether in the case of visual experiences, of feeling happiness, or of dream experiences. According to Dennett, there is nothing called consciousness involved in these sorts of *experience*. All these experiences are subjected to the physical or extensional description of the brain processes. For instance, dreams are usually understood as *real* conscious experiences. And since dreams can be remembered they must be conscious experiences. They are part of the thought processes, sensations, impressions. They occur somehow in the occurrence of consciousness. The physical explanation of dream experiences can be given by Rapid Eye Movement (REM) and the function of memory. Moreover, there is also a little activity in the visual processing system. Memory, which plays a vital role in dream experience, unconsciously takes impressions from our experiences.

The unconscious awareness is a part of peripheral conscious experience. If we bring the center and periphery distinction, as Searle suggests, we are conscious of the thing which is at the centre of our consciousness whereas we are unconscious of the peripheral objects of consciousness. We unconsciously experience the peripheral details and they are unconsciously stored in the memory. So what is important is the *capacity* to recall the memory in order to reproduce the experiences subsequently. This capacity is a physical feature of the function of the neural processing of the cerebral system. Recollecting data from memory and experiencing it reveals a conceptual relationship between memory and experience. Dennett says, "A 'conceptual relationship' could be established between experiences and memory that avoided the difficulties heretofore encountered in such claim, as follows: The conceptual relationship is *not* between experiencing and subsequent subjective convictions of memory (the latter are not criterial) but between experiencing and something perfectly objective: the laying down thereupon a memory trace - for however short a time and regardless of subsequent success or faliure at recollection. The conceptual relationship would be identity. *Experire est recodare*."[19] This conceptual relationship is not a subjective attitude but an objective fact. And this objectivity can be explained in the physical terms. Dennett rejects the concept of the subjective attitude of dream experiences and thereby dissociates it from the real conscious experiences. This is because any sort of conscious experience will result in a subjective experience. The 'conceptual relationship' rules out the 'cassette theory" of dream experiences, which describes dream experiences as 'spuriously recalled' in our waking state. This process, in short, is defined as the empty process. Moreover, it denies the dream as experience. On the other hand, Dennett's conceptual relationship talks about the successive features of dream experience in particular and of conscious experiences in general. Like any other experiences, dream experiences too possess the necessary conditions of experiences, such as, *familiarity* and *continuity*.[20] Thus, the experiences, according to Dennett, are part of physical processes of the brain and not a part of the consciousness. Moreover, experiences with this physical basis can have not only a *personal accessibility* but also have *public accessibility*.[21] Public accessibility implies that there wouldn't be anything *hidden* or subjective about one's experience. It is the subjective attitude that keeps something specific to the very nature of subject's experience. And that attitude cannot be accessible to any other person. Dennett rejects this view, and says that objectivity about the process of experience is possible through the public accessibility to the extensional explanation, because there is no subjective feature involved in it.

This notion of public accessibility is more transparent in the case of Dennett's Multiple-Draft-Model (*MDM*). The *MDM* suggests similarity between the function of the human mind and those of the computer. The cerebral system as a vital part of the human organism is constituted of different sub-systems. The brain system functions in relation to different sub-systems. So there are multiple drafts which operate within an artificial system. Such an analogy is beneficial because it analyses *consciousness* from the point of view of language processing. This is given importance precisely in the sense that a linguistic or language speaking being is considered not only as a conscious being but also a rational being. Thus robots as information processing systems can also be characterized as intelligent systems. As Dennett puts it, "Of course, we are machines, we're just very, very sophisticated machines made of organic molecules instead of metal and silicon, and we are conscious, so there can be conscious machines–us."[22] The human thought process and language processing in the artificial systems are analogous to each other. The former is considered as a part of conscious activity whereas the latter brings out the notion that language processing is entirely a physical process. In the case of the conscious thought process, we are *aware of* our thoughts, at the same time there is physico-chemical process which goes on in our brain. If such parallel processes exists then brain is considered as a more vital controlling unit of what we call the *conscious-thought-process*. This is because the brain causes such activity. An artificial system shows the parallel processing that simultaneously goes on in the case of *language processing* during the operation of a programme. The simulation of a programme or software is nothing but an electro-magnetic process of the physical system connected with various sub-systems. The system has many sub-systems like, input and output devices, the central processing unit (CPU), the memory, etc. The input device helps in feeding the data into the machine whereas the output device shows the processed result. The CPU controls all the activities of the computer. It is the via media between carrying the input and processing it for the output through the help of memory and other subsystems like data structure, etc. And all the processing goes through the CPU including decoding the instruction as well as encoding the output. The CPU is also related to data structure and memory. Memory has two basic functions: First, it stores the binary codes of sequences of instructions for carrying out the process in the system. Secondly, it stores the binary coded data with which the system is going to work. So in the computer or any artificial system there are different levels of operations that take place within the structures which are analogous to the brain processes. Dennett says, "Representations apparently play roles at many different levels in the operation of the brain. I have already mentioned the possibility of codes representing information about the tension of eye muscles and so forth and these representations do not fall into the class of our beliefs. At another level there is an information we "use" to accomplish depth perception. Psychologists ascribe to us such activities as *analyzing depth cues* and *arriving at conclusions* about distance based on *information we have* about texture gradients, binocular interactions, and so forth. Yet it is nothing conscious that I do in order to perceive depth, and if you ask me what beliefs I have about texture gradients I draw a blank."[23] The neuro-physiological process is a necessary feature of all our activities whether it is the case of visual representations or the case of linguistic representa-tions. Explanation of the pattern of neurophysiological and physico-chemical process in the cerebral structure will help in explaining our experiences and behaviour. And these processes are in principle unconscious because we are not aware of what is going on in the brain.

Moreover, Dennett argues against the notion of consciousness or the unity of consciousness which is taken as the *central gravity* of our conscious thought experiences. Thoughts are not only conscious but are always there in the mental processes. There is a stream of thoughts which constitutes the mind or unity. And the ontology of the unity is named as *self*. A person's self-consciousness or consciousness about his thought process is part of the unity of a stream of thoughts. Dennett rejects such unity of the consciousness or the ontology of consciousness. The conception of 'conscious-thought-experience' is not significant at all. He holds the view that imagination of such a unity of consciousness is not a part of the stream of consciousness, rather it is an activity of the brain processes. On the other hand, the conception of the stream of consciousness is conceived as a mere operation of the brain. According to him, in order to understand what constitutes such a stream of consciousness, we must focus on the *unconscious* aspects of life. It is because consciousness itself would not be able to explain the phenomena completely. Just as solidity can be explained by the phenomena which are not solid, consciousness itself is caused by the brain, which is unconscious. Since the functions of the brain processes are unconscious, the cause of our awareness must be unconscious. As Dennett rightly points out, "your consciousness does not consist in the fact that your brain is inhabited by an inner agent to whom your brain presently displays, so far inability to find such a central agent in that bat's would not jeoparadise its claim to consciousness our claim is about to say what its consciousness was like."[24] So there is nothing like the Cartesian *inner agent* which itself is in principle conscious and all our activities can be explained through that principle of consciousness. And this inner agent or 'little main in the brain' what he calls a *homunculus* is nothing but a designed function of all faculties of brain.

All the sub-systems of the brain are interdependent and each one has certain specific functions So a machine behaves intelligently or a brain produces intelligent behaviour depending on the how system is designed. Dennett gives importance to proper coordination among the functions of the subsystems. And there is no dictatorial power or one "central meaner"[25] to control all the brain activities, rather the activities are functionally different and divided. Moreover, there is a causal process or the coordination involved in bringing out all other successive processes of the brain. And this creates an impression of a unitary power that controls all the internal processes. As he explains, "Instead of such a single stream [there must be central Headquarters] (however wide) there are multiple channels in which specialist circuits try, in parallel pandemoiums, to do their things, creating Multiple Drafts as they go. Most of these fragmentary drafts of "narrative", play short-lived roles in the modulation of current activity some get promoted to further functional roles, in swift succession, by the activity of the virtual machine in the brain. The seriality of these machines (von Neumannesque character) is not a "hardwired" designed feature but rather an upshot of a succession of the coalition of these specialists."[26] Thus there is no centrality at all insofar as the consciousness is concerned. That is, consciousness has no centre to which one can relate all of one's behaviour. On the contrary one can say that the behaviour is being caused by the different subsystems that are working together. Their correlation is a part of their interdependency. The subsystems or the modules are interdependent because their function is determined by their specific capacities. And neither of them is totally independent of all but the function of one succeeds the other in the simultaneous process. To explain the structure or the design of the subsystems is to explain the unperceived processes that go on in the system.

To explain the designed stance of the system is to explain the *myth* of the inner agent or the little man in the brain. The myth is about the conscious mental life. According to Dennett, it is purely a Cartesian myth. But the Cartesian method of explaining the self or consciousness would not help us in finding out the solution to the problems of consciousness. Rather it generates self-deception.[27] Descartes presupposes a conscious self as a *central meaner* in order to explain all conscious activities. What is real, according to the Cartesians, is the consciousness of the self, as it is the ground of all our epistemological enquiry. But this ontology is never fully explained by the Cartesians. Therefore, Dennett emphasizes, "Only a theory that explained conscious events in terms of unconscious events could explain consciousness at all."[28] Unconscious events are events about the brain processes. Once we are able to explain distinctly the function of each of the neurons, synapses and axons along with their physico-chemical processes then the *miracle* of consciousness can be fully exposed. He says, "The illusion that consciousness is the exception, comes about, I suspect, because of a failure to accept this general feature of successful explanation. My explanation of consciousness is far from complete. One might even say that it was just a beginning, but it is a beginning, because it breaks the spell of enchanted circle of ideas that made explaining consciousness seem impossible."[29] Here in Dennett there is no circularity involved in explaining consciousness through consciousness. Rather, for him, the theory is successful by pointing out what consciousness really is, by changing the whole set of the Cartesian tradition. In Cartesian categories there are metaphors like, Cartesian Theatre, Central Meaner, etc., which have no reference. On the other hand, Dennett considers his theory *non*metaphorical in the sense that the approach is both *literal* and *scientific*. It is literal because it has its own metaphors like, software, virtual machine, multiple drafts, etc. The metaphors can be taken from observation and experiment. Dennett writes, "All I have done really, is to replace one family of metaphors and images with another, treading the theater , the witness, the Central Meaner, the Figment, the software , virtual machines, Multiple drafts, a pandemonium of Homunculi. It is just a war of metaphors, you say - but metaphors are the tools of thought. No one can think about consciousness without them, so it is important to equip yourself with the best set of tools available. Look what we have built with our tools. Could you have imagined it without them?"[30] In this connection one can say that Dennett tries to *deconstruct* the Cartesian theory of consciousness both in the light of the discoveries in the brain sciences. That will eliminate certain myths that are present in the Cartesian theory of consciousness. The Cartesian tradition is reflected in the phenomenological method of analyzing the whole concept of conscious mental life which has been unsuccessful in explaining the mental life. Hence Dennett suggests that a crucial aspect of a complete explanation of consciousness must bring out the unconscious neurophysiological processes of the organism. That is, it must be heterophenomenological in its approach. Heterophenomenology explains consciousness from the standpoint of neurophysiology as well as from the angle of interaction with the environment in which the organism has developed.

III. What is it like to be conscious?

Dennett's deconstruction of the theory of consciousness presents a serious puzzle to the reader as regards the appropriate method of studying consciousness. It is because heterophenomenology tries not only to dissociate features of consciousness like intentionality, pehenomenality, etc., from consciousness *per se*, but also explains away the ontology of consciousness as the underlying principle of conscious mental life. So the Dennetian methodology stands in contrast to the Searlean method of analyzing consciousness. The Searlean method may be called *autophenomenological* in the sense that it emphasizes the phenomenological features of consciousness, i.e. intentionality, subjectivity, and phenomenality, as the intrinsic features of consciousness.[31] It considers the ontological basis of consciousness and therefore of the conscious mental life. Its ontology is from the *first person point of view*, whereas the heterophenomenolgical method sees the ontology of mental life (or brain life) from the *third person point of view*. The approach of explaining the phenomenon of consciousness from the third person point of view reveals the real cause of consciousness and thereby it reaches at an *objectivity* or objective analytical viewpoint, of consciousness. The *first person point of view* associates the phenomenon of consciousness with a person. That is to say, the objectivity of consciousness is grounded in the very nature of a *conscious being*. So being conscious has to be understood from the different aspects of the conscious features of conscious beings.

Now one must inquire into the specific features of a conscious being. Consciousness is a *species' specific* feature of living organisms. So the manifestation of consciousness varies from species to species insofar as the living organisms are concerned. But human beings as conscious beings have a specific feature, i.e. have conscious experiences. Thus conscious experiences are a basic part of the human conscious life. As Nagel puts it, "Conscious experience is a widespread phenomena. It occurs at many levels of animal life, though we cannot be sure of its presence in simpler organisms and it is very difficult for us to say in general how to provide evidence of it. No matter how the form may vary, the fact that an organism has conscious experience *at all* means there is something it is like to *be* that organism."[32] The specificity of consciousness in the case of human beings' conscious experience signifies the subjective characteristic of mental states and experiences, i.e., about the subjective feelings as an outcome of our conscious experiences. It is fundamental and highly specific that each human being has a uniqueness of seeing or experiencing things. Hence, it is important to understand the very nature of subjective experiences. This subjective experience is a part of the phenomenal feature of consciousness which is otherwise known as *qualia*.

Are these subjective experiences or qualia real? This question is seriously debated in the contemporary philosophy of the mind. Some admit that qualia or the phenomenality of experience is one of the features of consciousness like intentionality and reflexivity. So it is important to note that qualia cannot be easily explained away. Norton Nelkin advocates the disassociability thesis with regard to these key features of consciousness, i.e., intentionality, phenomenality and reflexivity. According to him, these are the functional properties of consciousness. The dissociation of these functional properties is possible because these features are not always reflected in our consciousness or conscious experiences. As a result, it makes consciousness noncomposite. Whenever, we talk about consciousness, these features appear as the composite features of consciousness. Nelkin writes, "These features can, and often do, occur together compositely in human experience, each of the first two can exist independently of each other and of apperception. Because they frequently co-occur" He further states, "there will be less reason to think that they are co-features of a non composite, invisible state."[33] Phenomenality and intentionality are central to conscious experiences as they are represented propositionally. Propositional representation takes place in language.

Nelkin also rules out any necessary relationship between intentionality and consciousness. For him, the functional interrelationship of intentional or propositional representations is mechanical rather than semantic. Intentionality as an intrinsic feature of propositional awareness exhibits not only the aboutness, but also the semantic interrelationship of our phenomenal awareness. Propositional awareness is related with the reflexivity of consciousness. Thus there is a semantic bond between the states of consciousness and their linguistic expressions. This happens in the case of normal human perceptions. For example, when someone near a *bank* says the bank is good, one can understand the meaning of the term 'bank' which the speaker refers to. But when the word 'river' is uttered to a blind man, he automatically co-relates it with the notion of the 'bank'. There he certainly means the 'river bank', and not the 'bank meant for transaction of money'. Here though the semantic relationship of the two concepts is prominent, the notion of apperceptual awareness is ruled out. The same thing happens in the case of 'creative thinking'. Creative thinking is not an intentional act. A good piece of poetical thought comes to a poet in a flush which cannot be called an intentional act. Because even if one is intentionally or consciously thinking of writing something he may not produce a good poem. That is to say there no rational process involved in it. Rational processes are much in need in reasoning and solving difficult sums, but they are not part of the artistic creation. It is precisely because rational processes takes place outside the realm of apperceptual awareness. This gives the plausible impression that apperception can be dissociated from intentionality. Similarly, in the same case of a blind sight-view, Nelkin dissociates intentionality from phenomenality saying that it has both experimental and theoretical difficulties. For instances, the spell-check in the computer follows the *lexical* method, and its function is a part of the mechanical process of the programme installed in the computer.[34] So it does not have genuine intentionality. Importantly enough, this dissociation has to be realized in order to understand the nature of consciousness. In his words, "Once we realized the possibility of these dissociations, we recognize that many of our beliefs about consciousness are in error. The conclusion drawn is that the all three previous attempts failed to find a complete definition of 'consciousness', because there was no state of 'consciousness' not because consciousness is an empty term, but because there are at least three separable and often even dissociated states, each of which is called 'consciousness'."[35] One must agree with Nelkin that consciousness is not an empty term and also that there cannot be a complete definition of consciousness, because conscious-ness is an *widespread* term. Especially when we take Nagel's notion of consciousness into consideration

The notion of dissociability can be further analyzed with reference to the functionalists' interpretation of the qualia or the subjective conscious experiences. According to the functionalists like Shoemaker and Dennett, qualia is neither associated with intentionality nor with conscious-ness. There can be a complete explanation of qualia without any reference to consciousness or *conscious thought experiences*. Moreover, the functionalists' interpretation goes against the Searlean conception of *intrinsic qualia* i.e., subjectivity or qualia is necessarily related with the consciousness. Furthermore, we would like to focus on functionalists' explanation of qualia in order extend the dissociability thesis.

IV. Shoemaker's Description of Quasi Qualia

We have already discussed Searle's conception of phenomenality of consciousness as one of the intrinsic properties of the conscious mental states. The qualitative feature of consciousness signifies the notion of qualia. Qualitative feature refers to the first person conscious experiences, i.e. subjective attitude of experiencing things as something and also representing them accordingly. For example, my feeling about sunset and sunrise could will be different from the someone else's & feelings of these things. Thus each one has his way of experiencing things. Qualia thereby can be represented from the first person *point of view* and therefore it has only the first person ontology.

Functionalists try to naturalize the qualia advocating that qualia can be scientifically explained. Shoemaker talks about *quasi qualia* and gives a functional description of it. His functional interpretation of qualia is anti-intentionalistic. That is, qualia is not an aspect of intentionality or conscious experiences. It is functional in the sense that the process of such qualitative experiences remains in tact even if the person undergoes some physical operation. Qualia as a *specific property* or properties of conscious experience can be explained not by itself but by its relationship with other functional mental states of similar as well as dissimilar varieties. The realization of these specific properties is possible because of the causal correlation with other qualitative states. Shoemaker points out, "Now functional states are properties which can be said to have physical "realizations". A physical state or property *realizes* a functional state or property in a particular creature if in the workings in that creature, it plays a 'causal role' definitive of that functional state or property, i.e. if it creates causally in the required ways with inputs, outputs and other internal states of the creature. Given the same in which they are functionally definable qualia can we have physical realization, which in principle we could discover by physical investigations."[36]

The physical investigation will reveal how the qualia or quasi qualia states are produced and how they are being related with each other which would further help in determining the specific qualitative property. Furthermore, the process of generating qualitative states includes three successive steps; i.e., qualia before experience, qualia during experience and qualia after experience. The individuation or determination of quale of particular mental states is the power of the object, which is constituted by the disjunctive characteristics of the micro-structural properties of the object. This according to Shoemaker, is the intrinsic power of the object of experience. Further explained, successive experiences constitute a *qualitative space*.[37]

Qualitative space is a structure of phenomenally similar and dissimilar qualitative states. Shoemaker writes, "The phenomenal similarities and differences amongst our experiences reflect the structure of our quality space; the phenomenal similarity of experience is a function of the proximity in our quality space of the stimuli that are normally elicit them. And our quality spaces have the structure they do in part because we evolved to be sensitive to certain similarities in the world, ones that are relevant to our needs. In consequence of this, there is a correlation between certain phenomenal similarities between our experiences and there being certain objective similarities between causes of these experiences."[38] The phenomenal similarity plays a key role in bringing out the relationship between the quality space of the neural structure of the brain and the qualitative properties of the objects. There is no intentionality involved in this relationship. It is because the intentional features of qualitative mental states presuppose the phenomenal features as constituents of intentional mental states. It is possible in the case of a conscious being to assimilate the similarities and differences of qualia that she or he gathers from various stimuli of external environment.

In order to state that qualia are constituents of intentional reference, Shoemaker makes the distinction between two types of similarities. One is *intentional similarity* and another is *phenomenal similarity*. Giving priority to phenomenal similarity, Shoemaker writes, "However, I shall argue that the awareness we have of intentional content of our experiences, of how things look, feel, etc., involves an awareness of qualia. My basic strategy is to argue that my awareness involves an awareness of a kind of similarity between experiences – call it "phenomenal similarity" - which cannot be equiated with "intentional similarity", i.e., with having the same or similar intentional or representational features, of which we are aware of, in virtue of which they stand to one another in relation to phenomenal similarities and differences. These will be qualia."[39] Qualia as the constituents of phenomenal similarity has no relationship with intentionality, precisely because the *accessibility* to the object's qualitative features in particular and an object in general is not determined by the feature of *intentionality*. Rather when an object looks like or is felt like something, then it is the phenomenal features of the object that determine the content of one's accessibility of the object. He says, "If I am aware that my experience is "as of" something red, I am aware of the intentional property of it. But that would not be a quale, for qualia are supposed to be non-intentional features of experiences that somehow underline their intentional features."[40] A person's awareness of an object is determined by the quale of the same object. And the quale of an object of experience determines the intentional content. Since quale is an underlying property of one's object of exper-ience and determines the intentional content of experience, the explanation of quale will also be an explanation of the *intentional content* of it.

In fact, the non-intentional version of qualia reveals the non-intrinsic association of qualia with consciousness. There is nothing called *conscious-qualia-experinece*, according to Shoemaker. The functionality that determines the qualia is completely the function of the neurological processes of the brain. The *quality space* is part of the physical structure of the neural network, and producing such a *space* is a part of the innate capacity of the brain. Since neurological processes are in principle non-intentional, that establishes by definition its non-intentionality. As Shoemaker says, "Likewise, insofar as we are detectors of the phenomenal similarity amongst experiences, we are detectors of phenomenal qualities, the qualia, in virtue of which these hold. Of course, we might, as Smart says, know that experiences are alike without knowing what 'neurological' properties they have in common ; and we might do this even if it is in virtue of sharing these neurological properties that they are alike—even if the qualia in virtue of which they stand in their similarity and difference relationships are identical to neurological properties. But this would be a matter of knowing the similarity relations, without knowing in virtue of properties they hold; it would be a matter of knowing the similarity relations without knowing these properties *under their neurological descriptions*."[41] Since the quality space is identical with the neurophysiolgical structure of the brain, it is the function of the neurophysiology of the brain organism to detect the quale of experience. Moreover, the neurophysiological function of the quality space not only determines the quale of experience but also produces the qualitative representational states, i.e. the quasi-qualia states. That can be symbolically represented as: P_s & P_{ex} $[x = n_1 \vee n_2 \vee n_3] \rightarrow S_1 \rightarrow B_s$ Our innumerable formulations of quasi-qualia states cause a family of belief states. We can call them 'Network' of belief states. Insofar as the quasi-qualia with consciousness are concerned, they are inaccessible to consciousness. Shoemaker argues; "As I see it, the requirement of accessibility to consciousness is not due to a special link between the notion of qualitative character and consciousness, but rather to a general link between the notion of consciousness and the notions of the family of folk-psychological states with which the notion of qualia is intimately bound up. It has become part of received wisdom that much, indeed most, of what goes on in the mind is unconscious. It is not my aim to keep this for obscuring the fact, which until recently was obvious to everyone that there is an important sense of it which is the essence of folk-psychological states inaccessible to consciousness."[42] This clearly shows folk-psychological states, like belief, desires, intention, etc. are *identical* with the neural states which reveals a close general link between them. And this has been advocated mostly by the functional identity theories. Neural states belonging to the functional quasi-qualia states and events not only determine the quale of the experience but also the quale of the emerging states. This whole process of emerging qualitative states and detecting the quale of the brain states (or folk-psychological states) is an unconscious process. So there is no accessibility as such possible.

V. Dennett Qunining the Qualia

Dennett, on the other hand, does not deny the qualia as an experiential property. It is the experiential property which determines the content of experience. However, he nullifies the specific feature of qualia as a property of conscious experience. "Qualia are supposed to be special properties, in some hard to define way. My claim - which can only come into focus as we proceed - is that conscious experience has no properties that are special in any of the ways as qualia have been supposed to be special."[43] Because the qualia have been defined as not only subjective properties but also as ineffable, intrinsic, private, directly or immediately apprehensible to consciousness.[44] This characterization of qualia does not explain what qualia in reality are.

The subjective or first person point of view of experiencing phenomena has nothing to do with subject's way of experiencing them. That is, representation of qualia and their specific relationship with the subject is defined from the stand point of the first person subjectivity. Dennett rejects such an approach and advocates verificationistic standard of measuring qualia. That is, firstly, the representational feature of objecifying qualia has *third person* objectivity and secondly, their neurophysiological structure is commonality as another underlying feature of defining qualitative conscious experiences. This view denies precisely the 'philo-sophical fantasy' about qualia. Rather, as he puts it, "Qualia are not even something about which nothing can be said, 'qualia' is philosopher's term which fosters nothing but confusion and refers in the end to no properties or features at all."[45] Dennett's third person's perspective relates qualia with the neurophysiological functions of the brain. To say that our subjective experiences of colour, beauty, etc., embody *quale* is externalistic rather than internalistic. Dennett says, "For if it is admitted that one's attitudes towards, or reactions to, experiences are in any way degree constitutive of their experiential qualities, so that a change of reactivity amounts to or guarantees a change in the property then those properties, those 'qualitative phenomenal features', cease to intrinsic properties and in fact paradigmatically extrinsic, relational properties."[46] They are externalistic in the sense that the secondary quality experiences are not things in the mind, rather the science of qualia, in the case of colour, actually shows the cause of external lighting reflection as conditions responsibility for generating such experiences. Moreover, these varieties of sensations have an impact on the brains states and processes which in a way helps us in determining different quale in different experiences. The comparative analysis of two shades of one colour may be an example. [47]

Qualia as non-relational intrinsic properties must have objective features. For example, bitterness, redness, etc. An eatable tastes bitter to normal persons because of its objective bitter properties. And the property can be tested and specified. But if we say it is intrinsic and it has different tastes to different normal persons then it sounds ambiguous.

So qualia are not non-relational intrinsic properties. Dennett says, "Why not give up intrinsicality as a second order property altogether, what intrinsicality might be? Until such time the instance that qualia are the intrinsic properties of experience is an empty gesture at best; no one could claim that it provides a clear, coherent, understood prerequisite for the theory."[48]

According to Dennett, man's consciousness itself has been developed in an evolutionary process. In other words, this is acquired for discriminating external conditions which impose on the human organism. Hence, the internal structure of qualia in a particular environment may have only a causal explanation. For instance, in the case of pregnancy, Dennett cites, mere identification of someone who is pregnant does not really explain anything about quale of pregnancy, rather it is an *empty gesture*. "But once we've figured out the requisite mechanical conception [of pregnancy] we can see how conception is the cause of pregnancy, and informativeness is restored. In the same spirit, we might identify qualia, by definition as proximal causes of our enjoyment and suffering (roughly out) "[49]

Whether qualia are private sense experiences can be publicly judged by attaching a perfect neuro-scientific device into human head. And that will certainly provide the causal explanation of the visual experiences which we are calling qualia. Thus this verificationistic approach of Dennett proves that the phenomenon of inverted qualia is nonsense. It is because the mechanism is sufficient to explain how qualitative experiences occur, according to inverted qualia. As he points out, "you would certainly be able to detect that the way things looked to you now was very different and we would even have a proper scientific explanation of why this was: the neuron cluster of visual cortex that "care about" colour, for instance would be getting their simulation from a systematically shifted set of retinal receptors."[50] Hence, according to him, the heterophenomenological study of qualia is necessary because this not only enables us in determining qualia that are ascribed to different functions of brain processes, but also it will help us in making differences between one's prior experiences and present experiences.

Can qualia be named as epiphenomena? To say that 'x' is an epiphenomenon means 'x' exists, but does not have any effect in the world. Being an epiphenomenon x cannot exist on its own, that is, cannot be self-determined. Then how is its assertion possible at all? According to Dennett, qualia as epiphenomena owe their origin to the brain. They are basically the byproducts of our brain processes. Dennett rightly puts, "When a philosopher summarizes that qualia are epiphenomenal properties of brain states this might mean the qualia could turn out to be local variation in the heat generated by neuronal metabolism."[51]

However, Dennett rejects the *first person point view* of qualia as it makes the qualia subjective and private. He suggests, qualia being products of brain states are objective neurological phenomena. There they need to be looked at from the third person point of view. The representations of qualitative experiences can relevantly talked of only among the people who share these experiences. Because whenever one says the object looks red or sugar tastes sweet, these expressions are called qualia among a particular group of people. And the same thing does not make any sense to another who does not share it.

The above argument of Dennett's shows that qualia or the properties of conscious experiences can be explained bythefunctionofneurophysiologicalstatesandprocesses.Their functional description is a part of the heterophenomenological method of analyzing qualia as well as dissociating it from the notion of consciousness. The heterophenomenological approach is more in Dennett's theory of consciousness in general and his negating the qualia in particular. As Johnsen remarks, "The first of these concerns his general method for approaching the matter of consciousness, viz. '*heterophenomenology*'. He describes this method as clear 'neutral method of description' which is responsive to the need to construct the theory of mental events using the data the scientific method permits, which in turn requires that it be constructed from third-person point of view."[52] Since the problem of qualia is part of the general problem of consciousness, one may ask whether if *heterophenomenology* is a method of analyzing consciousness, it will it discard the first person point of view. The first person point of view does not deny that there are brain processes involved in having such subjective conscious experience but it emphasizes that qualia represent the first-person qualitative experiences of the phenomena. Radner focuses on the first person analysis of *heterophenomenology* and writes, "I shall argue that heterophenomenlogy as a study of conscious experiences of other subjects can be done either in a first person or a third person perspective. Both perspectives can have useful roles in scientific study of animal sensation and behaviour."[53] The first person account of heterophenomeno-logy includes two aspects of experience, i.e., *how things appear* (look, sound, smell, etc.) to the subject and *what is the subject's experience is like* or what it is like the subject to have experience. The essential character of both the aspects focuses on the *experience of* something whether the *view* is from third person or first person. It is because, as Radner further puts it, "When concerned with how the world appears to the subject, the heterophenomenologist attempts to give a picture of subject's surroundings from subject's point of view. When the inquiry centers on what it is like for the subject to experience the world the aim is to give a picture of what is going on in the subject's brain from the subject's point of view."[54] In every case of experience the brain processes occur but what remains specific for qualia is the experiential aspect of the subject. That is, the subject is *experiencing* something from his/ her point of view. And their experience is part of their own way of *seeing* things which give a first person account. Radner says, "The approach I am advocating may be called a *phenomenological stance*. One describes how the world appears to the organism if it had sensory experiences (third-person perspective), or how it would appear to me if I had certain features in common with it (first person perspective), in order to explain some aspects of the organism's sensory systems or of its recognitions of objects in its environment. As with the intentional stance the strategy can lead to successful predictions even if the ascriptions are not literally true."[55] It is because the *experience* of both first person perspective as well as the third person perspective can be thoroughly studied from the *phenomenological* perspective. The phenomenological stance of experience will tell us how the experiences are like. Depending upon the nature of experiences one can verify the simultaneous changes that occur in the neural processes of the brain. That is to also to specify in which circumstances the person is having a different experience and representing the experience accordingly. Hence, heterophenomenology has to be part of even the first person study of analyzing various qualitative conscious experiences.

Can we really specify the qualitative property of these experiences? The experiential property of this experience will not be captured by the scientific analysis of qualia. As Jolley and Watkins who try to analyse the ineffable feature of qualia write, "It is not simply that any scientific account of the mind or the brain will necessarily leave something out. Nor is it that we are blind to certain features that other creatures might be capable of seeing. The thought, rather, is that we can never capture propositionally, scientifically or otherwise, the richness or kind of information presented by experience."[56] These ineffable characteristics of qualia are favourable to the friends of qualia. It is because qualia always remain something specific or intrinsic to the very nature of conscious-experience of a person. Accroding to Jolley and

Watkins we should rather analyze the very nature of thought in which qualia are properties. For example, one's experience of seeing different shades of red. Once we point out the differences, we can easily point out the qualitative properties. It is true that by avoiding qualia we are not solving the problem of qualia. One may ask how can we distinguish the uniqueness of an experience from its family of experiences. To analyze this in our thought process one need to talk about the very essence of the experience which makes it different from other experiences. And that differentiating property is called quale of the experience which is embedded in each of our *conscious thought processes*. So to accept the conscious thought experience and simultaneously to discard its essential feature results in contradiction. The following remark of Jolley and Watkins sounds contradictory. Referring to Raffman they write, "The very significant contribution of Raffman's argument is that it provides a way to focus on, and to analyze, that thought. And we believe that once the thought is made clear, it is also clear that it can be resisted. By explaining what she wants explained without appeal to *qualia*, we have earned the right to pass by the qualia problem and meta-*qualia* problem in silence. Experience provides us with the knowledge of the world and contributes to our abilities to cope with that world, but none of this results from gaining phenomenal information. To put it another way: Experience is the best teacher, but it does not teach phenomenology, then what else could? There is just nothing that it is like to be a phenomenologist."[57] This remark sounds contradictory.

Thus precisely qualia are the part of the experience. Since the notion of *experience* occupies a central place in our discussion we must see what is the real nature of experience. That is, we must examine, whether the nature of experience in itself is a conscious thought processes as Searle advocates, or it is in principle an unconscious-thought process, as Dennett consistently argues. It is necessarily the case that experience has phenomenal properties. Therefore qualia have the essential features of phenomenal consciousness.

VI. Searle Against the Cartesian and the Dennetian View of Consciousness: Consciousness Restructured.

Biological naturalism as a theory of consciousness rejects both Cartesianism and functionalism. Consciousness can neither be rejected fully by the neruphysiological explanation of brain functions, nor can it be accepted as a pure spiritual or autonomous principle. Moreover, consciousness does not divide the mental phenomena from the neurophysiological processes of the brain. Rather, it stands as the *connecting principle* between the two realms, i.e. the realms of the mental and the physical.

The problem with Cartesianism lies in the problem of dualism. The Cartesian theory of the mind divides reality into two substances; the mental and the physical. The substances are in principle independent of each other and belong to two different realms. Physical objects are accessible to the laws of physics whereas the mental is beyond the explanation of the physical sciences. Consciousness is the essence of the mental, that is, the underlying principle of all mental phenomena. Consciousness, according to the Cartesians, has a metaphysical reality of its own independently of the physical reality. Against the dualistic world view, Searle writes: "The bankruptcy of the Cartesian tradition, and the absurdity of supposing that there are two kinds of substances or properties in the world, 'mental' and the 'physical' is something threatening to us and has such a sordid history that we are reluctant to concede anything that might smack of Cartesianism. We are reluctant to concede any of the commonsense facts that sound "Cartesian", because it seems that if we accept the facts, we will have to accept whole of Cartesian metaphysics."[58] Consciousness as the metaphysical principle is rejected by both Dennett and Searle. Both Dennett and Searle advocate the neurophysiological description of the mental. As we have discussed in the earlier section, Dennett's *SPL* model tries to explain the consciousness away from the discourse of the mental life. It is the neurophysiological functions which explain mental life. The neurophysiological function of the brain subject to scientific explanation. So there is no question of conscious-ness being something independent or hidden from the scientific explanation of the mental. As a result, the mental states and processes are found to be identical with the neurophysiological states and processes of the brain. Thus the mental is part of the physical reality and can be explained by the laws of the physical sciences. The idea of consciousness having a metaphysical reality is thoroughly rejected.

Searle is neither in favor of the metaphysical analysis of consciousness nor does he advocate reductionism in the way Dennett does. Searle finds Descartes' notion of consciousness as a metaphysical reality suspect. As a naturalists, he finds it difficult to accept the metaphysical notion of consciousness. He finds its objectionable that consciousness is posited beyond the physical or causal processes of the brain. However, he accepts consciousness as a noteworthy given. So, Searle remarks, "Any sort of mentalism that recognizes the obvious facts of our existence is regarded as automatically suspect. At the most extreme some philosophers are reluctant to admit the existence of consciousness, because they fail to see that the mental state of consciousness is just an ordinary biological, that is, physical feature of the brain."[59] The mental phenomena are not only real, but they are caused by the neurophysiological processes of the brain. Unlike Dennett, Searle is not rejecting consciousness. Consciousness, for Searle, is the essential feature of mental life and it emerges out of the brain processes. There cannot be a complete notion of conscious mental life without the neurophysiological functions of the brain. That is to say, brain function is the part of the causation and realization of the mental states.

So there cannot be a notion of consciousness that does not take neurophysiology into account.

Searle criticizes the use of Cartesian vocabulary in explaining the notion of consciousness. Descartes' categorization of reality as *res cogitans* and *res extensa* or mental and physical, is inherited by most of the philosophical theories of mind. Searle says, "The vocabulary is not innocent, because implicit in the vocabulary are a surprising number of theoretical claims that are almost certainly false. The vocabulary includes a series of apparent oppositions: 'physical' versus 'mental', 'body' versus 'mind', 'materialism' versus 'mentalism', 'matter' versus 'spirit'. Implicit in these oppositions is the thesis that the same phenomenon under the same aspects cannot literally satisfy both terms. Sometimes the semantics and even the morphology seems to make these oppositions explicit, as in the apparent opposition between 'materialism' and 'immaterialism'."[60] Thus the Cartesian vocabulary has fostered the illusion of the independence of the mental and the physical. Therefore, Searle says that the Cartesian dualism can be resolved if we can firmly reject the vocabulary of the opposition between mind and body and relate the mental with the physical. He says, "Thus we are supposed to believe that if something is mental, it cannot be physical; that if it is a matter of spirit, that it cannot be matter of matter; if it is immaterial then it cannot be material. But these views seem to me obviously false, given everything we know about neurobiology." (op. cit.) Neurobiology as the science of the living organism brings out the hierarchy in the different strata of brain functions. The cerebral structure of the brain can be divided into different sub-systems. Consciousness or conscious-thought-process belongs to the higher order of the brain functions. Thus the mental is related with the physical. Furthermore, consciousness is not an independent category, for Searle. It is a system feature. Human beings as conscious beings are systems and all the activities of human beings are a part of the functions of the system. Therefore, consciousness is also a system feature. Reformulating Descartes' dictum Searle writes, "Revising Descartes for the moment, we might say not only "I think, therefore I am", and "I am thinking being," but also I am a thinking being, therefore I am a physical being."[61] The thinking being is identical with physical being because thinking is the part of the physical processes of the brain. Brain is a higher order physical organism.

However, as a theory biological naturalism presents a holistic worldview by incorporating physical science as well as the biological sciences, and above all by scientific bringing consciousness into the realm of the scientific knowledge. Here the analysis does not eliminate consciousness, rather it reestablishes it in the natural world order. Consciousness is thus placed in nature. This worldview challenges both Cartesianism and materialism which oppose to each other. Searle says, "One group of philosopher sees itself as defending progress of science against the residual superstitions. The other group sees itself as asserting obvious facts that any moment of introspection will reveal. But both accept the assumption that naïve mentalism and naïve physicalism must be inconsistent. Both accept the assumption that purely physical description of the world could not mention any mental entities."[62] Theoretical rivalaries of this sort will not resolve the issue of dualism or explain the various features of mental life. The solution lies in the clarification of the defining features of mental and physical phenomena, of course, not by excluding one for the other but by relating them. That would be possible if we come out from the traditional framework and think a one word *a new*. That is, as he says, "I believe if we could forget the tradition, then the question as to the place of such states in nature would have an obvious answer. They are physical states certain biochemical systems, viz., brains. But there is nothing reductive or eliminative about this view. Mental states with all thier glorious or tiresome features –

consciousness, intentionality, subjectivity, joy, anguish and the rest - are exactly as we knew they were all along."[63] The Searlean thesis, thus, reestablishes the reality of consciousness and other mental features by rejecting the metaphysics of Cartesianism and physicalism. It is because Cartesianism advocates mentalism whereas the physicalists like Dennett try to build up a new thoery of consciousness for which consciousness is not only insignificant but also *explained away*. Biological naturalism preserves consciousness while explaining it scientifically.

However, Dennett and Searle see the significance of neurophysiology insofar as the explanation of thought process is concerned. But, for Dennett, the thought process is a neurophysio-logical processes of the brain, not a part of consciousness. It is therefore called unconscious-thought-experience. Neural activities are completely physical activities which have nothing to do with consciousness. So all our activities like sensations, feelings, experiences, language processing, decision making, etc. can have neurophysiological explanation. On the other hand, for Searle, these activities are part of consciousness. The emergence of thoughts or mental states is an emergence in which the basic properties of the mental are involved. Thoughts, in that sense, are not only conscious but also they are intentional, aspectual, phenomenal, etc. All our experiences represent these basic properties of consciousness. So experience is in principle conscious whether the experiencer is aware of it or not. When we are seeing something, we are really seeing one aspect of it that is presented to us. So phenomenality and intentionality are a part of the mental representations. For Searle, mental representations are intrinsically intentional. Thus the mental states are the states of consciousness. However, Dennettians, (including Shoemaker) not only play down the importance of *intrinsic* intentionality and phenomenality or qualia of conscious-thought-experience but also as a whole they deny the reality of consciousness. The Dennettian thesis therefore fails to explain his conscious phenomena are possible at all.

The functionalists, especially Dennett, admit the unconscious thought process in a Freudian way. These processes have a neurophysiological basis. These mental states are in principle unconscious. But Searle rejects this hypothesis, though he accepts the legitimacy of the brain functions. He admits an ontology of mental processes. At one level neurological processes cause conscious mental states and at another level the same mental states are being realized by the neural processing. So the emerging conscious states are causally dependent on the neurons, synapses and axons, of the brain. And the changes that occur in neural states and processes bring out a change in the thought process This process, for Searle, is an inevitable process insofar as the causation and realisation of the mental states and processes are concerned. As Searle writes, "There is a sense in which both are unconscious. But there is a big difference between them in that the structural states of my axons couldn't themselves be conscious states, because there is not anything mental about them. I assume for the sake of this argument that myelination of function essentially in the production of my mental states, but even if myelinated axons were themselves objects of expriences, even if I could feel inwardly the state of the myelin sheaths, still the actual structures are not themselves mental states. Not every unconscious feature of my brain that (like mylenation) functions essentially in my mental life is itself a mental feature. So there are two states in me, my belief and axon myelination: both have something to do with my brain, and neither is conscious. But only one is mental, and we need to get clear about what makes it mental and the connection between that feature – whatever it is – and consciousness."[64] Though neural functions of the brain help in causing and realizing the mental states, these states are called mental because they are conscious states. Consciousness plays the role of connecting principle between the function of neural processes and the function of conscious states. The function of mental states refers to both unconscious and conscious mental states. Moreover, the function is nothing but conscious-thought-experience. Thus, consciousness does play an independent role in making the unconscious mental states conscious. If signifies the accessibility of conscious mental states to unconscious mental states. For Searle's words, 'All unconscious states are in principle conscious, accessible to consciousness.'

Furthermore, the mental, for Searle, includes both unconscious and conscious mental states. It is because, one is not always conscious of or about all of his mental states. Searle writes, "Our idea of an unconscious state is that idea of a mental state that just happens then and there to be unconscious; but we still understood it on the model of conscious states, in the sense that we think of it as being just like a conscious state and as one that in some sense could have been conscious. Unconscious mental states are like objects stored in the dark attic of the mind. The objects have their shapes all along even when we can't see them."[65] To say that unconscious mental states have their shapes like the conscious mental states is to say that both have similar structural properties but some of them are conscious at a particular moment and some are not. In other words, the structural features that are embedded in the unconscious states are in the form of latency. As Searle clarifies, "The naïve picture of unconscious states confuses the causal capacity to cause a conscious intentional state with a conscious state itself, that is, it confuses the latency with its manifestation. It is as if we thought the bottle of poisoning on the shelf had to be poisoning something all the time in order really to be poison. To repeat, the ontology of the unconscious is strictly the ontology of a neurophysiology capable of generating the conscious."[66] Though the structural properties of the conscious and unconscious mental states are the same, there is only a difference of forms; form of latency and form of manifestation. Conscious states are manifested in the form of representational or intentional states. That is, mental states are a part of the conscious thought experience. Experiencing thoughts means one is conscious about his mental state or states. To say that one is not thinking at present about something means he is not conscious about that now. Unconscious mental states posses all the features of consciousness but they are not just part of the conscious thought experience. Moreover, they are in principle conscious.

For Searle, neurophysiology is the ontology of both conscious and unconscious mental states. Since neurophysioloigcal processes are the cause of the emergence of consciousness, they are the cause of the unconscious mental states. To quote, "Well, the only fact that could exist while he is completely unconscious are neurophysiological facts. The only things going on in his unconscious brain are sequences of neurophysiological events occuring in neural architectures. At the time, when the states are totally unconscious, there is simply nothing there except neurophysiological states and processes."[67] Dennett also emphasizes the unconscious processes of the neurophysiology. It is the root of all of our conscious and unconscious activities or intentional and non intentional activities. However, Searle's thesis is different from Dennett's. Searle makes the distinction between two different levels insofar as the mental is concerned. One is the ontological level and other is the epistemic level. The ontology of the mental is neuropysiology whereas the conscious thought processing goes on at the epistemic level. Mental states at the epistemic level have aspectuality, intentionality, etc. whereas at the neurophysiological level there is no aspectuality, phenomenality, intentionality, etc. Searle remarks, 'The ontology of unconscious intentionality consists entirely in the third-person objective, neurophysiological phenomena, but all the same the states have an aspectual shape that cannot be constituted by such facts because there is no aspectual shape at the level of neurons and synapses.' Epistemic and ontological levels are interrelated; they are like two aspects of the same coin. Since conscious thought experience belongs to epistemic level, it can be given a first person account. Thoughts having all the structural properties are a part of conscious experience, and that form of experience has only first person objectivity. A person's, beliefs, and intentions are formed according to his/her interaction with the world. There is will be a qualitative difference between the mental states of one person in comparison with others. This qualitative feature of one's mental states is thereby treated as the subjectivity of consciousness. Qualia are a part of the subjective experience. They belong to the epistemic level of analysis.

Searle's ontology of consciousness posits the neurophysiological states of the brain as the basic ingredients which give rise to the mental states. The emergence of the mental states can be symbolically represented as: (Bsw)→n_1+n_2+n_3 [causal sufficiency]→ Rsw. The natural process lacks the aspectual and the phenomenal processes of the mental states. However, a paradox arises when we define these conscious state as unconscious states with all structural features, like intentionality, phenomality, aspectuality, etc. Properties of the mental states, according to functionalists, are physical and can be specified by the functional analysis. Functionalists are committed to this conception of unconscious mental states. They separate or dissociate consciousness deliberately from the brain states so that other features will not have either intrinsic relationship with consciousness or they could be treated as just epiphenomena. According to the functionalists, not only the dispositional capacity of brain processes which is unconscious, but also the conscious mental states are in principle, unconscious. Searle, however, rejects the functionalist claims. The neurophysioloigcal facts are always causally sufficient for any set of mental facts, someone with perfect causal knowledge might able to make the inference from the neurological to the intentional at least in those few cases where there is a law like connection between the facts specified in neural terms and the facts specified in intentional terms. But even in these cases, if there are any, there is still an inference, and the specification of the neurophysiological in neurophysiological terms is not yet specification of the intentional.[68] Thus Searle makes it clear that there is no identity relationship between the neural processing of the brain and conscious thought processing. A conscious thought process is an intentional act. And there is no reduction possible between these two levels of functions. That is precisely because the properties of mental states are different from the properties of the neural states. So there is no inference possible. Searle also writes, "It is harder but still possible to see how they are satisfied for unconscious states if we think of the ontology of the unconscious in the way I have suggested—as an occurrent neurophysiology capable of causing conscious states and events. But how can the nonconscious neurophysiology have apspectual shape and subjectivity right then and there? The neurophysiology does indeed admit of different levels of description, but none of these objective neurophysiolgical levels of description—ranging all the way from micro-anatomy of the synaptic cleft to large molar organs such as the hippocampus—is a level of aspectual shape or subjectivity."[69] Thus the presupposition of the Freudian conception only shows that unconscious-mental states have every other feature like subjectivity and intentionality without consciousness. In this regard, the only difficulty that the Freudian theory faces is that it is unable to relate unconsciousness with consciousness.

VII. Sealean Subjectivity: Towards an Ontology of Consciousness

As we have already discussed, subjectivity or the first

person attitude is an integral part of consciousness in the Searlean scheme. The conscious-thought-experiences have subjective attitudes or feelings. That unfolds qualia as part of the subjective features of consciousness. Therefore, there is only the first person accessibility to subjective states and their qualia. The subjective states unfold how the world is represented to each one of us and how we experience the world. That is, the form of experience is part of the subjective structure of one's mental states.

Subjectivity is not a self-conscious perceptual phenomenon. We cannot perceive our subjectivity in the Cartesian sense. As Searle put it, "there is no way in the model to observe the act of observing itself. The act of observing is subjective (ontological sense) access to objective reality. Though I can easily observe another person, I cannot observe his or her subjectivity."[70] Searle rejects the Cartesian accessibility or introspection as a method of seeing one's own mental states. According to him, conscious experience, for Searle, can only reveal the structural framework in which the subject is interacting with the world. In other words, a conscious being not only acts intentionally in the world but the world also reacts to the subject or there is a typical response from world-to-being. That is, there is an intentional interrelationship from the being-to-the-world and from the world-to-the being. As a result, there is no private world of consciousness because the privacy of the subjective attitudes gets dissolved by his constant interaction with the world. So there is no private ontology for qualia. We do share each other's feelings and thoughts, etc., otherwise it would be difficult for us to know each other. Moreover, Searle denies the Cartesian sense of privacy that Dennett ascribes to the quale of mental state. According to him, Dennett is wrong in calling the qualia private and incommunicable. Qualia are the objective features of the conscious mind. Searle says, "The whole idea of there being a observation of reality is precisely the idea of (ontologically) subjective representation of reality. The ontology of observation is opposed to its epistemology–precisely the ontology of subjectivity."[71] Subjectivity as one of the features of consciousness, thus, has different levels of function. And thus, the ontology of subjectivity is similar to the ontology of consciousness. Because subjectivity as co-feature of conscious-thought experience emerges along with the consciousness or mental state. So it is intrinsic to the consciousness not to the neurophysicological functions of the brain. By showing the intrinsic relationship of qualia with consciousness, Searle discards the notion of naturalizing qualia. It's because that will result in the naturalization of consciousness.

Sturgeon clarifies the epistemic aspect of qulia or the subjective feature of consciousness. According to him, qualia need a conceptually homogenous explanation which will adequately explain qualia in terms of qualia alone – "qualia are conceptually *sui gneris*."[72] Since qualia is ascribed to the experiences of mental life, the explanation of qualia seeks a property explanation. The property explanation of qualia has two dimensions: (I) the causal explanation of constituting properties causing a discriminatory role; (ii) the generative explanation which mainly focuses upon the 'target property' as a specific property must be needed to know 'how it is generated' or non-causally generated from the conscious experiences.[73] Qulia as a *sui generis* feature of conscious experiences disallows the exhaustive explanation of qualia through the causal dispositional capacity of brain processes.

However, Sturgeon does not deny fully the causality involved in explaining qualia. But how far can causality can be entertained in explaining the relationship between qualia and the dispositional states of the brain? This further leads to the basic question: How is the quale of an experience being constituted and applied to conscious experiences. Sturgeon describes this problem with reference to two types of connections namely, *epistemic connection* and *cannonical connection*. The epistemic connection is defined as the constituting liasion for a *concept* as it is, whereas, the cannonical connection is a sort of link between the concept and the mental states. The role of epistemic connection, on the other hand, is to separate mental states from the concept or concepts. [74] For example, concept "Red" is different from 'Q'-Red, because the latter is known through the former. But to talk about 'Q'-Red mental state one must see the cannonical relation between the concept red and the *quality* of seeing object. That typical *quality* or quale of the object may be called the *target property* to be explained by the application of the concept. However, in the case of the epistemic connection one sees the conceptual difference between the concept and the mental states or *belief* states.

Sturgeon's notion of fixing up belief states is different from Shoemaker's conception of fixing up the belief states for determining the properties of qualia. That is, belief states are put in the form of disjunction and they are processed by the causal power of the neural processes to determine the quale of a belief state. Rather, fixing up such belief states, for Scott, "We cannonically apply 'red' [concept] by forming belief states about our environment on the basis of visual experiences. Hence, the manner of belief fixation through which red is cannonically applied is not a visual belief fixation. Rather it is *introspection*."[75] Introspection or reflexivity as one of the features of conscious experience that helps in scrutinizing the differences between the appearance of the things and the reality of correct fixation of belief. Moreover, determining the quale of an experience through the application of concepts is a conscious activity. Thus applying the concepts by following introspection for the analysis of qualia signifies the intentionality that is involved in the process of conscious experience. In this regard, consciousness is always projected as the structural and composite phenomenon with the basic properties like intentionality, pheomenality or qulaia and subjectivity. And these properties cannot be logically dissociated from each other insofar as the conscious-thought-experience is concerned.

Though biological naturalism advocates neurophysiology as the ontology of the mental, still it argues against the functionalists' notion of neurophysiology as ontology. Functionalists like Dennett reject the notion of consciousness as real and as having any ontological status. Dennett reduces the mental phenomena to the function of the brain processes. There is only one ontology so far as the science of the mental phenomena is concerned, and that is neurophysiology. Searle accepts the reality of the mental. He writes, "My own approach to mental states and events has been totally realistic in the sense that I think there really are such things as intrinsic mental phenomena which cannot be reduced to something else or eliminated by some kind of reduction. There are really are pains, tickles and itches, fears, hopes, desires, perceptual experiences, experiences of acting, thoughts, feelings, and all the rest."[76] Neurophysiology constitutes only one aspect of the reality of the mental life because it causes consciousness including various other mental features. We, however, experience the phenomena of mental life because they belong to the realm of consciousness. This is with regard to consciousness as an evolutionary phenomenon having its own *life*. That is, it has its own *structure* and *function*. Neurophysiological aspects and the conscious aspects of the mental life have only a certain functional relationship insofar as *causation* and *realization* of the mental states are concerned. But they are structurally independent of each other having their own respective properties. The properties of the mental states are different from the properties of the neurological process of the brain. The neurophysiological process of the brain is a higher order physical processes. They are both real. Searle writes, "On my account mental states are as real as a biological phenomena, as real as lactation, photosynthesis, mitosis, and digestion. Like these other phenomena, mental states are caused by biological phenomena and in turn cause other biological phenomena."[77] So the reality of the mental is not denied at all, since consciousness is a fundamental property of the mental is real.

Biological naturalism, thus, explains *consciousness* as an evolutionary property of the human organism. Besides, the consciousness in the non-human organism is also an evolutionary property. There is therefore hierarchy in the manifestation of consciousness in various organisms. To quote Searle, "Apparently, it is just a fact of biology that organisms that have consciousness have, in general, much greater powers of discrimination than those that do not. Plant tropisms, for an example, which are light sensitive, are much less capable of making fire discriminations and much less flexible than, for example, the human visual system. The hypothesis I am suggesting then is that one of the evolutionary advantages conferred on us by consciousness is the much greater flexibility, sensitivity, and creativity we derive from being conscious."[78] The life in the case of human beings or *consciousness* in the human beings is a higher order property. Conscious beings are not only sensitive to the environment but also they change their behaviour according to the change in the environment. This change occurs not only in the physical structure of the organism but also in the realm of the mental. It shows a high degree of flexibility on the part of the conscious organism in its adjustment with environment. Besides, creativity is another of the higher order features of human consciousness. Creativity is manifested in language using, emotion sharing, creativity in art and science, etc., which demand definitely a *higher order consciousness* rather than having mere sensitiveness. Human beings are sensitive to their environment not in way, say, the ants are. Human behaviour is more sophisticated than of the behaviour of animals. Hence, there is a hierarchical order in them. And there is hierarchy in the emergence of the manifestation of conscious behaviour. Consciousness is a higher order property. The higher order consciousness has no specific limits. All forms of art, literature and religion manifest different levels of consciousness. This reaffirms Searle's theory of emergence of consciousness.

Notes and References

1. L.Wittgenstein, *Notebooks: 1914-1916*, second edition, (eds.) G.H. von Wright, G.E.M. Anscombe, Basil Blackwell, Oxford, 1979, p. 82.
2. He discusses it extensively in the chapter-7 "Mind, the Brain and the Soul", See Paul Johnston, *Wittgenstein: Rethinking the Inner*, Routledge, Oxford, 1993, p. 209.
3. Searle, *The Rediscovery of the Mind*, p. 128.
4. *Ibid.*, p. 130.
5. *Ibid.*, pp. 130-131.
6. *Ibid.*, p. 131.
7. *Ibid.*, p. 132.
8. *Ibid.*, p. 135.
9. *Ibid.*, p. 138.
10. *Ibid.*, p. 139.
11. *Ibid.*, p. 140.
12. *Ibid.*, p. 141.
13. David Rosenthal, "Two Types of Consciousness," *The Philosophical Studies*, Vol. 49, 1986, p. 330.
14. Daniel C. Dennett, *Content and Consciousness*, Routledge and Kegan Paul, London, 1969, p. 4. (Henceforth CC)
15. Daniel Dennett, "Toward a Cognitive Theory of Consciousness", *Brainstorms*, The MIT Press, Massachusetts, 1986, p. 153. (Henceforth *Brainstorms*)
16. Dennett, *CC*, p. 111.
17. *Ibid.*, p. 94.
18. *Ibid.*, p. 95.
19. *Ibid.*, p. 144.
20. See, *Ibid.*, pp. 144-45.
21. Dennett advocates three different varieties of "accessibility"; I) the personal, ii) the computational and iii) the public. The computational accessibility is about different features of functions of the sub-subsystems; it includes the execution and the operation of the programs. See, Dennett's "Towards the

Cognitive Theory of Consciousness," p. 153, So far as accessibility criterion is concerned, pain as a conscious experience can be explained not by any personal account of expressing pain, but by accessing to the physical processes of the body including the nervous system that are involved in suffering pain. See, his *CC*, p. 94.

22. Dennett, *Consciousness Explained.*, pp. 431-432. (Henceforth, *CE*)
23. Dennett, *Brainstorms*, p. 46.
24. *Ibid., CE*, p. 445.
25. *Ibid.*, p. 288.
26. *Ibid.*, p. 253-54.
27. *Ibid.*, p. 454.
28. *Ibid.*, p. 455.
29. *Ibid.*
30. *Ibid.*
31. Cf. Hetrophenomenological (HP) method of studying consciousness opposes the view of autophenomenology (AP) advocated by Brentano and Husserl. AP advocates the first person perspective of studying consciousness whereas HP proceeds from the third person point of view. See Daisie Radner, "Heterophenomenology: Learning About the Birds and Bees, *Journal of Philosophy*, Vol. XCI, No. 8, August, 1994," The p. 389. (Henceforth *Heterophenomenology*)
32. Thomas Nagel, "What Is It Like To Be A Bat?" *The Philosophical Review*, Vol. 83, 1974, p. 436.
33. Norton Nelkin, *Consciousness and the Origin of Thought*, Cambridge University Press, Cambridge, 1994, p. 417. (Henceforth *COT*) He also talks about it in his paper, "What is Consciousness?" *Philosophy of Science*, Vol. 60, 1993. Cf. See, pp. 430-31.
34. Cf. Nelkin talks about Dixcon experiment and also about the congruent and incongruent causes of concept relationship. In congruent cases the first and third stings of word are related. For instance, the polysemous words: hand, palm, and wrist. See, *COT*, p. 155. He says, "the 'semantic' priming is not really fully semantic, that while based on semantic features, the processing is just merely a kind of lexical assiociative, merely mechanical process, not characteristic by intentionality." See, "What is Consciousness?" p. 424.
35. Nelkin, *COT*, p. 8
36. Sydeny Shoemaker, "Inverted Spectrum", *The Journal of Philosophy*, vol. 79, no.7, July 19992, p. 372.

37. Shoemaker, "Qualities and Qualia: What is in the Mind?" *The Philosophy and Phenomenological Research*, Vol. 50, 1990, pp. 117-121.
38. Shoemaker, "Qualia and Consciousness", *Mind*, Vol. C, no. 4, 1991, pp. 518-519.
39. *Ibid.*,p. 516.
40. *Ibid.*, p. 515.
41. *Ibid.*, p. 517.
42. *Ibid.*, p. 513.
43. Dennett, "Quining Qualia", *Mind and Cognition: A Reader*, ed. William G. Lycan, Basil Balckwell, Cambridge, 1990, p 520. (Henceforth, *QQ*)
44. Cf. *Ibid.*, p. 523.
45. *Ibid.*, p. 524.
46. *Ibid.*, p. 533.
47. See, "Qualia Disqualified," in *CE*, pp. 371-375. Also see, *QQ*, p. 539.
48. Dennett, *QQ*, pp. 539-540.
49. *Ibid.*, p. 386
50. *Ibid.*, p. 391
51. *Ibid.*,p. 405
52. Bredo Johnsen, "Dennett on Qualia and Consciousness: A Critique", *The Canadian Journal of Philosophy*, Vol. 27, No. 1, March 1997, p. 48.
53. See, Daisie Radner, *Heterophenomenolgy*, p. 389.
54. *Ibid.*, pp. 390-391.
55. *Ibid.*, p. 398.
56. Kelley Dean Jolley and Michael Watkins, "What is it like to be a Phenomenologist?" *The Philosophical Quarterly*, Vol. 48, No. 91, April 1998, p. 204.
57. *Ibid.*, p. 209.
58. Searle, *RDM*, p. 13.
59. *Ibid.*
60. *Ibid.*, p. 14.
61. *Ibid.*, p. 15.
62. Searle, "The Place of Intentionality in the Nature" , *Synthese*, Vol. 61, 1984, p. 9.
63. *Ibid.*, p. 10.
64. *Ibid.*, p. 154.
65. Searle clarifies that "This is clearly true, for example, in Freud, whose notions of both what he calls 'preconscious' and 'unconscious' states is built on the rather a simple model of

conscious states (Freud 1949, esp. 19-25) As it is most naïve, our picture is something like this: Unconscious mental states in the mind are like fish in the deep sea. The fish that we cannot see underneath the surface have exactly the same shape they have when they surface. Fish don't lose their shapes by going under water." See, *RDM*, p. 152.

66. *Ibid.*, p. 172.
67. *Ibid.*, p. 159.
68. *Ibid.* p. 158
69. *Ibid.*, p. 169.
70. *Ibid.*, 99.
71. *Ibid.*
72. Scott Sturgeon, "The Epistemic view of Subjectivity", *The Journal of Philosophy*, Vol. XCI, no.5, 1994, p. 225.
73. *Ibid.*, 223
74. *Ibid.*, p. 227
75. *Ibid.*, p. 228
76. Searle, *Intentionality: An Essay in the Philosophy of Mind*, The Cambridge University Press, Cambridge, 1983, p. 262.
77. *Ibid.*, p. 264.
78. Searle, *RDM*, p. 109.

Chapter - III

NATURALIZING INTENTIONALITY

The structure of consciousness would remain incomplete without the analysis of the notion of *intentionality*. Intentionality as a feature of consciousness plays a vital role in *explicating* and *constituting* the structural network of mental states and experiences. Since intentionality is embedded in the very nature of our conscious activity the explication of the structure of consciousness itself presupposes intentionality. Similarly, it constitutes the structure in the sense that phenomenality and subjectivity presuppose intentionality. Moreover, as we have discussed in Chapter II, consciousness is related to the various aspects of life. Intentionality, in fact, unfolds those relationships. That is to show that intentionality as an underlying property of consciousness unfolds the various dimension of consciousness, i.e. the *aboutness* or *directedness* of consciousness of the mind to the world. Above all, it unfolds the relationship of the conscious beings with the world, that is, how the beings are part of the world. Now we must know what is there in the consciousness or the mind which causes this intentionality or directedness? This chapter mainly tries to answer this question by focusing upon the *content* or the essence of intentionality. As Lyons puts it, "Intentionality covers those characteristics of the mental activities on account of which those activities are said both to have a content that contains information about something beyond the content of the activity, and to involve a particular sort of attitude towards that content. Moreover, it is a peculiarity of the mental content that it is necessarily 'perspectival'."[1] The notion of content basically tries to reveal those aspects of intentionality where intentionality not only gets explained but also shows the perspective in which it goes beyond the content, i.e. to the world. Thus, the definition describes the content as the embodiment of directedness. Thus the intentional content is embodied in the directedness of consciousness towards the world.

This chapter is divided into five sections. The first section focuses exclusively on Searle's notion of intentionality and how it is reflected in the notion of perception, action, and causation. The second section is devoted to discussion, of Fodor's notion of intentionality with reference to his notion of semantic evaluation of the content of intentionality. In the third section, the discussion is on Dennett's notion of *as-if* intentionality. The fourth section focuses on the neo-phenomenological interpretation of Searle's concept of intentionality. The concluding section highlights the how Searle naturalizes intentionality by intentionalizing causality.

I. Searle's Theory of Intentionality : A linguistic perspective

Intentionality, according to Searle, is an intrinsic feature of the mental, especially conscious-thought-experience. As Searle defines, "Intentionality is the feature of certain mental states and events that consists in their (in a special sense of these words) being *directed at*, being *about*, being *of* or representing certain other entities and states of affairs."[2] Intentionality is a property[3] of all the mental states and events which represents something about the world. And that representational feature is a part of our conscious activity. Moreover, for Searle, certain not all the mental states are intentional. Some mental states are non-intentional because they don't have specific object of reference. Mental states with specificity of reference can be called genuinely intentional states, like desire, intention, belief, etc. They are intentional because they represent something in the world. Whereas, sudden feeling of joy, or being frightened are not intentional because they are not directed to anything. Those mental states are not proper intentional states. In other words, the representation of mental states must have some object of reference for the *direction of fit*. That discolses the directedness embedded in the mind-to-the world. As Searle puts it, "What is a belief really? is taken to mean: what is a *qua belief*?, then the answer has to be given, at least in part, in terms of the logical properties of the belief: a belief is a propositional content in a certain psychological mode determines mind-to-world direction of fit, and its propositional content determines a set of conditions of satisfaction. Intentional states have to be characterized in Intentional terms if we are not to lose sight of their intrinsic Intentionality."[4] Condition of satisfaction is an outcome of the logical properties of the representation of the intentional states of a person. That means, there is already an intentional act involved in the very process of representation. In other words, the intentional act of an agent is to represent his mental states in such a way that it should be effective to carry our action. Thereby, intentionality is already acting in the process of representation. Moreover, the logical properties of the intentional states consist in the *psychological mode* and *propositional content*. Psychological mode of a person determines his relationship of aboutness, i.e., how his mind or mental states are related with the world, which results in bringing about the mind-to-the world *direction of fit*. Whereas, the propositional content of the intentional states determines the *condition of satisfaction*. Furthermore, the content of an intentional state is not determined by one intentional state alone. Rather, the content of condition of satisfaction is determined by the interrelationship with a group of intentional states. In Searle's words, "Intentional states with a direction of fit have contents which determines their condition of satisfaction. But they do not function in an independent and atomistic fashion, for each intentional state has its content and determines its condition of satisfaction only in relation to numerous other intentional states."[5] These numerous mental states have functional correlation with each other. Their functional relationship is nothing but intentional relationship. It is a part of the conscious activities of the person to represent his mental states. Searle, therefore, says, "We might say that his intention refers to these other Intentional states in the sense that it can only have the condition of satisfaction that it does, and thus can only be the intention that it is, because it is located in the Network of other beliefs and desires. Furthermore in any real life situation, belief and desires are the only part of a larger complex of still other psychological states; there will be subsidiary intentions as well as hopes and fears, anxieties and anticipations, feelings of frustration and satisfaction. Searle points out, "I have been calling this entire holistic Network, simply the 'Network'."[6] It is not just one mental states is related with other and together constitutes the network of intentional or mental states. But the network is just one aspect of the intentional or conscious activities of the person. It is because; a representation of intentional sates involves lot of other conscious features like feelings, anticipations, hope, etc. For example, when someone is lecturing to his students his feeling is expressed in his speech. Unless he cares the students the students may not be attentively listening to him. It is a part of the teaching activity that one tries to know the feelings of students. And, of course, the teacher anticipates that his teaching should be effective, so that the students will do well. In this connection, there are lots of psychological factors involved in the representation of a lecture. In a single representation there are lots of mental factors involved, and that precisely makes the intentional representation complex.

Now the question arises: How is this complex mental activity revealed? The structure of consciousness does not provide complete answer to this question. It only shows the structure of mental states having certain basic properties at the micro level. How do the micro properties or the logical properties of intentional states get unfolded? It is through language. Intentional states are expressed in language. More precisely, the *speech act* expresses the intentional representation of the mental states. There is an isomorphism between the structure of the intentional states and the structure of their linguistic representation. The structural isomorphism shows there is a logical relationship between the two structures. That is, there is continuity between the propositional content and the illocutionary force of the linguistic representation and the representational content and the psychological mode of the intentional states. Searle says, "If I am right in thinking that intentional states consist of representative contents in the various psychological modes, then it is at least misleading, if not simply a mistake, to say that a belief, for example, is a two term relation between believer and a proposition. An analogous mistake would be to say that a statement is a two-term relation between a speaker and a proposition. One should say rather a proposition is not the object of a statement or belief but rather its content."[7] That is to say, the content is the essence of intentional states, is concealed to the conscious thought processes, till it gets manifested in the expression. It is not the content alone, but also the mode of speaking or believing is reflected in the very act of as well as the in the part of content formulation. So there are logically correlated with each other. For Searle, content which is a realized in its manifestation in linguistic representation but content is not identical with it. The content is the intentional property of mental states, which in essence embody *intentionality*.

Mental states are biologically more primitive than the language use. Searle remarks, "By explaining Intentionality in terms of language I do not mean simply that Intentionality is essentially and necessarily, linguistic. On the contrary it seems obvious that infants and many animals that do not in any ordinary sense have a language or perform a speech acts nevertheless have intentional mental states. Language is derived from Intentionality and not conversely. The direction of pedagogy is to explain intentionality in terms of language; the direction of logical analysis to explain in terms of Intentionality."[8] Language is an instrument of thought process and thereby it is also an instrument of expression of thoughts. Since intentionality is essentially correlated with all of our conscious activities the content formulation is also an aspect of consciousness. So intentionality is logically prior, insofar as the representation is concerned. Thus, for Searle, language is secondary to the intentionality or the content of intentional states. As he writes, "The forms of realization of an Intentional state are just as irrelevant to its logical properties as the forms in which a speech act is realized are irrelevant to logical properties. The logical properties of Intentional states arise from their being representations, and the point is that they can like linguistic entities have logical properties in a way stones and trees can have logical properties) because Intentional states unlike linguistic entities and unlike stones and trees, are representation."[9] Searle stresses on the continuity of the content as the logical property of intentional states to its representation. Though the intentional states and expressions are only two different forms where the content of both the forms remain same. Furthermore, one can apply Searle's notion of latency and manifestation of unconscious mental states and conscious mental states to the form of intentional states and their expressions. Insofar as the realization of the content is concerned the form is not important. Rather, the properties of the intentional states are significant because the properties are intrinsically related to consciousness. And consciousness is the basic feature of human beings. All the forms of intentionality including the content formulation are part of the basic features of consciousness. Searle explains these forms of the content of intentionality by explicating the notion of perception, action, and causation.

Insofar as the content of intentionality is concerned, it is vividly reflected in visual form of experience. Perceiver's vision is directed towards the object of perception. According to Searle, the perceiver is not only seeing the object but also experiencing it. Seeing being a part of *conscious experience* is intrinsic to the mind. Searle says, "Both belief and visual experiences are intrinsically intentional phenomena in the minds/ brains of agents; the ascription of these states and events is to be taken entirely, not just as manner of speaking, nor as short hand for a statement describing some more complex set of events and relations going on outside the agents."[10] For him, experience is a conscious activity. And the intentional feature of experience is clearly shown in the case of visual and thought processes. These are the two basic forms of mental representations. As Searle puts it, "There are perceptual experiences; they have intentionality; their intentional content is propositional in form; they have mind-to-world direction of fit; and the properties which are specified by their Intentional content are not in general literally properties of the perceptual experiences."[11] Though experiencing these properties of consciousness is an inner activity but the properties are reflected in the form of propositional representation of mental states and experiences. Propositional representation is a form of *transformation*[12] that takes place from our visual form of experience to the verbal form of representation. And verbal representation unfolds the content of the experience. One single content can be represented in various forms of linguistic or verbal representation. So the transformation mainly focuses on the different descriptions of the experience. Searle writes, "There is an additional syntactical argument for the same conclusion. Just as verbs of desire take the temporal modifiers that requires to postulate an entire *proposition* as the content of the desire, so the verb "see" takes spatial modifiers that under natural interpretation require us to postulate an entire proposition as the content of visual experience."[13] This argument of Searle shows a logical compatibility between the visual experience and its verbal representations. This facilitates the transformation of the visual experience into verbal representations. This logical transformation entails the notion of *causal self-referentiality that* is involved in the very process of experiencing the content.

The causal self-referentiality is involved in the process of transformation. It is because of the structural similarity between the properties of the visual experience and the properties of linguistic representation. The causal self-referentiality is caused by the intentionality of consciousness and reflects on the intentionality or *aboutness*. The referentiality properties reveal the condition of satisfaction. As Searle rightly says, "The verbal representation that I have just given of the visual intentional content is not in any sense a *translation*. It is rather a verbal specification of what the intentional content requires it be to be satisfied. The sense then in which the visual intentional content of self-referential is not that it contains a verbal or other representation of itself: it certainly performs no speech act of reference to itself! Rather, the sense in which visual experience is self referential is simply that figures in its own condition of satisfaction."[14] Linguistic expression is not, thus, identified with the content of the intentional states and experiences. It is because the content posits the notion of *aspectuality* and *phenomenality*. When a person sees thing, he *sees* the thing *as* something or some *aspects* of it. It is always specific to the person's point of view. And that specificity is intrinsic to the conscious experiences which constitutes the content of experience and determine the condition of satisfaction. The expression of content in terms of language reveals the content but it does not represent it completely. The self-referentiality is a part function of content formation and thereby it is part of consciousness and intentionality.

Similarly, the content is also embedded in action. The intentionality in the case of human action is equally posited with its logical properties. The content of action is part of the structural framework of the intentional states and processes. The processes of intentional states or content signifies transition, i.e., a content persists from prior intentional states to the present intentional states. Because, intentional sates cause action, and each action is a consequence of the realization of the intentional states, which is a cause of that action. Searle says, "My intention is satisfied iff my action represented by the content of intention is actually performed."[15] So it shows that the content of an action is revealed the action of the agent and by performing the action the agent experiences it. Experiencing the content of intentional states, as the cause of action is part of conscious experiencing which results condition of satisfaction. However, every action presuppose two things such as *prior intention* and *intention in action*. The prior intention reveals the structural framework of intentional states. Planned action is constituted of many sub-intentional states, which determine the very course of action. And sub-intentional states are put in a sequential order where one follows the other. On the other hand, intention in action is part of realizing the very process of action. As Searle makes the difference, "All intentional states have intention in action but not all intentional action have prior intentions. I can do something intentionally without having formed a prior intention to do it, and I can have a prior intention to do something and yet not act on that intention."[16] Searle emphasis here is on the realization of the content of action. Insofar as the content of action is concerned it is expressed is the very process of intention of action. It is because each action whether intentional on non-intentional will have *intention in action*. That is, a person will have a reason to describe his cause of performing the action. Prior intention of actions changes because the agent doesn't find suitable conditions of representing the intention. As a result, the intention of the agent changes. The change is always context dependent. Moreover, it is the *intention of action* which reveals the real content of action. That is, it involves two things, the intentional component of action which represents intentionality showing how mind is affecting the world; secondly, the condition of satisfaction action performed (includes the bodily movements) by the agent is realized by the agent. Thus, the conceptual connection between them is: [Prior Intention]→*causes* [Intention in action]→*causes* [bodily movement].

Furthermore, Searle considers an action as a unit, represented by prior intention, which includes the experience of acting, and the intention in action. For example, prior intention represents the whole of action along with the conditions of satisfaction but intention-in-action only presents the action without representing it. Representation is part of experiencing the intention.[17] Prior intention and intention in action are causally self-referential even though they look outworldly different. The whole unit of action is the intentional object of prior intention, whereas the bodily movement is the intentional object for intention in action. Intention in action determines only conditions of satisfaction. In this regard there can be only a conceptual difference between prior intention and intention in action. As Searle puts it, "prior intention causes intention in action. But transitivity of intentional causation, the prior intention represents and causes the entire action, but intention in action presents only bodily movement."[18] As we have mentioned earlier, the transitivity of actions refers to a sequential process. That is, intentional states follow up one another in sequential order. Searle remarks, "Where we have a sequence of causal by means of relations the initial term of which is an experience of acting, the Intentional content can include each of the various steps – the intention can be, for example, to break the vase by means of hitting it with a hard object, by means of moving the hard object, by means of moving the hands holding the hard object. But the steps beyond the movement of the hand are all causal steps and the same causation which is part of the content of the experience in manipulation be observed in cases where there is no manipulation."[19] From the frequent observations of the happenings of two different phenomena, i.e., the process of one phenomenon is resulting in producing the another phenomenon. We find that there is the entailment of causal relationship between the two phenomena. Each intentional state is the cause of producing action as an effect. Our observation of one event causing some other event is not just simply observing the sequential order of the events but also experiencing the relation of causality. It is because the causal relationship that follows from experiencing such events is part of the content of one's experience. Thus Searle extends the notion of intentionality to cover the notion of causality.

Experiencing the causal relationship is part of the conscious thought experience. The explanation of causation, according to Searle, undergoes an intentional process, i.e.; intentionality is presupposed in the mind-to-world and world-to-mind relationships. Searle *intentionalizes* the notion of causality. Intentionalization refers to the structural explanation of mental states causing the actions as well as realizing the very notion of intention-in-action, which is the content of action. As we have discussed already intention in action is a part of the conscious process of action. An intentional state causes action is nothing but a feature of mental causation. Experiencing the intentional transitivity of an action is the same as experiencing the causal order of the mental states causing other bodily movements or action. Searle rightly says, "I get direct experience of causation from the fact that part of the Intentional content of my experience of acting is that it causes the bodily movement, i.e., it is satisfied only if bodily movement is caused by it; and I get a direct experience of causation from the fact that part of the Intentional content of my experience of perceiving is caused by the object perceived, i.e., it is satisfied only if it is caused by the presence and features of the object. Now, what counts as the conditions of satisfaction of my Intentional events are indeed determined by intentional events, but that intentional event in fact satisfied is not itself part of the content. Actions and perceptions are in my account are causal and Intentional transactions between the mind and the world, but that the transactions are actually taking place in not up to the mind. And indeed this fact is a consequence of the fact that there is nothing subjective about causation. It is really there."[20] Causation is internalized in the case of action and perception. Experiencing the content of the causal order means experiencing the changes that occur in the phenomena of causation. It also happens that one particular intentional state brings out another mental state or states. This is called as experiencing the mental states and events. In both these the experiencing the phenomenon of change means to capture the content of change occurring in the phenomena of action and perception. And, moreover, experience in both the cases is part of our conscious activity. So experience includes intentionality.

However, causal explanation is usually understood as a relationship of cause and effect. For instance, when a particular billiard ball *A* hits at other billiard ball *B*, it generates movement in B. Here, *A* is the cause of generating such movement in *B*. So there is a causal relationship between the two events; event *A* is causing the movement in event *B* but before *B*'s movement both are in their respective states. If the similar changes occur in a regular basis, i.e. whenever a billiard ball [b^1] hits another billiard ball [b^2] then there will be certainly a movement in the ball, which is hit. This is how we precisely talk about a causal law. Searle, however, makes a distinction between the notion of *causing* and the *causal relations*. For him, causal relations operate within the events, i.e., a *causal force* acting within the very nature of things. In other words, causal force of an entity signifies its potentiality to bring out certain effect. The neurophysiologi-cal processes of the brain have the *causal capacity* to generate conscious mental states. Causal force is embedded in the very nature of object. Another example is that of milk *causing* curd. Milk has the potency of causing curd, which is something different from what milk is not. Thus, the notion of *causing* shows that both are logically independent of each other. It is because, properties of milk or neurological process are different from the properties of curd and conscious mental states respectively. Moreover, at the same time, all the things in the earth are gravitationally attracted to the centre of it. That is to say the gravitational force is operating in every field of existence. The force shows that there is a causal relationship that is operating in the universe. Within the universe there are many things, which are *causing* some other things. For Searle small 'causal relations are holding only between the events, but causal relation exists between things which are not events'.

The notion of intentional causation, as Searle suggests, is a relationship between the cause and effect; effect is not an entailment from the cause. Rather, it is a logical relationship that holds between the interrelationship between the intentional states and the conditions of satisfaction. Searle writes, "The experience of something red, when satisfied, is not literally *red*, but it is literally caused. And the paradoxical aspect of the asymmetry is this: on my account the concept of reality is a causal concept. Part of our notion of the way the world really is, is that its being the way it is causes us to perceive it as being that way. Causes are part of reality and yet the concept of reality is itself a causal concept."[21] As we have discussed earlier phenomenality and aspectuality of the objects of experience are intentional. Intentionality is logically presupposed in the case of all experiences. And so is the notion of causality. The cause of our *seeing* or experiencing the object *as* something is a feature of intentionality. It is because the intentional representation of it results in direction of fit, i.e. the mind-to-the world relationship. However, he also suggests that not all cases of intentional causation involve self-referential intentional content. The intentional causal conditions that he puts forwards are as follows: To quote:

"1. Either (a) *x* is an intentional state or event and *y* is (or a part of) the conditions of satisfaction of x.

2. or, (b) *y* is an Intentional state or event and *x* is (or a part of) the condition of satisfaction of *y*.

3. if (a), the intentional content of *x* is a causally relevant aspect under which it causes *y*, if (b), the intentional content of *y* is causally relevant aspect under which it is caused by *x*."[22]

This notion of causal capacity between *x* and *y* or *y* and *x* shows the referential feature of the causal capacity of the phenomena of causing. Insofar as mental causation is concerned the self-referentiality is the causal capacity of the intentional states. Realisation of intentional states results in condition of satisfaction. So both causing something and realizing it have same locus, i.e. they are intentional features of consciousness. The conception of causal experience and experiencing causality refers to the causal nexus related with content of experience. Searle writes, "The causal nexus is internal to our experience and not to its object. On my account one does not observe the 'necessary connection' between events, rather one event, e.g., my experiences of acting, is a causal intentional presentation the of the other event, or i. e.g., the movement of my arm and the two together make up the composite event, raising my arm."[23] When someone is intending to raise his arm to convey some message to his fellow beings; his intending is a conscious activity and act of raising arm is also a conscious activity of the person. When he conveys the messages by raising his hand, his intention is satisfied.

Thus, according to Searle, intentionality is intrinsic to the structure of mental states and its various forms are revealed in the forms of experiences like perception, action, and causation. For Searle, these forms of experiences are realized because they are the very features of intentionality. So, intentionality plays a double role, at one point it is reflected in the visual experiences, intention-in- action and mental causation. And secondly, realizing the state of intentionality which it results in conditions of satisfaction one understands the notion of intentionality *per se*. In other words, *self-referentiality* is the logical feature of intentionality. Conscious beings' mind is not only directed about the states of affairs of the world, but also the whole of iteration or participation of a being in the world reveals that the world is acting on the mind of conscious beings. Searles theory of intentionality tries to unfold this essential *link* between mind and the world. The link can be called the *connecting principle*. Moreover, intentionality by itself revealing its form becomes an independent feature of the mind. Since intentionality is intrinsic to consciousness, it never becomes independent of consciousness *per se*. Rather, intentionality as such is the basic feature of consciousness. And the form of one has to be reflected in the forms of other. It is precisely because intentionality is one of the intrinsic features of structure of consciousness. So there cannot be intentionality beyond the structure of mental states or consciousness. Moreover, the question arises, 'Can we explain away the notion of intrinsic intentionality?' That is, can we separate intentionality from consciousness? According to the functionalists like Jerry Fodor, and Daniel Dennett, the separation of intentionality from consciousness will not only help in explaining intrinsic intentionality but also prove that there is nothing specific about the very nature of consciousness *per se*. Searle, who advocates such a theory of intrinsic intentionality has been criticised by Fodor and Dennett. Insofar as the intrinsic relationship of intentionality and consciousness is concerned, for Fodor and Dennett, there is no such intrinsicness. It is only an *as if* relationship which appears to be between them.

II. Functionalists Plea for Intentionality : Fodor on the Mental Content

The functionalists' notion of intentionality is defined as the physical property of brain states. It is physical because the mental states are identified with the neurophysiological states or intentionality is called the higher order property of the physical states. And the functional determination of the physical brain states will help also in determining the properties which are involved in those states. Intentionality being the property of mental states could be determined by its functional characteristics. Determining the functional feature of intentionality is to explain its relationship with mental states. Mental states are not intrinsically intentional. Fodor tries to explicate this particular notion of intentionality by bringing out the analogy between the mental thought processing and the language processing of the machine. Thinking or thought process is a rational process. There is always a reason for what we think and do. The structure and process of thought reveal the logical sequence of how thoughts are arranged and one follows the other. This process can be called a rational process. It is analogous to computers' language processing. When a computer tries to solve a problem there is also a process involved in receiving the input data and manipulating it and giving an appropriate output. It thereby follows a rational pattern for analyzing the problems and solving it. For functionalists the rational feature of machines explains the intentional behaviour. In this regard, the intentionality is not a primary feature to be counted so far as the rational ability of men and machines is concerned.

However, Fodor cites three things in his analysis of the content of the mental states: firstly, mental states are semantically available; secondly, mental states have causal powers; thirdly, the implicit generalizations of common sense psychology or belief-desire psychology are largely true. Fodor's notion of semantic evaluation does not involve intentionality in its function. Intentional content becomes the part of the causal properties of the mental states. Causality is the very feature of mental states through which all mental states are anchored with each other. In this regard, our explanation of any behavior whether linguistic or physical is referred to mainly to the belief, desire are intentional states. As Fodor writes, "Beliefs are kinds of things that are true or false; desire and kinds of things get frustrated or fulfilled; hunches are kinds of things that turn out to be right or wrong; so it goes. I will assume that what makes a belief true (/ false) is something about its relation to the non-physical world (and not - e.g.,- something about its relation to other beliefs unless happens to be belief about beliefs) Hence, to say of a belief that is true (false) is to evaluate that belief in terms of relation to the world. I will call such evaluation semantic."[24] Beliefs and desires are the representational states of the mind, i.e., they represent the state of affairs in the world. But their realization is dealt within the mental life. Realization results in condition of satisfaction, of these states. The content of mental states cannot be evaluated by isolating it from other mental states. Evaluation takes place within the network of the mental states.

Fodor's thesis of semantic evaluation differs from the Searlean way of realizing the content of the mental states. Though both Fodor and Searle talk about the role of the network of mental states. It is because Fodor emphasizes the causal power of the mental states through which mental states are related with one another and secondly the content is local to a mental state. It is local in the sense that determining the content of mental states is not to take all the mental states into account, rather it is *fixed* with that particular mental state. The causal power of mental state manifests in the form of behaviour impinging on the environment. Impingement is a matter of participation the world, i.e., one is interacting with the environmental events. As Fodor writes, " Commonsense acknowledges chains of thought is thought as species of complex mental events. A chain of thought presumably a causal chain in which one semantically evaluable mental state gives rise to other; a process that often terminates in the fixation of belief."[25] The process of evaluation of content of mental states shows that the mental states causally connected. That is, one mental state interacts causally with other mental states. This causal interaction explains how the mental states are into being and acquire the content they have.

So the causal power and the causal nexus of the network of mental states is something intrinsic to the brain. Moreover, this causal power reveals that the intentionality or semanticity of the mental content is not intrinsic to the mental states *per se*. As Fodor says, "If the semantics and intentional are real things, properties of things it must be in virtue of their identity with (or may be of their supervenience on ?) properties that are themselves *neither* intentional *nor* semantic. If aboutness is real then it must be really something else."[26] Thus, for Fodor, intentionality is derived from the brain processes themselves which are causally connected. The crux of the problem, therefore is: 'there is no place of intentional categories in physicalistic view of the world; the intentional cannot be naturalized' . There is, thus a *non-semantic* and *non-intentional* way of explaining the very nature of content. And this could be possible through the causal power of each mental state. To describe the brain process through causality is not to eliminate intentionality or *aboutness* of mental states but to naturalize it. Naturalization is nothing but the causal explanation of the mental states. And intentionality has to be causally explained. Since causality is the property of the brain states and processes, the ontology of intentionality is the ontology of the causal power of the neurophysiological states and events of the brain.

Each mental state called token representational state embodies certain causal power along with some information. The causal power of the token representational states is to establish connection with other token representational states. The information that a token state carries is always about something. To identify the content of the information of a representational state is to identify the causal linkage of it. For example, to say that *x* is taller than the *y*, one knows the height of *x* and also knows the height of *y*, which refers to two interrelated token states about *x* and *y* respectively. And to determine the height is to know the content of the representational state, i.e., the meaning of tallness. Moreover, these token representational states can be symbolically represented. Fodor writes, "Here in barest outline, is how the new story is supposed to go: you connect the causal properties of the symbol with semantic properties, via its syntax. A syntax of a symbol is one of its higher order physical properties."[27] Syntax represents the structural features of language. So the syntactic representation of token mental states gives a formal structure in which they causally function. So to put each token state in a causal sequence and transforming each state of experience into mental representation is possible because of mental processes. According to Fodor, "mental processes are causal sequences of transformations of mental representations. It follows that tokenings of attitude must correspond to tokenings of mental representations when they - the attitude tokenings - are episodes in mental processes. If the intentional objects of such a causally efficacious attitude tokenings are not explicitly represented, the RTM is simply false. I repeat for emphasis: If the occurrence of a thought is an episode in a mental process, then RTM is committed to the explicit representation of its content. The motto is therefore, No intentional causation without explicit representation."[28] The explicit representation of a representational state will show how content is specific to the token state. For instance, wining the competition is one's desire. This desire is a collection of many token representational states. To know the content of that wining desire, one must see what are other contents of token representational states, which could result in the form of wining *desire* representational states. In other words, the wining desire as a token representational state can be explicitly distributed in the form of many sub token states. As a result the explicit representations of mental states not only help in the *symbolic* representation of token states but also to locate how the content is localized in each token state.

The specific content of each representational state can be called a token state having *narrow content*. It denotes to particular referent. But it has the causally affecting power, which relates to other mental states. So the specific content is a *locally supervening* feature of that mental state. In other words, content is context dependent. Fodor writes, "Well, to return to causal powers of water - utterances (water - thoughts) of Twin's: It is true that when I say 'water' I get water and when my twin says 'water' he gets xyz. But that is irrelevant to the question about identity of causal powers, because these utterances (/ thoughts) are being imagined to occur in different contexts (mine occurs in a context in which local potable is H_2O, his occurs in a context where local potable is xyz."[29] Thus, I could have been offered *xyz* when someone asks me water if the phenomenon has occurred to me the way it has occurred to my twin's. The content of the mental states of water differs for me and for my twin because both of our representational states have occurred in two different contexts. So the causal power of the mental states is counterfactually conditioned.

Since the content of intentionality is to relate the representational states with the world, it reveals the intentional property that a mental state embodies. Fodor, calls it *relational property*. And the semantic evaluation depends on certain relational properties. The content of a mental state is determined with regard to some of the interrelated mental states but not involving all the mental states as whole. Moreover, we have already talked about the explicit representation of the mental state, which is otherwise known as individuation of mental states. This individuation is a part of the process of semantic evaluation where other mental states are related. But then the question arises: How can we individuate the content of a mental state as distinguished from the contents of other mental states? According to Fodor, the individuation is *nonrelational* and it is *called solipsistic individuation.,* " In particular, though it is a point of definition that solipsistic individuation is nonrelational, there is nothing to stop principles of individuation from being simultaneously relational and individualistic. Individualism does not prohibit the relational individuation of mental states; it is just says that no property of mental states, relational or otherwise, counts taxonomically unless it affect's causal powers."[30] Solipsistic individuation does not deny the notion of evaluating the local content or the narrow content of a mental state with relation some other related mental states. But it only emphasizes the aspects of methodological solipsism that 'psychological states are individuated without respect to their semantic evaluation.' In this regard, what is important for semantic evaluation of content by incorporating the relational and individualistic aspects is the *causal power* of the mental states. Thus, precisely to talk about the content of intentionality is to talk about the affecting feature of the causal power of the mental states.

Furthermore, it is already assumed, by Fodor that mental states are in principle causally efficacious. This causal power of the mental states not only runs the process of evaluating the content or individuating the content but also it explains the very notion of intrinsic intentionality. That is to say, intentionality is causally explainable. Explaining, how the causal powers are part of the mental states, Fodor writes, "Given what causal powers are, preserving the principle constrains the way that we individuate causal sequence. In the case of behavioural consequences of the attitudes, it requires us to individuate them; in the ways what violates the commonsense taxonomies. So be it."[31] The commonsense taxonomy does not follow the causal order or the sequential arrangement of the mental states. Since each mental state can be individuated and causally related; the causal relation helps in explaining the intentional behaviour. Because intentional attitude of behavior is a part of the intentional or what Fodor calls the causal properties of the mental states. Moreover, taxonomizing is a part of the causal efficacy or causal power of the mental states. That is to say, self-taxonomization of the representational states is a part of the causal efficacy of mental states. Therefore, he writes, "Causal explanation is one human preoccupation among many; individualism is your constitutive principle of science, not of relational taxonomy *per se*."[32]

Now it is important to focus on the process of causally efficient mental states for the explanation of rationality. Since, Fodor finds that information processing and thought processing are analogous, it would be therefore interesting to describe how the representational machine states function to explain the intentional behaviour. It is not that mind can only behave intentionally, rather the behaviour of the computer can also be characterized as intentional. Intentionality does not exclusively pertain to the mental, it can be artificial, that is, it can also be ascribed to machine. Fodor writes, "the mind is conceived as an organ whose function is the manipulation of representations and these, in turn, provide the domain of mental processes and the (immediate) object of mental states is what is to see the mind as something like computer."[33] In the case of information processing one must know the manipulation and processes involved in a system's behaviour. Because a system is not just an input receiver and output producer. Besides, the different units of the machine function together in a harmonious way. The function of all the units subsumes different functions of input system, memory, transducer, central control system, etc. According to Fodor, "Computational processes are, by definition, *syntactic*, a device which makes information available to such process is therefore responsible for its all format as well as its quality."[34] Each token mental state can be syntactically represented in the machine. The processing of the representational states is called *encapsulation*. The internal representations are encapsulated through the input system and stored in memory. As he says, "Input systems function to get information into the central processes; especially they mediate between transducer output and central cognitive mechanism by encoding the mental representations which provides the domain for the operation for the latter."[35] Thus the process simultaneously occurs in the different aspects of units in the system and also has mediation among the units during the processing. Moreover, what is more important is to know the processes of internal representations which get transformed into some representational states. This process is carried out without affecting the content of the propositional attitudes. This is quite possible, because the system has a *qua* language which preserves the syntactical and semantical content of the propositional attitude of the representational states. He says, "The system of internal representation constitutes a (computational) language. Qua language, presumably having syntax and semantics; specifying the language involves saying that what properties are in virtue of which its formulate and things in the non-linguistic world. I have no idea what an adequate semantics for a system of internal representation will look like; suffice that, if propositions come in at all, they come in here. In particular, nothing stops us in specifying a semantics for the IRS by saying (*inter alia*) that some of its formulae express propositions. If we can say this then we can make sense of the notion that propositional attitudes are relations to propositions, with internal representations doing the mediating."[36] *Qua language*, thus, helps in transforming the input representational states to its specific output representation. That is, the algorithm as qua language encodes the representation and also decodes the representations. Content of the representation is not lost in the process of encoding and decoding. It is the basic function of the qua language or algorithm for "informational encapsulation of the input system, is the essence of modularity."[37] Fodor's modularity thesis thus states that the mental life is the congregation of different modules. It is a system of modules.

A modular system functions within a specific domain, i.e., the system is 'domain specific'. The domain specificity of a system helps in encapsulating maximum number of representational states to make the database. This is otherwise known as the *fixation of belief.* A chess-playing computer will have the specific data regarding the game of chess which would be different from computers that are used is a banking organization. Because each deals with specific problem, their representational states, which are encapsulated in the computer will be different. Moreover, the programme that is designed by taking all the belief states of a specific domain assists in matching the particular input with proper output. Furthermore, fixing the belief is analogous to perception. The way perception brings out action, the fixation of belief does the similar job in the case of input-output relationship. As Fodor remarks, "on the decision theoretic story, there is something special about the relation between perception and action: perception affects the behaviour in much of the same way the other cognitive processes (e.g. thinking) do, namely, via the fixation of belief."[38] Perception is taken as the necessary case of formulating the data of belief states. Beliefs are considered as knowledge states. One's perceptual states are determined by his belief states.

The decision that is taken up usually through belief (knowledge) data base is the manipulation of the data The nature of decision-making strategy in the case of artificial system lies in the principle of choosing the best possible data for the output. Especially in the case of the chess playing computer, the system makes the best possible move from the fixed or mapped states. It follows the optimal condition for not only making the best possible move but also it desires to defeat the opponent. Thus in its behaviour the system shows its *rationality*. Because, mostly the decisions that are taken in the domain of human psychology are optimal. By choosing the best option one justifies his/ her rationality. In the case of decision-making rationality is ascribed to both to the man and the machine.

Intentionality is explained by Fodor at the level of the thought process or information processing. And it is possible because of the qua language. The function of qua language has to be described in terms of nonintentional and nonsemantical terms. Since qua language is a higher order property of the brain, and the brain is a physical organism, the property of its can also be physical. Like all other physical phenomena the properties of the brain can be accessible to the physical laws and explained by them. Thus precisely content determination has a psychophysical basis. That is to say, though content belongs to the psychological realm, its syntactic characterization in principle pertains to the realm of physics. In other words, content can be fully instantiated nonsemantically, nonintentionally and nonteleologically. As Fodor says, "In fact, they are psychophysically specifiable.

Physchophysics is the science that tells us how the content of the organism's belief box varies with the values of certain physical parameters in the local environment. And it does so in nonintentional, nonsemantical vocabulary: in the vocabulary of wavelengths, candle powers, retinal irradiations and the like."[39] To identify the content of token representational states is to identify also the specific properties of it. For example, I have seen different shades of colour red; there are certain similarities that I found in each shade of red and I too see the certain differences which make them different token red shades. Blood red differs from rose red. And rose red is different from crimson red. But the properties of all red shade can be physically or mechanically determined which need not be based on any psychological explanation. The local content of one class of events can thus be specified after measuring out their commonality or similar properties, which they all possess. Psychophysics generalizes the observed properties of the same class for a reliable connection. Fodor writes, "And psychophysics guarantees a reliable causal covariation between observable properties of the apparatus and the tokenizing of the concepts in the belief box (if psychophysics didn't guarantee this correlation these properties of the apparatus wouldn't count as, observable). And reliably causally covaries with is, I suppose fairly transitive; transitive enough for the purposes at hand."[40] If the properties are not observed then their causal relationship will be at stake. Only the observable properties of the brain states can be causally featured so that their function in the belief box or in the network can be instantiated. And then their interrelationship will be causally determined. Thus, it naturalizes the intentionality, especially the intentional content of representational states by explain-ing it through causality. Causal explanation eliminates totally the subjective content of the seeing and *seeing as,* as person specific conscious feature. Content, thus, can have a mecha-nical explanation and also it can be ascribed to a machine.

III. Dennett : Looking Beyond the Realm of Fodorian Qua Language

Dennett finds Fodor's theory of intentionality is inadequate. The inadequacy results from deficiencies of the causal function of the mental states. Though Fodor propounds non semantical and nonintentional ways of explaining the notion of intentionality still his scheme which advocates the causal power of the mental state does not state further how the mental states are causally efficacious? The qua language is inadequate to explain the causal power of the mental states. The explanation of qua language and mental states must go beyond the syntax of has to be extensional rather than intentional. It is because intentional explanation presupposes the notion of consciousness where intentionality has a specific role. There cannot be any structure of mental states possible without the notion of consciousness. The extensional description provides possible scientific explanation taking both physics and physiology into account. Fodor's notion of qua language not only syntactically describes the content but also justifies the commonsense psychology. Dennett calls it *propositional attitude psychology*. Mental states are informational states and they can be linguistically represented. He rejects the Fodorian realism about the function of mental states, because the prediction of human behaviour is intentionalistic in its approach. And secondly, the intentional explanation of the mental states does not explain 'what the attitudes are'?.[41] This is precisely an anti-realistic stand that Dennett takes up. Moreover, the propositional attitude psychology is inadequate to predict human behaviour. It gives only a stereotypical description of the causal features of behaviour, which fails to recognize the person's intention. It only deals with limited data. Most importantly, it never emphasizes the relevance of neurophysiological aspects of the brain which are vital to the explanation of mental behaviour.[42]

Though Fodor talks about the functional description

of the mental states with reference to the artificial systėms, still it strictly confines to the algorithmic process of cognitive states. Qua language will itself not be to define the intentional feature of the system. The best thing it does is that "It (brain) could be designed to approximate the impossible task; to mimic the behaviour of impossible object (the semantic engine) by capitalizing the close fortuitous moment between structural regularities—of the environment and its own internal states and operations—and semantic types."[43] Brain as biological system is more sensitive to the environment. Its constant interaction tries to incorporate many new changes that occur in the environment and develops its function automatically. Biological developments are, thus, considered as evolutionary development. And so far as the brain function is concerned, Dennett says, "Evolution has designed our brains not only to this but to evolve and follow strategies of self improvement in this activity during their individual lifetimes."[44] Designing stance basically emphasizes the constant modification in the very structural activities, which evolves in the process. This process is an ongoing process where the revision of any single function takes place. This version leads to further development in brain activity. The qua language fails to reflect this activity of the brain. Thus, what is more important for Dennett is the *organizational capacity* of the brain. Mental or cognitive states are real but their function is dependent of the function of the neural network of the brains or the hardware struc-ture of the systems. This is what Dennett calls *instrumen-talism.*

Instrumentalism provides foundation to the belief-desire psychology. Answering to Fodor, in this regard, Dennett differentiates himself from the classical (traditional) instrumentalism and explains belief, desires and other propositional attitudes through various neurophysiological parts, states and processes. Therefore it answers all the 'hard ontological questions'. In this regard, intentionality or intentional stance can be ascribed to a system depending on how a physical system has been construed. What is important is its structural configuration. As he writes, "One can view the intentional stance as a limiting case of design stance: one predicts by taking on just one assumption about the design of the system in question: whatever the design is, it is optimal."[45] Optimal feature is intrinsic to the design stance or to the physical features of the organic system. For example, intentionality is ascribed to the chess playing computer and strategy making computers for their optimal feature. Optimality feature depends on how the systems are designed. The scanning out and choosing the appropriate output from the mapped data structure in the case of the Blue chips or Praram 10000 will certainly be more advanced than the mere data processing system. In the advanced systems many programmes can run simultaneously. That shows the complexity involved in the designing structure of the machine. Dennett writes, "A purely intentional system can be so complex, and yet so organized, that we find it convenient explanatory, pragmatically necessary for prediction, to treat it as if it had beliefs and desires and was rational. The chess-playing computer is just that, a machine for playing chess, which no man or animal is; and hence its 'rationality' is pinched and artificial."[46] Rationality is a feature, for Dennett, is not specifically related to the belief-desire psychological explanation. It is a part of the systemic feature. Since the system itself is artificially developed rationality or optimality features are not specific to the biological species. Hence developing the more and more sophisticated machines will simply explain away the specific features that we ascribe to human beings. Dennett, thus, alters the approach of optimality to explain the intentional feature of system behaviour. As he writes, "Rather we will find whatever mechanistic regularities there are in the functioning of internal systems whose design approaches the optimal (relative to some ends). In seeking knowledge of internal design our most promising tactic is to take out intelligence-loans, endow peripheral and internal events with content, and then look for mechanisms that will function appropriates with such 'messages' so that we can back the loans. This tactic is hardly untried."[47] Once we know the mechanical regularities we can well explicate the very nature of the intentional feature of the system. Intentional features like optimality or rationality result in the mechanical functions of the system as a whole. The events like information processing is a part of the whole activity of the control mechanism of system. For instance, a multi-media computer displays the pictures and at the same time describes them. So, sound and picturizations are the functional features of the system. In the case of information processing the cognitive states also function in the peripheral aspects of the system. Moreover, what Dennett really means is that it is physical mechanisms which control the various functions involved in information processing. Information processing as a linguistic activity cannot be fully described by the algorithm or qua language. Since content determination occupies the vital aspect of information processing, Dennett gives priority of the designing stance as cause of intentional stance.

Intentional stance or intentionality as system feature is ascribed to physical structure of the system. The ontology of content is intrinsic to the physical-structural aspects of the system. According to Dennett, "one can only ascribe content to a neural event, state or structure when it is a link in a demonstrably appropriate chain between the afferent and efferent. The content one ascribes to an event, state or structure is not, then, an extra feature that one discovers in it, a feature along with its other, extensionally characterised features allows me to make predictions. The extensional characterization in terms of physics and physiology should be susceptible to explanation and prediction without any recourse to content, meaning and intentionality."[48] Since intentionality is characterized as the physical property of the contents of the mental states and events are physically determined. This is possible through the help of physics and physiology. It is because neurophysiology deals with the physico-chemical processes of the brain. Once we see how the various functions are taking place at various stages of *thought processing* there would not be any essential feature left to explain. And the explanation can be given fully without taking account the mental states and processes. Intentionality, according to Dennett, needs a causal explanation. It tries to explicate more and more about the micro level structure of neural configurations of the entire cerebral system. And it also explains, how neural network generates the intentional features. But what is emphasized by Dennett, is not the intentionality as such but the capacity of the system to generate it. Moreover, this systemic capacity is not just specific to the human beings but it can be artificially reproduced. Since intentionality is a physical property of the brain organism there is no question of mind as an independent entity. There is no logical gap between the mental and the physical realms. Rather, the physical structure is only reality. Dennett emphasizes extensionality because the hypothesis advocates the causal efficacy of the brain organism and how it reacts to the environment. It lays down the foundation for the causal explanation of intentionality.

However, the extensionality thesis takes the designing stance as the cause of intentional stance. The designing aspect is important in the sense that rational behaviour emerges out of the design stance. Optimality in this stance is related with the rational behaviour. But optimality is a relative concept since it is realized with a system of ends. Since, rationality occupies the central place in the design of intentional system, as Dennett argues that, "if rationality is the mother of intention, we still mean intentional systems from the criteria that give them life, and set them up to their own. Less figuratively, if we are to make use of the concept intentional system in particular instances, as some point we must cease *testing* the assumption of the systems rationality, adopt the intentional stance and grant with further ado that the system is qualified for beliefs and desires."[49] That is to say, whether it is rationality or intentionality what is important is the physical structure of the system under consideration. And it is the source of both rational and intentional behaviour. Rationality comes prior to the ascription of intentionality because by seeing rational behaviour we are ascribing intentional feature to it. The designing aspects of such a rational function include two prerequisites: (I) the environmental impact within which the system or an organism has developed or evolved. And (II) the self-choosing capacity of the system for survival.[50] Dennett talks about artificial systems which can self-generate the capacity by its constant interaction with the environment. In the process of interaction, the system not only chooses to survive but also chooses to act according to certain ends. So the system has to have *self-sensory capacity*. And once we realize the function of these varieties of robots there would not be any difference between the 'biological species' and the 'survival machine'. In both the cases we have something common that is the physical structure; a non-representational and non-intentional capacity that generates certain intentional (physical) properties. As he states, "We are artifacts, in effect, designed over the eons as survival machines for genes' that cannot act swiftly and informedly in their own, our interest as we conceive them and the interest of the genes may well diverge – even though were it not for our genes' interest, we would not exist, their preservation is our original *raison d'être*, even if we can learn to ignore that goal and device our own *summum bonum*, thanks to the intelligence of our genes have installed in us. So our intentionality is derived form of the intelligence our genes have installed in us. So our intentionality is derived form of intentionality of our "selfish" genes! They are Unmeant Meaner, not us!".[51]

Dennett's emphasis here is that to learn about the real cause of our being conscious or to behave intentionally is not because there is something conscious and an intentional entity present in us, but to learn this deeper fact we have to go to the basic structural components of the organism and their functions. And the physical structure is neither itself conscious nor it is in principle intentional. As he remarks, "Presumably Fodor *et al* would be content to let me say this, since after all, the two-bitser is just an artifact. It has no intrinsic, original intentionality, so there is no 'deeper' fact of the matter we might try to uncover. This is just a pragmatic matter of how best to talk, when talking metaphorically and anthropomorphically about the states of the device."[52] The notion of original intentionality or intrinsic intentionality that is ascribed to a system's behaviour is just a metaphorical way of stating a fact. Since an artificial system behaves rationally, we can also ascribe the original intentionality to the system. In the case of robot sharing certain beliefs is an *objective* and *real* intentionality because this notion of intentionality can be stated from the third person's point of view. So there is nothing hidden or *deeper* fact about intentionality *per se* which cannot be scientifically explicated.

IV. Neo-Phenomenological Interpretations of Searle's Intentionality

Searle's theory of the notion of intentionality is naturalistic which opposes the phenomenological interpretation of intentionality. However, as we have already seen, his interpretation is quite different from the functionalist's approach of intentionality. It is also important to note how he differs from the transcendentalists' like Husserl on the concept of intentionality. First, I would briefly discuss Husserl's theory of intentionality and see how the Neo-Husserlians have interpreted Searle's thesis on intentionality.

Husserl, the founder of Transcendental Phenomenology, has developed a theory of intentionality. Intentionality, for Husserl, is the essential property, which reveals the structure of consciousness. It unfolds the various intentional structures of the *cogito*. The structure of consciousness here referred to is that of the "lived experience". Each experience is a conscious experience and is logically connected with other experiences such that totality constitutes a *stream of consciousness*. And, the conscious experiences are called *logical acts* which include thinking, knowing, etc,. Though intentionality is placed within the circle of consciousness yet Husserl characterizes it as non-psychological and *transcendental*. And his phenomenological approach to intentionality includes various dimensions, such as epistemological, methodological and ontological.[53] But, insofar as the "lived experiences" are concerned, as Hopkins puts it, "Husserl's essential investigations of lived experiences of categories find that they always manifest specific objective significance of thought, know and grammatically expressed, an intentional 'directedness toward'."[54] This logical acts of *lived experiences* contain two modes of intentionality, i.e. the *actionable* and *non-actionable* mode of exhibiting directedness. At the actionable mode the consciousness is simply directed towards the object or objects, like in the case of perception, whereas at the non-actionable level it is *reflexive* in its feature and at the same time encompasses the background field of intentional objects. And this further clarifies the ontological basis of intentionality.

In the Husserlian framework, however, the intentionality in the case of transcendental reduction is more important, because it exhibits the *structure of consciousness* where Husserl considers the possibility of transcendental consciousness without its relation to the external, natural objects. As Husserl rightly points out, " it is completely empty of essential components, it has absolutely no explicable content, and it is in itself indescribable: pure ego and nothing further."[55] Bringing forth a theory of intentionality within the transcendental schema, Husserl tried to provide a proper interpretation to intentionality as such. Husserl discarded the usual understanding of the notion of intentionality. As Hopkins further elaborates, "Husserl's intentionality is not a 'concept' in the usual philosophical sense. This is to say, for Husserl the term 'intentionality' does not designate a general concept that is universally applicable to either experience or meaning of experience as such. But rather, the meaning of the term intentionality is 'phenomenological' in the decisive sense of its referring to essential structures of various domains of methodologically uncovered lived experience Husserl's account of intentionality has as its prerequisite *both* reflections that are critical (in the phenomenological sense) and the various pregiven domains of experience, (*Efahrung*) that are subsequently pheno-menally uncovered by these reflections."[56] In other words, intentionality must not simply be understood as directedness, i.e., consciousness is directed towards the world. But intentionality also signifies the reflexivity of consciousness, i.e. consciousness of consciousness. Thus, intentionality objectifies the *conscious-thought-experience*.

The objectivity of *conscious-thought-experience* or the structure of consciousness is guaranteed by the *content* theory of intentionality. This content of intentionality explicates the logical structure of consciousness or *lived experience*. Content Theory of Intentionality or *CTI* is different from Object Approach of Intentionality or *OAI*. In the case of *OAI* the notion of intentionality is defined as having causal efficacy. And causality is part of the physical law through which intentionality can be explained. CTI thus talks about the primacy of content as the mediating and objectifying notion which makes *act* intentional. That is, it is the content which confers intentionality. And it is the content that determines the object. But now the question arises: How is the content located in the act itself? As we have already pointed out, are two dimension of intentionality: at one level intentionality is embedded in consciousness in reaching at the object. And at another level intentionality helps in determining the object through the application of content.[57]

This intrinsic feature of content of intentionality seems to be quite difficult to make out. It is because the content of the act is not based on the empirical or natural principle. But what is important here is to note that Husserl's conception of the very idea of *content of consciousness* and *relation of intending* are *sui generis*. As MacIntyre and Smith put it, "At any rate, our present point is simply this: since contents have intrinsically pointing character, an act will be intentional—directed toward something—just in virtue of having content, whether a corresponding object exists or not."[58]

Describing the act content relationship further, Husserl introduces two important concepts; *Noesis* and *Noema*. They are interdependent on each other. The act of *noesis* logically implies the object or *noema*. They are the inseparable constituents of the structure of *lived experience*. The phenomenological understanding of *noema* and *noesis* is given not through the ordinary sense-object perception, but by the *act of experiencing* the object in the perception. Here the act of perception is different from the object of perception. The former refers to the reflexive conscious experience whereas the latter is merely the intentional object of experience. The reflexive mode of conscious experiences presupposes the existence of *noema*. *Noema* and *noesis* are two aspects of the phenomenal content of experience. *Noesis* is the *act of intending* the object, and so the object is presented in the act. *Noema* is usually conceived through the way the *object is presented*. And it also includes the comprehensive notion of several ways of presentations of the same object to the agent. They write, " each noema includes an ideal correlate of the generic 'way' in which the subject is conscious in an act."[59] It is because the agent's experience of the object varies from context to context: the relationship is the way the agent becomes aware of the objects. The fundamental component of *noema* is the logical essence of the object presented in the consciousness. In short, the constituting component of *noema* is the logical essence. It is twofold in character: at one point it refers to the particularity of the referent, since every representation has distinctive *noematic* content. And, at another point, it includes the generality of qualities expressed in general terms, because generality refers to the commonly shared features.

The ontology of intentionality reveals the transcendental structure of consciousness.That is pure consciousness or transcendental consciousness as the background ontological support for the whole description of intentionality. The transcendental feature of consciousness in phenomenology has to be understood not only through the method of *bracketing* or suspending the belief, which is an intentional act. But the notion of intentionality remains an intrinsic co-feature of consciousness in the case of *epoche* as well as in the realm of transcendental consciousness. The objectivity of transcendental consciousness is guaranteed by the notion of intersubjectivity.

Searle's content theory of intentionality has received two divergent interpretations from the contemporary phenomenalogists; Ronald McIntyre and J.N. Mohanty. McIntyre evaluates Searle's theory as having 'close affinity' to Husserl's transcendental theory of intentionality, whereas, Mohanty claims that Searle advocates an *existential* or causal account of intentionality. According to McIntyre, Searle takes intentional content as the central notion of his theory of consciousness.

Since the *Intentionality* (1983), Searle's exclusive focus is on the *logical properties* of intentionality rather then its ontological structure, though he specifically discusses the notion of the Background. As representationality is treated as one of the *internal property* of intentional states, and the representation of such a states of mind gets satisfied if and only if its representation *fits* into to the states of affairs in the world. McIntyre questions the very function of intentional content, because it is the content which relates the mind with states of affairs, and also determines the *causal-self-referentiality*. And it is also true that *content* needs to be presupposed always, "to explicate the intentionality of mental states [then, that is] to describe its content not its object."[60]

As we have already discussed that the content of *causal-self-referentiality* implies the transitivity of intentional causation relating the intentional states with the condition of satisfaction. But this transitivity does not unfold really the causality *per se*, according to McIntyre. He also says, "Searle seeks to elucidate Intentionality only in terms of what is intrinsic to mental states. What counts for Intentionality for Searle, is not really causality *per se* but causality as *represented* in the condition of satisfaction of certain kind of mental states, by virtue of special feature of their Intentional contents."[61] What follows consequently is the necessity of describing the notion of content itself. And, that precisely gets unfolded in the discourse of meaning. 'Searle's analysis enlarges the traditional notion of meaning of content with demonstrative elements and replaces my externalist treatment of demonstrative content with an internalist one'.

Relating Searle's internalistic approach of content theory of meaning to the Background condition, McIntyre claims that the Searlean Background is close to the Husserlian thought. McIntyre mainly emphasizes the linguistic background of human beings where the whole gamut of linguistic activities plays a significant role. The semantic activities and the mind-world relationship are significant in the sense that it is only through the linguistic component of intentionality, that intentionality gets reflected in the representation and participation of being in the world. As McIntyre puts it, "That Intentionality requires a Background in Searle's sense does not mean that Intentionality can (logically) take place only in creatures with physical bodies, nor does it mean that Intentional relations involve, even in part, the body's physical relations to its environment. That I have certain set of Intentional states and that I, have a Background do not logically require that I be in fact in certain relations with the world around me."[62] McIntyre stresses upon the Being's relationship with the world. For him, Searle's linguistic background cannot be similar to the Hedeggerian conception of being-in-the-world. Rather, Searle is Husserlian in his approach.

Mohanty's interpretation of Searle's concept of Intentionality is different from McIntyre's interpretation. According to Mohanty, the theory of intentionality has to incorporate some sort of *transcendentalism* in order to be free from naturalism. The naturalistic intentionality emphasized by Searle is inadequate. It fails to account for how intentional phenomena are possible. Therefore, Mohanty advocates a theory called "transcendental constitutive intentionality" incorporating both the phenomenological and the empirical and historical components.[63] This precisely unfolds the relationship of content with the subject. Thus, ontologically speaking, for Mohanty, intentional content being the source of our various intentional experiences presupposes a transcendental ground. He also argues for the autonomy of content. The content has to be autonomous in the sense that it cannot be causally conditioned. It must be logical and transcendental. It cannot be collapsed into a propositional or linguistic content, either.

Insofar as the content theory of meaning is concerned, Mohanty tries to show how meaning is rooted in the unalterable facticity of worldly experiences. This historisist worldview of Mohanty does not disown transcendentalism altogether, but brings about a harmony between historicism and transcendentalism. They are not two different domains rather they belong to one[64]. As he puts it, " transcendental consciousness and empirical consciousness are distinct and different; the latter one is individualized, the former is a pure *eidos* with no individuating traits within itself. *However,* such a conception does not accord with the empiricist motif of Husserlian thought, with its thesis of "wonderful parallelism" between the empirical and transcendental, and the claim that with *epoche* nothing is lost but everything reappears with a "change of signature."[65]

The notion of 'intentional content', for Mohanty, plays a significant role in the semantic framework of phenomenology. Mohanty emphasizes the phenomenological perspective of the content which embeds the content in the act of consciousness. At the same time, he rules out the causal or naturalistic account of the content theory. Because the naturalistic perspective of intentional content does not explain how content is possible. As Mohanty explains," when I am thinking of an object *O*, I am not thinking of the content of my intentional act, but I am thinking of *O*, an intentional content *C* is involved."[66] Furthermore, for the knowablity of intentional content, Mohanty suggests two important points: I) it can be expressed in language, but the very notion of awareness of intentional content with relation to subject is *non-propositional*. Thus the relationship of the intentional content to its subject is *subjective*. II) "The principle of phenomenological accessibility." It signifies the aspectuality of the object represented to the subject.

The logical structure of intentional content, according to Mohanty, has threefold composition; they are, *physical, psychological, and social.*[67] The naturalistic perspective also includes all the three aspects. But interestingly, the stress upon the each aspect varies according to the intensity of the dominance of *causal laws*. The "constitutive theory of intentionality" gives comparatively less importance to the first two aspects. But social aspect relating to its expression in language is given prominence. As Mohanty writes, " For the present, the point to insist upon is that while a subject's way of thinking (perceiving and acting) may have been socially determined, i.e. the social context provides a clue to understanding *why* a subject's intentional content is what it is, it, no more than the physical context, does not enable us to ascertain *what* content is."[68] Then the question arises how has the content to be comprehended? Answering to this question, Mohanty stresses upon the ontology of intentional content. However, there is only an indirect route to the ontology. He says, "A study of consciousness and its intentional content provides no direct route to ontology. However, since any ascription of features must be via an intentional content, no ontology can overstep the limits of a theory of intentional contents."[69] Besides, as we have already pointed out, the content finds its locus within the *expression* or representation itself, it is not simply identified with the *meaning of the expression*. On the other hand, Mohanty gives unique characterization of the intentional content, which differs from the Fregean and Husserlian notion of *sense* and *noema* respectively. That Fregean sense—be they linguistic meanings or not—are intentional content of certain sort, contents of certain mode of consciousness that may be called "understanding" of linguistic expression.

The phenomenological notion of *understanding* of the very nature of intentional content is not significantly different from the usual linguistic conception of understanding. Understanding brings out a unique experience, which embodies a sort of causal transitivity of the experiencing of things and the content of it. However, the strict phenomenological notion of experience involves both Kantian notions of *passivity* and *activity* in its discourse. Mohanty remarks, "experiencing is characterized by passivity and receptivity, a felt causality belongs to the very content of the experiencing; the bang of noise is heard as impinging on one's auditory sensibility."[70] Phenomenological notion of intentionality, thus, strongly emphasizes the intrinsic relationship of the consciousness with intentionality. In other words, consciousness is in principle intentional. It is not only reflected in the various forms of conscious activities is realized in the process of experience itself. In this regard, to talk about the consciousness is to talk about the experiencing subject. The phenomenological subject is a conscious being *acting* in the world. The beings' conscious participation in the world is due the fact that intentionality is the basic feature of consciousness. So being intentional and being consciousness are one and the same.

V. Intentionality Naturalized: Searle towards the onto-logy of Intentionality

So far we have discussed two divergent models of theorization of intentionality. Intentionality as explained by the functionalists like Fodor and Dennett can be completely naturalized. Intentionality, like any other physical phenomenon, is explained within the physicalistic framework. It is the physical property of the neuro-physiological functions of brains which can be causally explained. Strictly speaking, according to functionalists, intentionality is of the brain but not of the consciousness. The explanation of brain-features explains away consciousness. On the other hand, phenomenological theory of intentionality is completely *non-causal*. In this framework, intentionality is an intrinsic feature of consciousness. The explanation of intentionality as an essential feature of consciousness is a non-causal one. It is not a physical phenomenon. It has then to be accorded an autonomous status. In this regard, one can say that the phenomenological interpretation of intentionality is the thesis and the functionalist's view of intentionality is the antithesis. In this sense, Searle's theory of intentionality can be taken as an intermediate position. Searle neither strictly follows the causal explanation of intentionality nor does he accept completely the transcendental theory of intentionality. Rather he tries to *naturalize* intentionality and *intentionalize* causality. Intentionality, according to him, can be explained without giving primacy to the brain functions. It is important to note that for Searle, intentionality is a property of consciousness. Thus it is embedded in the conscious thought process or intentional states.

We have already discussed Searle's *intentionalization of causality*. But we have still to discuss the naturalization of intentionality in the Searlean scheme and to relate it with the notion of intentional causation. By naturalization of intentionality Searle means, in general, that intentionality has to be placed within the realm of *nature* as a whole. It is therefore made intrinsic to consciousness which itself is a part of nature. So there is no question of separating intentionality from consciousness. Fodor and Dennett try to eliminate intentionality *per se* by evaluating the content through *qua* language and identifying the content with neural states and events, respectively. The common thesis that they pursue is that intentionality is a physical property and that it can be ascribed to an artificial system. It is precisely because the artificial systems behave rationally that accounts for explaining the optimal and intentional features a system holds. Searle answers two things in his theory of intentionality. First, insofar as the ontology of intentionality as a mental feature is concerned behaviour is the necessary and sufficient condition of its existence. Second, to say that a computer is behaving intelligently is not to assert that it has the mental states like the human beings. Mere behaviour is not enough; the system must be originally connected with behaviour. He write, "It is only because connection between behaviour and the causal structure of other organisation that behaviour is at all relevant to the discovery of mental states in others." [71] That is precisely because Searle ascribes the basic mental features, like consciousness, intentionality, subjectivity, phenomenality, etc. only to human beings. A machine however sophisticated it may be, wouldn't possess the intrinsic features that conscious human beings do have. Behaviour in the case of human beings is not causally defined, rather it's *intentional*. The behaviour is caused by the intentional states of the mind such as; desire, intention and belief. Thus the intentional description of the behaviour embodies the notion of *intentionality*.

Although we ascribe intentional stance to the computer behaviour in the case of its intentional strategy while considering its rational-choice, still we cannot ascribe *intrinsic* intentionality to it. This point can be discussed by taking a general standpoint which Schmidtz talks about when he offers strategies for fixing rational behaviour. They are optimizing strategy and satisfying strategy. As he defines two such strategies: "An optimizing strategy places limits on how much we are willing to insist in seeking alternatives. A satisfying strategy places limits on how much we insist in finding before we quit that search and turn our attention to other matters."[72] Insofar as our ascription of rational choice to an artificial system is concerned, the optimizing strategy seems to be the more appropriate strategy. In other words, when we ascribe intention to the computer then its intentional move is always directed towards the optimal feature. Which is in a way a limiting case in comparison to the intentional behaviour of human being. For Searle, on the contrary, the human intention is not always conditioned by other factors. It is free in that if exercises options that are available. Human beings follow the satisfying strategy and exercise their *free will*. Will is not causally bound. Freedom of will is one of the features of human beings. Each conscious or intentional act is caused by the intentional states and intentional states carry the conditions of satisfaction.

On the other hand, the optimizing strategy, which comes closer to Fodor's conception of rational choice relies on the conception of *belief fixation* and preferences. Choice making is causally defined.[73] This choice making is typical of the internalists. Since the internalists' conception of rational choice functions within the framework of 'belief and preference', its approach minimizes the inquiry. As Staz and Ferejohn points out, "the conception of human rational agency in terms of maximizing over a complete and consistent set of preferences is not psychologically realistic."[74] The internalists' approach which Fodor adheres to show minimizing condition of the function of belief states. The cognitive states that are mapped in the computer are fixed. The machine making its choice is fixed within the limited mapped informational states. The more reasonable approach, according to them, is that the "objective of rational-choice" must be intentionally characterized. Though they themselves accept the viability of existence of mental states such a belief and intentions, does not brand them as internalists. However, what is more essential for a rational-choice theory in order to be explanatory is that it must possess the 'semantic relation' to individual decision making. To say that decision making must involve the *semantic relation* is to say that intentionality has to be figured in the very process of decision realization. It is the *semantic content,* which basically unfolds the intentional relationship between the representational states of the mind and the world. Searle precisely emphasizes these aspects of intentionality which are semantic in character. Syntax based content is defined as having causal relationship among the representational states. Their syntactical representation gives the formal structure of the representational states. And the structural function is causally determined. Searle is against this Fodorian notion of syntax of the mental states.

In the Fodorian schema each token state can have a symbolic representation. And their symbolic representation is completely syntactical in nature. On the other hand, the content of the state is determined by qua language. Qua language keeps the syntactic and semantic content of the representational states unaltered. That is, the input-output relations can be precisely carried out through the proper algorithm or qua language. This process of receiving the input states and producing the output states can be otherwise called a sort of ***translation***, which the algorithm in the computer does. In this connection, Hillary Putnam's views on functionalism are worth mentioning. He says, "For any human society, there is a possible other society which is more sophisticated, which has modes of conceptualizing and describing things which members of the first society cannot understand without years of specialized study. What is often said is true, that all human language are intertranslatable; that does not mean that we can translate a current book of philosophy or paper in clinical psychology into the language of a primitive tribe without first coining a host of new technical language. It does not mean that we could tell any 'smart' native what the book in philosophy 'says' and have him understand (without years of study). Often enough we cannot tell members of our linguistic community what these discourses 'say' so that they will understand them well enough to explain them to others."[75] Each study of a particular domain has its own vocabulary, call it its language. That is, it uses its own terms, which are specific to the facts of that domain which cannot be translated into another language concerning a into different domains. However, to formulate a new language for our purpose is to create a *second language*; a language with its specific syntax and semantics. But the language (qua language) which translates the mental representations completely deals with syntax, not with semantics. Since the content is specific to the semantical aspects of the language, the question is how could the syntax exclusively accommodate the semantic content. If qua language is completely a syntactical language then how can the semantic content be explained? As Searle justifies, "even if my thoughts occur to me in strings of symbols, there must be more to the thought than abstract strings, because strings by themselves cannot have any meaning. If my thoughts are to be about anything, then the string must have a meaning, which makes that thought about those things. In a word, the mind has more than a syntax, it has semantics."[76] If thought processing is analogous to the information processing in the computer and the process is purely syntactical in its form, then how will the symbols have meanings. To have meaning means the symbols have the semantical content, which relates the token symbolic states to the world. So there is semantic content in the process of thought itself. Moreover, if content can be included in the token itself then question arises as to how the content is put into the syntactical form of the mental states. How is the content formulated? The functionalist's interpretation offered by Fodor and Dennett fails to explain intentionality because consciousness has no role to play for defining intentionality or the content of intentionality.

Philip Cam in his paper "Consciousness and Content Formation"[77] discusses the defects of the functionalists theory, according to him, functionalists fail to explain how consciousness is possible. Functionalists like Fodor and Dennett deny the realistic basis of consciousness. As he remarks, "So far I am criticizing functionalism for its failure to give us a realistic account of experience, but I have not shown that structuralists can do better. Let us suppose, indeed, the psychobiologists had cracked the neural code, could identify the neural micro structure of a given internal representation, and that a psychobiological account what goes in our heads was on offer. That still would not give guarantee a place for consciousness or experiences of any thing of that kind."[78] Cam rejects Fodor's explanation because of its over emphasis on the qua language without explaining the causal autonomy. And secondly, Fodor only says the qua language is a higher order property of brain states without explaining the proper connection between the syntactical states of mind and the neural structure. On the other hand, Dennett only emphasizes the sub-personal level of analysis of the neural networks. Content, in Dennett, is identified with neural states and events. It does not have any intentional explanation rather the content can have only an extensional account by explaining the various functional aspects of the neurological structure of the brains or the subsystems of the brain as a whole. And there is no role for consciousness insofar as the content is concerned. Content is a physical property and it can be mechanically explained or measured. In this connection there is nothing specific or intrinsic about intentionality as such. For Cam, even if we apply the best scientific instruments to know the neural functions of the brains we cannot know how the content is formulated. It, at best tells us how the physical process goes on in the different parts of the brain. The realistic account would be to accommodate experience, and how it is being realized by a conscious being. Functionalists do not focus much on *experience*. Experience is a conscious feature of human mental life which the functionalists dismiss as irrelevant.

The realistic account, for Cam, is to incorporate both neurobiological aspects as well as the conscious feature of the neurobioloigcal structure of the brain. His approach is rather holistic, in the sense he rejects the duality and takes both neurophysiological functions of the brains and consciousness as unique features of experience. Moreover, his intention is to capture how the content is realized by conscious being or experiencing subject. He writes, "Apart from the neural activity that directly subserves my mental life, my brain is monitoring all sorts of stimulus conditions, operating feed back loops, and so forth, all providing a contrast flow of organized activity. In its afferent aspect, we may call this activity 'detection'. Detection is an activity of essentially hardwired mechanisms, in which the plasticity required for content-formation would be inimical to proper functioning."[79] Detection is a physical process of the brain system. It only shows what processes go on while the mind is stimulated by the external stimuli. On the other hand, it would not say how the content is revised, in the sense that when one person is experiencing different shades of red colour he can very well distinguish the differences among the colour shades. While seeing different shades he is experiencing different content of red shades. And it also happens that content gets revised in the formulation itself. What is important here is that we are not aware of the physical process that is involved in it. Content is consciously revised. Cam rejects the Frueadian notion of unconscious formulation of content.[80] Experiencing something is a part of conscious activity. Realizing the content of experience is also a conscious process. As he argues, "I shall argue that experience or consciousness is the formulation of content. In order to avoid the misunderstanding, perhaps I shall stress that I am identifying consciousness not with content formulation. Whatever they are, contents are not events, and even if they have the origin in experience their retention is not in general restricted to the duration to that experience."[81] Experience itself is a continuous process. It is because conscious states of experience cannot be tokened. To specify each content or states of experience separately may lead us to the functionalists' way of formalizing the content. Consciousness can be thus understood as a linking bond implicitly presented. He also says, "I take it that if experience is the formation of content, then there is no experience without content formation and no content formation without experience". This is possible because the formulation itself is a conscious or intentional activity. In the case of intentional representation of experience there is no division between content formulation and experience. It is because the experiencing subject is not just experiencing but the content formulation is an aspect of conscious process of experience as such. Cam also writes, "And, finally, this suggests not only the possibility that consciousness is the lying down of contents or trace formation but also how we might begin to explain what would otherwise seem to be a variety of counter examples to this claim. I find this is an attractive line of thought especially given both the difficulties and importance of a given reality to the experiencing subject."[82] Cam relates consciousness with content formulation focussing on the notion of experience. It is consciousness, which links with varieties of experiences that a subject encounters. This link, of course, is a sort of reflection, which helps in revising the content.

However, Cam does not explicitly talk about notion of intentionality, which is to be the basic feature of consciousness. It is the intentional property of consciousness which sets up the relationship between the mind and the world and between experience and the things experienced. The act of experience is an intentional act. Thus, Cam's thesis comes closer to the Searlean theory of intentionality. Intentionality in Searle is a specific feature of conscious being. Searle extends the notion of experiencing subject by explicating the intentional feature of consciousness. For Searle, it is intrinsic because it is biological in nature. It is specific to the human beings. He says, "intrinsic intentionality is a phenomenon that humans and certain other animals have as part of their biological nature. It is not a matter of how they are used or how they think of themselves or how they choose to describe themselves. It is just a plain fact about such beasts that, for example, sometimes they get thirsty, or hungry, they *see* things, *fear* things, etc. All of the italicized expressions in the previous sentence are used to refer to intrinsic intentional states."[83] Intentionality is basic to the biological organism. It is not just that the brain functions produce certain cognitive states and those cognitive states bear intentionality. The very fact that human beings are *feeling* hungry and feeling joy etc. and expressing that state of *experience* shows that the whole of the organism is involved in the process of generating such intentional states. As Searle as says, "It is convenient to use the jargon of intentionality for talking about systems that do not have it, but they behave as if they did. I say about my thermostat that it perceives changes in the temperature; I say of my carburetor that it knows when to enrich the mixture; and I say of my computer that its memory is bigger than the memory of the computer I had last year. All these attributes are perfectly harmless and no doubt they will eventually produce new literal meanings as metaphors become dead.". (op.cit)In the case of thermostat, carburetor and computer we ascribe intentionality because they seem to us *as if* their function has intentional form. This ascription is not literal or real. We can very well make distinction between the men and the machine. Machine is an artifact because it is created by the human beings. The information processing computer which possesses cognitive states does not itself has the capacity for generating intentionality. So, according to Searle, functionalists who suppose that machine can have intentionality is a myth. On other hand, if at all we ascribe intentionality to computer or any artificial system then it is of second order intentionality or as if intentionality. It is precisely because first order intentionality is specific to the human beings. It is primary in the sense that all the artifacts are dependent on the human intentionality. Artifacts are conscious creations of human beings. And every conscious act is an intentional act to serve certain purpose of human beings. In that sense artificial systems are used as means to realize certain ends.

Moreover, the very notion of *understanding* the experience itself is an intentional act. In other words, human beings as intentional beings are conscious of whatever experience they have. Supporting the Searlean standpoint Nemirow writes, "Understanding what a pattern is like is but a special case of understanding what an experience is like, which we may generally characterize as the set of abilities to recognize, remember, and imagine a kind of experience."[84] For Nemirow, it is not just neurological states and processes which are important for determining the content of visual experiences. Rather the whole mechanism of understanding involves interrelated abilities. And we cannot strictly talk about such abilities excluding consciousness. It is precisely because the very act of acquiring any skill or stance in the case of human beings is an intentional act. And skill develops at certain point after constant revision in the process of practice. Searle names this ability as the Background. The very conception of Background in Searle's theory of mind, indeed, explicates the naturalistic standpoint, whereas the analysis of the logical properties of intentionality refers to the Network of intentional states and processes. Insofar as the explanation of intentionality is concerned both the Network and the Background are essential prerequisites. They provide adequate support for the concept of intentionality. We have already discussed how the intentional states constitute a complex Network for realizing the condition of satisfaction, for the realization of one intentional state is possible with relation to other mental states. It is a totality of states where some of them are unconscious and some are conscious. On the other hand, the Background, for Searle, is a non-intentional physical capacity. As Searle puts it, "I believe that anyone who tries seriously to follow out the threads in the Network will eventually reach at bedrock of mental capacities that do not themselves consist in Intentional states (representation), but nonetheless form the preconditions for the functioning of Intentional states."[85] Intentional states are representational states. According to Searle they themselves are not sufficient enough to unfold the form of intentionality. The capacity is rather embedded in the non-representational feature of the brain. Thus the intentional states presuppose non-intentional states as the bedrock of the Network. Searle introduces the notion of the Background, which includes non-intentional and non-representational mental states. He rightly says, 'The Background is a 'preintentional' in the sense that though not a form or forms of intentionality it is nonetheless a precondition or set of preconditions of intentionality.' The function of intentional states will have two logical properties; the psychological mode which results in condition of satisfaction and the direction of fit which refers to the intentionality. Moreover, for Searle, whenever we intend to perform certain actions or represent some intentional states our intentionality will have two things, i.e. *knowing how* and *knowing that*. When I pass an order to my driver, "Bring the vehicle" he carries my order in a conven-tional way. He brings the vehicle, parks at the gate, waits for me and opens the door, etc. Here driver knows the things, that is, knows the procedure *how to do* with things. So knowing the things means we are already aware of the facts regarding how the whole process goes on. In this regard, Searle makes a division of the Background. The geography of the Background has two aspects, i.e., deep or biological and other is local or social. Driver's learning about the obeying the order is social background. Social background of being reflects how he does the things that he has learnt from the society. Thus, the background has a conventional or social aspect and a biological aspect. And both the aspects are related to satisfy the conditions of intentionality, which is shown in the forms of knowing *how the things* are and knowing *how to do things*.

However, both the aspects of the background focus on the nature of beings. That is, the very nature of being, that is, how a human being is biologically structured and socially related. Its biological aspect is a major distinct feature which differentiates the machines having an intentional stance. Intentionality revealed in the case of machine or a computer will not be biological. Biological aspect of the origin of intentionality refers to the human brain system and function. The human organism definitely possess certain stances, has the capacity to do things. It has capacity to self-generate intentional states and contents. Its general capacity, on the other hand, includes the whole of physical and linguistic activities. And they can be explained through the non-intentional and non-representational capacity of the Background conditions of human beings. As Searle says, "All conscious intentionality—all thought, perception, understanding, etc. determines condition of satisfaction only relative to certain capacities that are not or could not be part of the very conscious states. The actual content by itself is insufficient to determine the condition of satisfaction."[86]

Now a fundamental question arises as to what sort of relationship a non-intentional and non-representational Background holds with aspect to intentional states or the Network of intentional states and processes, since the intentionality only pertains to the latter not to the former. But Searle rejects the whole Cartesian notion stating that there should not be any metaphysical presuppositions regarding the mental as 'continuous inventory process of conscious mental states,' and there will be certainly a *category mistake* if we draw a dividing line between the Network and the Background. Because the Background is the 'sustaining principle' of the Network. Therefore, Searle categorically states, "The thesis of Background has to be rewritten to get rid of the presupposition of the mind as a collection, an inventory, of mental phenomena, because the occurrent reality of the mental as mental is consciousness."[87]

Literally speaking, the Background refers to the physical capacity of the brain processes which is an evolutionary phenomenon that an organism is sustained with. That is, the very nature of intentionality is such that " *Intentionality occurs in a coordinated flow of action and perception, and the Background is a condition of possibility of forms taken by the flow.* The flow of intentionality tends to rise to the level of the Backround ability it reaches all the way down to the bottom of the ability." [88] Thus, Searle treats intentionality as a persisting feature intrinsic to both *conscious-thought-experience,* (i.e. the function of intentional states) and the Background. It is because one always intends to act, or have desired to represent his mental states to get satisfaction. Intentionality persists in his experiences of realizing the conditions. Above all what is more important to note here is the capacity to represent or think or experience the conscious or intentional states. This particularly refers to the Background conditions of the human beings, which is unconscious, non-representational and non-intentional. Moreover, intentionality is the connecting principle between the conscious-thought-experiences and the unconscious Background capacities. Since intentionality persists in the function of conscious-thought-process it tries to build up the skill or stance. In other words, through practices different skills can be developed; because of the person's own intentionality. And this form of intentionality rises from the bottom of conscious thought to reach at the Background level. On the other hand, the same background or *the developed skill* helps in representing the intentional states in a specific way. When a skier practices he follows all the rules and advice of his coach. The skier always has intended to learn to win the race. At one level of his learning he reaches to a level of perfection and at that time he represents his skills and applies own techniques to win the race. So intentionality is present in both the cases, i.e. for developing the stance or skill as well as for representing it.

It is to be noted that the holistic version of the Network of Intentional states is supported by non-intentional non-conscious Background. Brain processes cause conscious intentional states but the latter cannot be reduced back to the former. As Searle writes, "There is no occurent to an unconscious Network of Intentionality that holistically supports its members but that requires further support from the Background To have a conscious thought, one has to have the capacity to generate a lot of other conscious thoughts. And these conscious thought further requires capacities for further application."[89] In this regard, intentionality is intrinsically related to the consciousness or conscious states. The emergence of consciousness is nothing but the emergence of the conscious mental states. So, there is a simultaneous emergence of the properties out of the neurophysiological process of the brain organism.

Intentionality ultimately has the physical background. But it is to be noted that brain processes are not intentional as Dennett and other functionalists presuppose. Rather intentionality occurs at that level of consciousness. If there is no consciousness or conscious thought process then there is no intentionality at all. Thus, precisely their intrinsic feature refers to the necessary relationship of the properties with the structure of conscious states. The ontology of conscious states where intentionality is the basic property refers to the neurophysiological structure and function of the brain organism. Brain is a physical system in the case of human beings has developed in the process of evolution.

The biological naturalism of Searle consistently advocates that consciousness is an evolutionary phenomenon. Consciousness has evolved in the natural process of biological evolution. It, thus, has a place in nature. And so is the intentionality. There cannot be intentionality outside the realm of the consciousness in particular and nature in general. Hence intentionality has place in nature itself. Hence, Searle is not a transcendentalist in the above sense so far as the ontology of the intentionality is concerned. Rather, he is biological naturalist as distinguished from a functionalist. He does not reduce intentionality to be physical extensional state of the brain. Although he says that the brain processes cause intentionality along with its other co-features of consciousness, still he strictly differentiates the brain processes from mental states. Both are logically independent. Intentionality is a property caused by the brain process but it cannot be *reduced to* the brain process. Intentionality has its independent function in relation to consciousness or conscious thought processes. But its function is not dependent from the neurophysiological processes. According to Searle, intentionality is more fundamental and primary. But insofar as the human mental life is concerned intentionality has a specific role. In short, it is a human *specific feature* reflected in the various activities, linguistic as well as the physical. Thus, Searle naturalizes the notion of intentionality.

Notes and References

1. William Lyons, *Approaches to Intentionality,* Clarendon Press, Oxford, 1995, p. 1.
2. John Searle, "Intentionality and Its Place in Nature," *Sysnthese,* vol.61,1984. p. 4.
3. Searle writes in his Intentionality that "Intentionality is a property of many mental states and events by which they are directed at, or about or of the subjects of the states of affairs in the world." Here Searle does not make any distinction between the property and features both are part of the mental states in particular and consciousness in general. See *Intentionality,* p. 1.
4. Searle, *Intentionality,* pp. 14-15.
5. Searle, *Intentionality,* p. 141.
6. *Ibid.*
7. *Ibid.,* p. 18.
8. *Ibid.,* p. 5
9. *Ibid.,* pp. 15-16.
10. Searle, "Intentionality and Its Place in the Nature", p. 4.
11. Searle, *Intentionality,* p. 45.
12. See, Wittgenstein, *Zettel,* ed. G.E.M. Anscombe, and G.H. von Wright, Basil Blackwell, Oxford, 1967, sects.433-434.
13. Searle, *Intentionality,* p. 41.
14. *Ibid.,* p. 49.
15. *Ibid.,* p. 9
16. *Ibid.,* p. 85
17. I have elaborated it in my M.Phil. dissertation, "Searrle's Concept of Intentionality" submitted to Dept. of Philosophy, University of Hyderabad 1996, p. 20. For clarification also see, Searle' s *Intentionality,* p. 93.
18. *Ibid.,* p. 95
19. *Ibid.,* p. 129.
20. *Ibid.,* p. 130.
21. *Ibid.,* p. 131.
22. *Ibid.,* pp. 122-123.

23. *Ibid.*, p. 125
24. Jerry Fodor, *Psychosemantics: The Problem of Meaning in the Philosophy of Mind,* The MIT Press, Massachusetts, 1987, p. 11. (Henceforth, Pshychosemantics)
25. *Ibid.*, p. 12.
26. *Ibid.*, p. 97
27. *Ibid.*, p. 18.
28. *Ibid,* pp. 24-25
29. *Ibid.*, p. 35
30. *Ibid.*, p. 42.
31. *Ibid.*, p. 44
32. *Ibid.*, p. 45.
33. See Fodor's *Representations*, especially the chapter on "Propositional Attitudes" , p. 203.
34. Fodor, *The Modularity of the Mind: An Essay on Faculty Psychology,* The MIT Press, Massachusetts, 1983, p. 40.
35. *Ibid.*, p. 42
36. Fodor, *Representations*, p. 200.
37. Fodor, *MoM,* p. 71.
38. Fodor, "Why Should the Mind be Modular?" in *Reflections on Chomsky*, ed. Alexander Geroge, Basil Blackwell, Oxford, 1989, p. 14.
39. Fodor, *Psychosemantics*, p. 113.
40. *Ibid.*, p. 119.
41. Dennett, *Intentional Stance*, p. 71.
42. *Ibid.*, p. 48.
43. *Ibid.*, p. 61.
44. *Ibid.*,p. 63.
45. *Ibid.*, p. 73.
46. Dennett, *Brainstroms*, pp. 7-8.
47. *Ibid.*, p. 15.
48. Dennett, *Content and Consciousness*, p. 78.
49. Dennett, *Brainstroms*, p. 19.
50. Dennett, "Evolution, Error and Intentionality", *Intentional Stance,* 296.
51. *Ibid.*, p. 298.
52. *Ibid.*, pp. 293-294.
53. I have elaborated these three dimensions of intentionality in the chapter "Two Models of Intentionality: Husserl and Searle" in my M. Phil. dissertation: *Searle's Concept of Intentionality: A Study,*

submitted to the Department of philosophy, University of Hyderabad, July 1995.

54. *Ibid.*, p. 33.
55. Ronald MacIntyre and David W. Smith, *Husserl and Intentionality*, D. Rediel Publishing Company, Holland, 1982, p99.
56. Hopkins, B., *Intentionality in Husserl and Heideggar*, Kluwer Academic Publishers, Dordrecht, 1993, p. 42.
57. MacIntyre and Smith, *Husserl and Intentionality: A study of mind, meaning and language*, D. Reidel Publishing Company, Dodrecht, 1982. p. 106.
58. *Ibid.*, p. 107.
59. *Ibid.*,p. 131.
60. Ronald McIntyre, "Searle on Intentionality", *Inquiry*, 1984, p. 471.
61. *Ibid.*, p. 475
62. *Ibid.*, p. 480.
63. Cf. J.N. Mohanty, *Transcendental Phenomenology*, Basil Balckwell, Oxford, 1991, p. 84. (Heanceforth IP)
64. J.N. Mohanty, "Husserl's Transcendental Phenomenology and Essentialism" in *The Possibility of Transcendental Philosophy*", Martinus Nijhoff Publishers, Dordrecht, 1985, pp. 209-11.
65. *Ibid.*, p. 208.
66. Mohanty, *T.P, Ibid*, p. 68.
67. The physical aspects includes the specific function of sense organs which are most indispensable part of acquiring sensations; whereas, the psychological aspect refers to the genetic characteristics of the human beings including backgournd of learning, habits, and the memory. Social facets of the logical structure are more prominent in the sense that it is briefly the domain of language. *Ibid.*,p. 83.
68. *Ibid.*, p. 85
69. *Ibid.*, p. 88-89.
70. *Ibid.*, p. 93.
71. Searle, *RDM*, p. 77.
72. David Schmidtz, "Rationality within Reason", *The Journal of Philosophy*, Vol. LXXIV, No. , September 1992, p. 451.
73. Staz and Ferejohn talks about internalist's notion of rational choice. Fodor's notion of rational choice making comes closer to the internalists in this regard. See, Debra Satz and John Ferejohn,

"Rational Choice and Social Theory," *Journal of Philosophy*, Vol. 91, No. , Feburary 1994, p. 73.

74. *Ibid.*, p. 47. They too reject the "Radical Externalists" notion of rational choice. Radical Externalists deny the causal efficacy of mental states. p. 75.
75. Hilary Putnam, *Representation and Reality*, The MIT Press, Massachusetts, 1989, p. 89.
76. Searle, *Minds, Brains and Science*, Harvard University Press, Cambridge, 1984, p. 31.
77. Philip Cam, "Consciousness and Content Formation", *Inquiry*, Vol. 27, 1984, pp281-297.
78. *Ibid.*,p. 384.
79. *Ibid.*, p. 392.
80. See, *Ibid*, pp388-390.
81. *Ibid.*, p. 384.
82. *Ibid.*, p. 395.
83. Searle, *RDM*, p. 79.
84. Lawrence E. Nemirow, "Understanding Rules," *The Journal of Philosophy*, Vol. 92, January 1995, p. 35.
85. Searle, *Intentionality*, p. 143.
86. Searle, *RDM*, p. 189. Aslo see, *Intentionality*, p. 175.
87. *Ibid.*, p. 187
88. *Ibid.*, p. 195
89. *Ibid.*, p. 190

Chapter - IV

LANGUAGE, REPRESENTATION AND MEANING

The structurality of content as a basic aspect of the structure of consciousness or intentional states remains concealed unless we discuss the notion of language or linguistic components thoroughly. It is language which reveals its own content in its function. And thereby it discloses the inbuilt components of the structure of mental states. One may ask, how does the structure reveal its composite features? As we have already discussed in the previous chapter, the structure of conscious thought is such that it is directed towards the world. The directedness is an intrinsic feature of intentional states. Language represents the mental states. Thus, representationality is the basic characteristics of language or linguistic activities.

Language has a role to play in the constitution of experience, understanding, meaning and truth. Moreover, linguistic activities include the totality of language use. In brief, language not only exhibits the very structure of mental representations but also exhibits the complexity of mental states. Furthermore, the linguistic activities are conscious activities. Hence the ontology of language can be traced along with the ontology of consciousness.

This chapter brings out some of controversial discussions regarding the naturalists' conception of the mind and its relationship with language. It tries to highlight the Searlean thesis that language is a part of human mind or consciousness. So linguistic activities are no doubt conscious activities. The first section brings out the Searlean conception of language and meaning. In the second section we discuss the Chomskyan and Fodorean notion of language focusing on how they separate language from consciousness. In the third section we talk about Gillett's notion of semantic representation in relation to the Fodorean kind of mental representation. The fourth section brings out the Intention based semantics keeping in the mind that the very exercise of meaning is not only intentional but also conscious. It discloses how intentionality is part of the linguistic discourse. In this section we discuss the two divergent interpretations of the Gricean semantics by focusing on the views of Schiffer, Loar and Avramedes. It also focuses on Millikan's view way of doing away with the notion of intrinsic intentionality from normal linguistic discourse. In the fifth section we discusses the Searlean concept of linguistic meaning by reestablishing the notion of intentionality. Moreover it deals with the Searlean response to other theories of meaning and language. The concluding section talks about the structural isomorphism between language and consciousness thus establishing unity between them.

I. Searle's Concept of Language and Meaning

Language, according to Searle, has biological origin and it can be understood as biological phenomena from the evolutionary point of view. Language has evolved in the natural process. And it is the part of human mental life. Both mind and language are part of the evolutionary history of biology. Moreover, the fact that human beings think and use language is a specific feature of human beings. It is also the case that the process of thinking involving language shows the intrinsic relationship between language and mind. However, for Searle, if one considers the *language use* in particular, then from the evolutionary point of view, the biological development of human mental life shows that mental states are logically prior to their linguistic expressions. Language or the linguistic expression of mental states causes later in the evolutionary process. As he says, "From a evolutionary point of view, just as there is an order of priority in the development of biological processes, so there is an order of priority in the development of intentional phenomena. In the development language and meaning comes very late. Many species other than humans have sensory perception, and intentional action, and several species, certainly the primates, have belief, desires and intention, but very few species, perhaps only humans, have the peculiar but also have the biological form of Intentionality, we associate with language and meaning."[1] Language thus plays a vital role both at the internal level, i.e. at the level of thought processes and at the external level, i.e., by expressing and communicating the thoughts or mental states. What is important here is that intentionality which is a basic feature of the conscious thought process persists without fail at the level of communication. In other words, intentionality as embedded in the very structure of thought gets disclosed by the linguistic expression of thoughts in communication.

Searle makes two important points about the biological origin of language. First, its biological development especially in association with the mental life unfolds the very function of mental phenomena. Second, being intrinsic to the mental life linguistic activities are characterized as intentional activities. Thus the mental phenomena or mental states and events not only have bearing on consciousness and thereby can be called intentional but also the very *experience* and *realization* of world unfolds the intrinsic feature of the linguistic content to consciousness. Consciousness, in this way becomes the ground for the linguistic activities like meaning and understanding.

Since Searle maintains a logical gap between intentional states of the mind and their linguistic representation, language *use* comes later than the inner function of the intentional states or the mental representations. Intentional states are *primitive* in Searlean terminology compared to their linguistic representation. In other words, the intentional form of language use, which is the very feature of expression of meaning, is secondary to the intentionality of the conscious thought processes. Intentional states are primitive and involve primitive form of intentionality whereas intentionality of the communicative language is a later development. Moreover, the communicative intention pertains to the social function of language. As Searle's naturalistic interpretation shows, the communicative intention is rooted in the natural form of intentionality. Meaning can be defined in terms of the function of mental states. In other words, the representational form of intentionality is not only logically prior but also it helps in defining the notion of communicative intentionality. As Searle puts it, "We define speaker's meaning in terms of forms of intentionality that are not intrinsically linguistic. If, for example, we can define meaning in terms of intentions we will be defined a linguistic notion, even though many perhaps most human intentions are linguistically realized."[2] The representational form of intentionality and the communicational form of intentionality belong to two separate levels of function. But the content of intentionality remains the same in both the levels of function. Only there is difference in *forms*; representational intention belongs to realm of the mental whereas the linguistic representation belongs to the realm of social. That is, language use is a part of the social communicative system where use of language expresses meaning. Language *use* reveals its social function in the linguistic framework of the society. Meaning, for Searle, in this regard is not exclusively a social phenomenon. It is related to the mental life of human beings. That is to say language use in the communicative framework cannot exclusively determine the meaning. Meaning rather can be defined in terms of the representation of mental states. Mental states or intentional states are expressed in language, so meaning is rooted in the psychological processes. Since each mental state has a biological origin, there is neurophysiological cause for the emergence of the mental states. The neurological processes of the brain cause the mental life of desires and intentions. The representation of such states has a psychological mode, which results in bringing out the conditions of satisfaction. Since mental states function within the network of other mental states each intentional state is connected in the web of other intentional states. Above all, there is a unity of the functions of such intentional network that determines the psychological mode of the intentional states. Thus the meaning of the linguistic expression derives from the psychological mode of the intentional states. As Searle writes, "on this approach the philosophy of language is a branch of philosophy of mind. And in its most general form it amounts to the view that certain fundamental notions such as meaning are analyzable in terms of more psychological notion such as beliefs, desires and intentions."[3]

Furthermore, the primary significance of mental states lies in the intentionality that is embedded in the different forms of the mental states and their linguistic representations. Thus intentionality is involved in mental representations of the intentional states and their linguistic representations. The source of this intentionality is consciousness. Consciousness is in principle intentional, that is to say, intentionality is an intrinsic feature of consciousness. So to talk about the forms of intentionality of mental representation and their linguistic expressions is to unfold that there is no such division between the intentionality of mind and that of language. Searle explains: "Meaning is a kind of Intentionality, what distinguishes it from other kinds? Speech acts, are kinds of acts what distinguishes them from other kinds?"[4] Answering these questions, Searle clearly holds two views on mind, which are different from other views on *Intention Based Semantics* (IBS). Searle's intentionality involved in the very discourse of meaning is different from the speaker's *intention* of representation. In other words, the linguistic meaning of expressions and sentences will have a general form of intentionality, which is different from the speaker's, own *intention* of representation. Intentionality involved in speaker's representation of a particular state of mind embodies a special form different from the mere linguistic representational form of intentionality. The emphasis is given to the speaker's intention of making a meaningful representation by uttering certain statements in a typical way. That shows the kind of intentionality there in the speaker's mind. But for Searle intentionality emerges out of the neurobiological processes of brain. So , the ontology of intentionality is the ontology of the brain processes. Thus the intention of representing certain state is logically related with physical process of the brain. In other words, in the course of linguistic exercises there is a parallel physical process going in the brain. Therefore, Searle says that the relation is from *physics-to-semantics.* Physics here refers to the physiological events that are taking place in the neural network of the brain. Semantics on the other hand deals with language and its use. The root of the intentionality of language use lies in the neurophysiology of the brain.

The connection between physics and semantics is established through the function of the network of intentional states. Searle is interested in the intentionality common to both language and mind. The structure of the intention states is the mind flow and the structure of the linguistic expression. Self-referentiality is the basic feature of the representation of intentional states. Behind any linguistic representation of a desire state for examples, the person seeks to have the result in mind in order to get his/

her desire satisfied. The intention of representation and thereby expecting its satisfaction involves two levels of intentionality. These two levels basically characterize the *structure of the intention*. As Searle puts it, "Level of the intentional state expressed in the performance of the act; level of intention to perform the act."[5] That is, the form of intentionality, which is contained in the intentional state, is identical with the act of intention of representation. Searle says, "The fact that condition of satisfaction of the expressed intentional state and the condition of satisfaction of the speech act are identical suggests that the key of the problem of meaning is to see that in the performance of speech act the mind intentionally imposes the same condition of satisfaction on the physical expression of the expressed mental state, as the mental state has itself— The mind imposes intentionality on the production of sound, marks, etc. by imposing condition of satisfaction of mental states as the production of physical phenomena."[6]

Searle makes the identity relationship of two forms of intentionality clear by making a gradation between *representational intention* and *communicative intention*. The representational intention is logically prior to the communicative intention. In the communicative form of the intentional content of mental state is expressed in language. Thereby intentionality is revealed in the form of language use. On the other hand, in the case of representational intention the person or the speaker tries to make out how better to formulate or articulate the representation itself, so that it would be suitable for resulting condition of satisfaction. In that sense, intending to express the mental states, one sees the relationship with rational and emotional aspects of mental life. The flow of emotion and rationaliza-tion in due course of communication shows the imposition of intentionality on the structure of the speech act. So the whole linguistic activity gets loaded with intentionality. Furthermore, it shows that the *conventional force* that exists in the social framework of *normal* language use or linguistic discourse is rooted in the human psychology. It is precisely because the psychological mode of every person blends up with the intentional states of linguistic expressions. And that determines the communicative intention. However, Searle makes a clear distinction between representation and communication. As he writes, "we need to have clear distinction between representation and communication. Characteristically a man who makes a statement both intends to represent some facts or state of affairs and intends to communicate this representation to his hearers. But this representing intention is same as communicative intention. Communicating is a matter of producing effects on ones' hearers but one can intend to represent something without caring at all about the effects of the hearer. There are therefore two aspects of meaning intention, the intention to represent and the intention to communicate. On the present account representation is prior to communication and representative intention is prior to communicative intention."[7] Representation intention is prior in the sense that the speaker decides or chooses before communication the means of expression of those states. It is not just that one is communicating but that his communication is meant to be such that it results in satisfaction. So the seeking of satisfaction condition is a part of the prior intention and that is an intrinsic feature of the function of intentional states. This precisely shows the two dimensions that are involved in the very nature of intentional states. That is, in the discourse of language use, linguistic representation not only expresses of the mental states but the speaker also desires for condition of satisfaction. It shows that the two ways intentionality or involved in the mental representation as well as its linguistic representation. For instance, when one passes order to his attendant he knows that his attendant will obey it. Or, when a leader addresses his followers, he intends to represent his idea in such a way that his followers get motivated by ideas and thus follow him. So the intention to address is to see that it brings the intentional satisfaction of the speaker. Thus the direction of intentionality in the case of self-referentiality would be from: Mind (language)→to→the world and consequently the condition of satisfaction shows world→to→the (language) mind. Self-referentiality unfolds the two ways of "direction of fit" that an intentional state possesses. Searle writes, "More precisely, he [the speaker] is trying to cause change in the world so that the propositional content achieves world-to-mind direction of fit, by representing the world as having been so changed, that is by expressing same propositional content with mind-to-world direction of fit. He performs not two speech acts with two independent directions of fit but one with double direction of fit, since he succeeds he will change the world by representing it has been so changed and thus satisfied both direction of fit with one speech act."[8] Self-referentiality unfolds intentional feature that exists between the two levels, i.e., levels of mental states and its linguistic presentation. And referentiality shows the continuity of flow of intentional content rather than division of the mental and the linguistic into two separate realms.

This conception of choosing to represent and to realize the intention of representation is a conscious activity. In the process of rationalization and selection we consciously think over different possible states and their perfect representation. So in that process of exercising that form of intentionality of the mind not only creates the *possibility* of meaning or interpretation but also realizes the *limits* of interpretation.[9] Such a mode of intentionality exceeds the realm of illocutionary condition of speech acts. Various forms of speech acts reflect on different dimensions of conventional forces that are embedded in the intentional discourses of linguistic activity. Intentionality exceeds the limits of conventional linguistic convention. In the regard, the scope of intentionality is larger, which, for Searle, goes beyond the realm of illocutionary acts. He says, "If the way language represents the world is an extension and realization of the way mind represents the world then these five must [i.e., five basic categories of illocutionary acts; assertives, declaratives, commissives, declaratives, expressives] derive from the same fundamental feature of the mind. The intentionality of the mind not only creates the possibility of meaning but it limits its forms."[10]

There are two things, which promptly follows from Searle's conception of self-referentiality of intentionality in the linguistic discourse. Firstly, linguistic activitie. are very much part of consciousness. Language processing or thought processing, so far as the human beings are concerned, is a feature of conscious activity. Intentional states are not only conscious but to have intentional states and to realize the condition of applying those states is nothing but a conscious activity. Secondly, there is relation between the individual structure of intention and the social structure of language function. Language is related with the social level of production of speech and social meaning. Social meaning structure signifies the social institution of intentionality. According to Searle, "their institution are constitutive rules, and how do they relate to prelinguistic forms of intentionality?"[11] The prelinguistic form of intentionality refers to the *background* condition, which helps in both generating the speech acts and in following the rules of speech act. In short, there cannot be any use of language without following any rule. For Searle, linguistic rules are *unconsciously* followed, but they can be intentionally defined. And their intentional explanation unfolds the relationship between the mental life of the linguistic being and the social linguistic rules.

According to Searle, meaning of a sentence or speech acts lies in the very content of sentence. It is the content of the sentence which not only unfolds the meaning but also justifies the condition of satisfaction. The content is the intentional content, which is a part of intentional states. Searle says, "Linguistic references is a special case of intentional reference, and intentional reference is by way of relation of fitting or satisfaction. It is not necessary to postulate any special metaphysical realms in order to account for communication and shared intentionality. The possibility of shared intentional content does not require any metaphysical apparatus any more than the possibility of shared walks."[12] Sense of the content or language is embedded in the language use, i.e., they are not of the Fregean variety which exists independent of the sentential expressions of language. The Searlean notion of content includes two things; firstly, it is context related, and secondly, the same content is intentional. The context dependence characteristics the normal linguistic meaning of expressions or of language use in general. That makes the agent's communication intention specific to certain contexts. In this connection, the Searlean intentional theory of meaning has a root in the subject's intentional states. Meaning is, thus, precisely internalistic. And the shared content is part of the intentional content of mental states.

Meaning can be analyzed through the intentional content. One has to see the root of the content in the mind itself. He writes, "If we are unable to account for the relation of reference in terms of internal intentional contents, either the content of individual speaker or the content of linguistic community of which he is a part, then the entire philosophical tradition since Fregeis mistaken and we need to start over some external causal account of reference in particular and the relation of words to the world in general."[13] The Searlean causal account of the origination of content shows the emergence of the intentional content with the formation of intentional states. In other words, human mind is intentionally acting upon the world. Moreover, the casual emergence of the mental states is in principle *intentional* because intentionality is an intrinsic feature of consciousness. So the conscious participation of human beings in the world is nothing but intentional. In brief, causality is intentionalized or can be intentionally defined. In that way it is context related or context dependent. As Searle illustrates the example of 'twin earth', one's mental content of 'water' on Earth differs from his counterpart's on the twin earth because what he sees as water on the Earth is different from his counterpart's as Twin earth. It is precisely because when he utters 'water' he means something like H_2O whereas his twin means it *xyz*, because their interaction with the phenomenon of water differs.

However, Searle also says, though two speakers belong to the same linguistic community and use the same language their content will differ with reference to their respective experience of the phenomenon. Each conscious being has his own way of seeing or experiencing things. It shows how one is associated with the phenomena. As Searle writes, "Though they have type identical visual experiences in the situation where "water" is for each indexically identified, they don't have type identical intentional contents. On the contrary, intentional content can be different because each intentional content is causally self-referential."[14] Though all the subjects belong to one linguistic community and share one particular concept, each will have his won way of experiencing the phenomenon. Their own experience or intention in action causes the subtle difference in the emergence of content. And that signifies the specificity of the speaker's representation. Self-referential condition is therefore specific to the speaker's intentional content. However, its general content, which is shared by all, remains the same. As Searle puts it, "Of course, our beliefs will be different in the trivial sense that any self-referential perceptual content makes reference to particular token, not to qualitatively similar tokens but that is the result we want any way, since you and I can share the visual experience what we share is a common set of condition of satisfaction, not the same token visual experience. Your experience will be numerically different from mine even though they may be qualitatively similar."[15] The difference is very subtle and each one will have some specific characteristics which consequently help in retaining *subjectivity*. That is to say, we cannot quantify the *first person's point of view* or specificity the of the subjective experiences.

II. Language of the Mind: Naturalists' separating Language from Consciousness

Chomsky believes that language has also evolved in the process of evolution. Mind and language are the natural aspects of the world order. His emphasis on the notion of language is quite significant. He writes: "Language serves as an instrument for free expression of thought, unbound in scope, uncontrolled by stimulus conditions though appropriate to situations, available for use in whatever contingencies our thought process can comprehend. This "creative aspect" of language use is a characteristic species property of humans."[16] It is through language that human mental life is expressed. Linguistic behaviour of human beings is not based on the behaviouristic principle of stimulus and responses. Rather, it is the natural property of the human beings. Human beings as biological organisms possesses certain rich components for acquiring language. Human beings thus are called linguistic beings.

The naturalistic study of language, for Chomsky, is an empirical or scientific inquiry into the unity of language and mind. Chomsky points out that "A naturalistic approach to linguistic and mental aspects of the world seeks to construct intelligible explanatory theories, taking as 'real' what we are led to posit in this quest and hoping for eventual unification with the 'core' natural sciences: unification not necessarily reduction."[17] Chomsky's scientific approach has been physicalistic, because he believes in the physicalistic worldview, i.e., the ultimate principle of physics can results in the unity of science. For him, the whole human organism is specifically designed to acquire language. The process of acquiring language shows the capacity of *growth* of language. Moreover, he supports the internalists' interpretation: "Internalists" naturalistic inquiry seeks to understand the internal states of an 'organism'. Language, being a specific feature of human beings grows through a process of development. The linguistic development takes place in the mind by the constant interaction with particular linguistic community. It is possible because of certain *innate* capacities of the organism. This innate capacity, for Chomsky, is called the 'generative grammar'. Generative grammar operates in two levels; *surface structure* and *deep structure*. As he writes, "it seems to me reasonable to propose that every human language surface structures are generated from structure of a more abstract sort, this will refer to us 'deep structure' by certain formal operation of very special kind called the grammatical transformations."[18] The surface structure reveals the very notion of language use or linguistic representation in the social level, whereas the deep structure helps in formulating or generating the linguistic representation. The function of grammatical transformation at the deeper structure helps in both linguistic experiences as well as giving a rational flavour to human intelligence. It has some specific properties; like phonological rules, principles of rule ordering, etc. which correlates with deeper structure. That, according to Chomsky, is called 'prelinguistic-symbolic-system'. This 'preliguistic-symbolic-system' is defined as having abstract structure of rules, which helps us in transforming or operating in our linguistic performances.

Chomsky relates the deep structure of the language with the mental states. The mental states which are linguistically identified are reduced to linguistic states. On the other hand, the linguistic states are also identified with physical brain states because mental states are themselves brain states. Thus there is no division between language and mind. According to Chomsky, "we may conceive of the mind as a system of 'mental organs', the language faculty being one, each of this organ has specific structure and function, determined by the general outlined by our genetic endowment, interacting in ways that are also biologically determined in large measure to provide the basis of our mental life."[19] Language formula-tion or the emergence of linguistic states in the mental life of human beings depends upon the function of various specific aspects of mental organism. And it is the biological capacity of the organism to produce or formulate the linguistic expressions.

Chomsky's notion of the 'appropriate idealization' to bring out the harmonious and necessary correlation between the 'mental organs' and the 'grammatical rules' shows his ambivalency regarding the methodological approach towards the theory of language as whole. As a naturalist, his contention of naturalizing the theory of language and mind remain similar to the physicalist theorization of the language and the mind. Though he admits that language has biological basis still the *unity* of the mental and the language is possible through physics, not biology. He argues that "Of course, there are differences; the physicist is actually postulating physical entities and process while we are keeping to abstract conditions that unknown mechanism must meet, we might go on to suggest actual mechanism, but we know that it would be pointless to do so in the present stage of our ignorance concerning the functioning of the brain."[20]

However, it is important to know whether Chomsky's conception of language or growth of language and the necessary correlation of language and the mental is *accessible* to the notion of consciousness. In other words, is his *innate* conception of language accessible to consciousness? Firstly, the notion of *accessibility* or the relationship of language with the consciousness has certain limitations in the sense that language has a physical structure. And secondly, language is generated because of certain rules according to which physical capacities. These physical capacities of language have nothing to do with consciousness. As he puts it, " a language is generated by a system of rules and principles that enter into complex mental computations to determine the form of meaning of sentences. These rules and principles are in large measure unconscious and beyond the reach of potential consciousness. Our perfect knowledge of the language we speak gives us no privileged access to these principles; we cannot hope to determine them by introspec-tion or reflection from within, as it were."[21] Mental activity is a completely physical activity. The emergence of the linguistic states is itself a higher order physical activity. And since the linguistic expressions are always in a structural form it is caused by the structural rules or syntax of the mind. Syntax is the underlying generative principle which formulates the language or linguistic representations. The question of consciousness thus does not arise with regard to the structure of language.

Jerry Fodor's conception of *mental representation* or language of thought comes closer to Chomsky's conception of generative grammar. Both emphasize the syntax as the essential component of structuring linguistic representations or expressions. Moreover, syntax is considered as the *language of the mind*. The syntactical feature of the language of the mind transforms the compositional feature of the linguistic representations. The compositional feature signifies the syntactical and the semantically contents of expressions. So it is the syntax alone which encodes and decodes the linguistic expressions while in the language processing.

Mental representations, according to Fodor, have two basic concerns, firstly, it must specify the intentional content of mental states, and secondly, the symbolic structure of mental states must define the functions of the mental processes. The specification of intentional content of mental states or cognitive states describes its relationship that holds between the propositional attitudes and the intentional content. Though the primary aim of advocating the notion of mental representations is to give a realistic account of propositional attitudes, we will not discuss the realistic and anti-realistic standpoints here.[22] Rather our aim is to know how the semantic content of the propositional attitudes is incorporated in the mental state or the network of mental states.

For Fodor, mental states are token neural states. All the token mental states are syntactically characterized. By characterizing the mental or cognitive states as purely syntactical or symbolic in their forms, Fodor does not undermine the semantic component of the propositional attitude of the mental states. Rather, the very function of the brain organism and the cognitive states is such that it has a specific mechanism which *transforms* the *representations* into the internal representations.[23] And all the cognitive states are known as internal representational states. Now the question arises, how are propositional attitudes made symbolic? Moreover, what is important here is to know the processes of internal representations which get transformed into some representational states. This process is carried out without affecting the 'content' of the propositional attitudes. This is quite possible, for Fodor, because the organism or the system has a ***qua language*** which preserves the syntactic and semantic properties of content of the propositional attitudes of the cognitive states. To quote: "Qua language is presumably having syntax and semantics; specifying the language involves saying that what properties are in virtue of which its formulae are well informed, and what relation obtain between the formulae and things in the non-linguistic world. I have no idea what an adequate semantics for a system of internal representation will look like; suffice that if propositions come in at all, they come in here. In particular, nothing stops us in specifying a semantics for the IRS by saying (*inter alia*) that some of its formulae express propositions. They are mediated relation to propositions, with internal representations doing the mediating."[24] This *qua language* of the organism is otherwise known as the *language of thought*. It has not only the capacity of transforming one particular representations to its symbolic or syntactic form, but also it constitutes the "cognitive architecture." The *language of thought* is a formula of having only the syntactic structure, meant for evaluating the semantic properties of the representations. Moreover, it claims two things, i.e., 1) "some mental formula have mental formula as parts; and 2) the parts are 'transportable'; the same parts can appear in lots of mental formulas."[25]

By *cognitive architecture,* here, Fodor means the causal network of the cognitive or mental states. This structurality of cognitive states unfolds a systematic causal relationship among the cognitive states which binds them together. And this capacity is a completely disposition capacity of the organism.[26] Furthermore, in his words, "Language of thought wants to construe propositional attitude tokens as relation to symbol tokens. (Token of symbols in question are neural objects.) Now symbols have intentional contents and the tokens are physical in all the known cases. And qua-physical-symbol-tokens are right sort of things to exhibit causal roles. Language of thought claims that mental states—and not just their propositional objects—typically have constitute structure."[27] Causal connections among the cognitive states are fundamental because they determine the content of the propositional attitudes.

Coming back to the second concern of Fodor, the symbolic 'cognitive architecture' defines the mental processes. Fodor maintains that there are two levels of functions insofar as the determination of content is concerned. They are the symbolic structure of mental states whose function determines the intentional content of the propositional attitudes and the other is the neural process. However, there is a causal relation between the two levels. They are causally related in the sense that causal law is applied to the function of mental or representational states. According to Fodor, each mental state is identical with a brain state. The mental or representational states have causal properties. These properties can be expressed through the 'vocabulary of physics'.[28] These physical properties are the primary properties of the mental states, whereas psychological properties possessed by representational states are 'causally inert'. Since those properties are inert they can be characterized as epiphenomenal in comparison to other dominant physical properties. Further the 'causal responsibility' is defined through the 'causal sufficiency'. Each representational state is causally sufficient enough to produce effect or to get related with other mental states. This causal sufficiency is characterized as causal law. Fodor points out that on this view the question whether the property *p* is causally responsible reduces to the question whether there are causal law about *p*. "[29]

Fodor clarifies it through two concepts, called, *productivity* and *constituency*.[30] The notion of productivity here signifies the collection of mental states and thoughts that constitute the mental life. More precisely, the productivity of thoughts is same as the productivity of language. The indefinite utterances of sentences in our speech presuppose that there are also indefinite existing thoughts.[31] This productivity of thoughts is really the mental capacity. And it designates the neurological structure of the brain organism. He writes: "whatever experiences engender such capacities, and the experiences have unknown Neurological Effects (these unknown Neurological Effects being mediated, it goes without saying, by the corresponding unknown Neurological Mechanism), and the upshot is that you come to have a very large but finite-number of, as it were, independent mental disposition."[32] This dispositional capacity not only *systematizes* our linguistic expression but it is also an ability to understand and learn language. The notion of systematization refers to the sequential followings in our linguistic behaviour. This corresponds to the different ways in arranging the 'sub-sentential constituents' and relating them with the meaning of the sentences. Productivity and systematicity are correlated which exhibit the adequate function of the mechanism.

Relating the symbolic structure of mental or cognitive states with the neural process, Fodor writes, "the causal roles of mental states typically closely parallel the implication structures of their propositional objects; and the predicative success of propositionalattitudes psychology routinely exploits the symmetries thus engenderedthe structure of attitudes must accommodate a theory of thinking; and that it is pre-eminent constraint on the latter that it provides a mechanism for symmetry between the internal roles of thoughts and their causal roles."[33] Thus, Fodor holds the identity relation between the neural events and states and with the linguistic or cognitive states. Moreover, propositional attitude of the cognitive states is dependent upon the causal efficacy of the neural states and processes.

Fodor suggests that connectionism is possible between the tokening symbols and the mental processes if and only if the semantic attitudes of thoughts are symbolically characterized. That is, "you connect the causal properties of a symbol with its semantical properties via its syntax. The syntax of the symbol is one of its second-order physical properties. to imagine symbol tokens interacting causally in virtue of their syntactic structures. The syntax of the symbol might determine the causes and effects of its tokenings in much the way the geometry of a key determines which locks it will open."[34] Thus, Fodor elaborates the role of *qua language* as basic to the mental process functions in transforming the representations to syntactical states and at the same time expressing them in speech. It also shows that qua language is the source of productivity of language use. The natural language which we speak is secondary to the qua language of the mental states. Furthermore, the semantic and syntactic components of natural language are getting reduced to the formal structure of qua language which is purely syntactical in nature.

In this way, Fodor's notion of mental representation not only tries to relate mind with the world through *qua language* but also uses the qua language for the 'evaluation of semantics'. Both Chomsky and Fodor strongly hold that language processing or the thought processing is a cognitive activity but not a conscious activity. We are not aware of how the *qua language* or *generative syntax* functions in the domain of mental representation. And this micro-level syntactical *language* is exclusively a higher order physical activity of the brain organism. The complete explanation of neurophysiology of the brain will explain the emergence linguistic structure which constitutes the essence of language. It not only rules out the role of consciousness in the thought process but also discards the other semantic features like intentionality as an intrinsic property of language.

III. Gillett's Semantic Representation: Consciousness Reconsidered

Gillett rejects the theory of mental representation advocated by Fodor in particular and the cognitive scientists in general who argue that thought processing or linguistic activity is not conscious activity. Mental representations of the Fodorian variety portray only the syntactic aspects of thought processes. Fodor is concerned only with the syntax of the language of mind. Thus syntax is the bedrock capacity of generating language which explains our linguistic behaviour. As Gillett puts it, "the cognitive activity of human beings can be understood as a set of transitions between causally structured inner states as specified by formal syntax and semantics. It embodies a strong claim that a calculus of formal symbolization and inferential would suffice to capture the essential of human thought."[35] This, according to Gillett, does not really explain the basic feature of 'representations'. The process of symbolization through the language of thought reduces the compositional feature of language to only syntax. Thus representation is purely syntactical. Representation as a part of human thought process can reveal its true nature when we emphasize both syntactical and semantical content of thought or language because they are basic constituents of the mental states.

Representations, as Gillett describes, is the representation of the world. It unfolds the relationship between the *mind* and the *world* where *language* plays an important role. Gillett does not deny the role of brain processes. Rather the 'central cortex' of the brain organism has certain essential functions to structure *concepts*. Concepts are linguistic and the ultimate ground for making representations possible. Furthermore, *semantic representation* emphasizes the notion of linguistic *meaning* which discloses the logical relationship between mind, language and the world. As Gillett systematizes, "...(a) language represents the world, and (b) the mind even if it is not dependent on language for its representational ability is able to express itself in language and use language to record its operations. The fact that cumulative human social experience and interpersonal activity makes an extensive contribution to linguistic meaning suggests that the adequate semantics for human psychology should play close attention to the activity of representation."[36] Semantic representation emphasizes two things; firstly, the formation of content or concepts by the neurophysiological function of the brain which helps in structuring thought processes. This is what Searle calls the micro level function of the language. Secondly, it also discloses how thoughts are represented in the language. Thought has the same structure as the language that functions in the social level. So in semantic representation there is a necessary relation between the function of language at the mental or psychological level and those at the social level. Gillett mentions three basic features that semantic representation includes; they are, "(i) flexibility in their effects, (ii) embedded in the activities of the organism, (iii) they allow recognition of degrees of likeness or connection between the information."[37]

The feature of *flexibility* characterizes the process of constant participation of human beings in the world as biological beings. In the process of constant participation the biological organism becomes attuned respond to the world, according to the situation present. This development is a natural growth in the organism because of its consistent interaction with environment in a multiple ways. Of course, the species not just interact but tries to overcome the environmental constraints in the interacting processes, which Gillett calls the *generality constraint*. That shows the potency of acquiring the concepts and its cognitive functions. As he describes, "the thinker is able to conceive of the same feature as common to number of situations and the same object as the potential instance of a range of predictive judgments, so there must be this flexible 'aspect seeing' attentional control and selectivity of response. But this is to be conscious."[38] Selecting to do something or *willing* is an intentional activity. Intentionality is associated with the will of consciousness. Thus, unlike Searle, Gillett emphasizes the notion of intentionality of consciousness acting independently of the causal function of the brain processes.

The second *basic* feature shows the representational criterion is intrinsic to the organism. The function of cerebral cortex is such that it links the structure of thought with that of the brain process. He sayes: "It is because the cortex enables us to form complex links between stimuli and to assemble significant stimulus patterns which are interwoven with action in a waryard different ways that we are compelled to speak of brain representing the world."[39] By structure the thoughts, here we mean, the conceptual patterns involved is thought i.e., how the concepts are structured and how they are expressed in language. That, briefly, unfolds the very function of intentionality and rationality as the conditions of judging the things and simultaneously generating the awareness of the environment. This is a sort of normative relationship developed by the capacity of cerebral cortex. As he writes, "We understand such an intentional behaviour by appeal to the conception and rules according to which structure her behaviour. And the brain activity concerned brings into full play the processing capacities that reside in the cortex."[40] This capacity of 'cerebral cortex' not only conceptualizes the sense-data but also provides the pre-conceptual relations and "preserve certain epistemological desiderata." Furthermore, Gillett makes three important points which explain the role of cerebral cortex: They are, firstly, the ascription of [perceptual] content to the mind. Secondly, the content is not inferred from the thought structure rather it is intrinsic to the 'role of basic-structure'. Thirdly, we are not able to represent the representations in the sense that there is a constraint in expressing them—"the constraints that operate upon subjects' conceptualizing and therefore to preserve a sense in which *what is there* dictates *what is sun*."[41]

The third basic feature which talks about the 'degrees of likeness or connection between information" describes the 'conceptual links' that help in building up the structure of thought and its relationship with content. And the pattern of connectivity is such that it is always open for modification within the environment in which it functions. Hence, the notion of mental representation used by cognitive scientists gives a narrow view regarding the language processing in the cognitive network of human mind. It does not reflect much on the convincing ground of content formation as the semantic representation does. Gillett writes, "representation as discussed in cognitive science is an abstraction from structured patterns of activity in a holistic web of brain function. In this abstraction, we still identify the key elements of an item of conceptual information by focusing on the central aspects of the *use* of the sign for the concept."[42] So the biological explanation of semantic representation can be proper to the idea of concept formation. Semantic representation takes consciousness as the fundamental principle for concept formation. Human beings are not only biological systems with certain dispositional features but also they are *higher order conscious being*. Searle, who argues in favour of semantic representation, writes, "Apparently it is just a fact of biology that organisms that consciousness have, in general, much greater powers of discrimination than those that do not. Plant tropism, for example, which are light sensitive are much less capable of making fine discriminations and much less flexible than, for example, the human visual system. The hypothesis that I am sugges-ting then is one of the evolutionary advantages conferred on us by consciousness is the much greater flexibility, sensitivity and creativity we derive from being conscious-ness."[43] Creativity is a specific part of human thinking. We think, imagine and try to comprehend the reality and its nature with the capability of our creative thinking. And all these are understood with reference to the semanticity that is present in the consciousness. Human consciousness is not only directed or about the things in the world but also human beings think and realize the thought consciously. Realization is a linguistic realization because we think in the same language, the language that we *use*. Thoughts are formulated by certain linguistic feature of the organism and they are also realized by the same feature of the organism. Being linguistic is something specific to the human mental life in particular and human life in general.

IV. Intention Based Semantics

The concept of representationality can be further elaborated by focusing on the nature of macro-level function of the language. The macro-level use of language consists in the very exercise of language in the domain of various linguistic activities. These activities describe the relationship between the language and the world. The world is represented in the language. Hence, philosophically speaking, the whole of our linguistic activities explicates the notion of *meaning*, i.e. the meaningfulness of the linguistic representation of the world. Interestingly, the conception of meaning discloses the complex relationship between language and the world.

Intention based semantics (*IBS*) holds the representational theory of meaning. It emphasizes the speaker's 'intention' as one of the basic features of meaning. Intention, like any other psychological state is entangled with the expressions in language. The linguistic expression makes the *intention* explicit. Grice, one of the early exponents of *IBS* proceeds with the assumption that meaning of an utterance has a functional aspect. That is, the functionality of language prevails within the domain of communication intention. C*ommunication intention* unfolds the shared *intentional content* by both speaker and the listener. Moreover, the function of communication intention produces an *effect* both in the speaker's *intention of representation* as well as in the hearer's *recognition* of that particular intention of the speaker. This notion of meaning can be interpreted as having "psychologi-cal experiences." As Anton Marty puts it, " the expression of one's psychological life, which is the exclusive and primary aim of intentional speech. What is rather intended is to influence or to control the unknown inner life of the hearer. Intentional speech is a special kind of action, which is essentially aimed at evoking certain psychological phenomena in the person."[44] That is, the discourse of meaning is based the psychological experience in the sense that the inner mental life or mental states are reflected in the linguistic representations and the same is realized in the realm of mental. However, the notion of intentional semantics is pertaining to the domain of psychological experiences, requires further clarification. We have to ask whether there can be an explanation of meaning without any reference to conscious psychological experience? The interoperation by Schiffer and Loar of *IBS* is naturalistic and meaning can be causally explained with reference the psychological states and functions. Whereas, Anita Avramides' interpretation of the *IBS* is non-naturalistic. It is close to Searle's interpretation precisely because the expression of meaning is a conscious activity. Before going to discuss the two divergent interpretations of the Gricean semantics left us discuss the main contention of Grice's semantics.

According to Grice, the meaning or the intention is entailed from the expression. Whenever one says something or utters a statement *x*, it is not that the person only means *x*, s(he) also knows that *y* must mean that *x*. this particular analysis of knowing the intention by meaning it, Grice calls a non-naturalistic way of defining meaning. It is non-natural in the sense that meaning is not a causal process. The natural or causal notion of intention based semantics is associated with behaviouristic and physicalistic mode of meaning analysis. The behaviouristic tendency always emphasizes a causal account of meaning, i.e., speaker's intention produces or causes a typical effect in the listener's mind, and thereby it maintains a conditional and causal approach to the analyzing communication intention.[45] As Avramides points out, "The causal theorists recognize that to account for meaning one must pay attention to the role of speakers and hearers. Their behaviouristic roots require that whatever it is speakers and hearers that is relevant to meaning should be accessible to observation."[46] The causal explanation of speaker's intention with reference to the intentional aspect of mental life gives a naturalistic interpretation of the notion of *IBS*. On the other hand, the non-naturalistic account of *IBS*, according to Grice, must deal with the explication of the notion like, 'means the same as', 'understands', 'entails' and so on and the utterances which are specifically 'informative or descriptive'.

Grice, however, in his notion of non-natural meaning, maintains that in the case of *IBS*, the speaker's intention of uttering sentences is to *induce* the audience and subsequently tries to see that the intention is well *recognized* by the audience. As he writes, "Shortly, perhaps, we may say that "A meant$_{nn}$ something by x" is roughly equivalent to "A uttered x with the intention of inducing a belief by means of the recognition of this intention."[47] To say that the hearer recognizes the intention of the speaker or that the speaker's intended utterances, in both the cases induce the hearer, is to produce an effect which gives rise to further psychological states by generating either pleasure or displeasure. In this connection, the accessibility to the domain of knowledge of each other's intentional states or cognitive states can be explicated in the framework of *communication intention*. Because in the process of communication the speaker does not utters just to induce, rather s(he) makes a *deliberate* attempt in *telling* and making the hearer to *think* over it in order to fulfill his/her intention. Therefore, the utterer thinks before s(he) intends to speak and also correlates his intentional states with other possible facts for the realization of the goal. This whole 'course of action', i.e. starting from the thinking to intending, intending to speak and intending to realize or fulfill the intention itself can be characterized as *intentional action*. Thus, it is a special case of forming an intention.[48]

However, in the case of IBS the content of intention of the speaker is realized in a particular linguistic domain. Language use or expression meaning is domain specific or context bound activity. The domain specifies the rules of the language use. There is fixity of 'reason' in the domain of *communication intention* which could be maintained precisely for the convenience of *recognition* of intention. Moreover, the reason for having such rules in the IBS is not a limiting factor, rather a constitutive condition for the coherent linguistic communication. As Grice points out, "This points to the fact for *x* to have meaning$_{nn}$, the intended effect must be something which in some sense is within the control of the audience, or the in the sense of "reason" the recognition of intention behind x is for the audience a reason not merely a cause ('reason for believing' and 'reason for doing')."[49] The rational way of believing and performing linguistic behaviour in the specific context follows specifically certain rules. For Grice, linguistic rules are conventionally defined. Convention here strictly signifies the specificity of language use within a particular context. That justifies the *reason*able discourse of linguistic exercise insofar as the *IBS* is concerned.

Schiffer's interpretation of *IBS* is based on the notion of sentential meaning. In explaining sentential meaning, Schiffer proposes that a sentence has a meaning if and only if speaker utters it, and its intention is recognized well by the hearer; then it is understood that the hearer *recognizes* the *meaning* of speaker's utterance. Thus intention is a derivative notion and persists parasitically within the discourse of communication itself. This conception of *intention* builds up a typical conventional framework, where the both speaker and the hearer shares some "mutual knowledge." And the sharing the *mutual knowledge* is an essential prerequisite for the *IBS*. Moreover, the functional aspects of intentional content show, whenever *x intends to produce a reason R* in the audience A. It *means x knows about the responses in A*. That is, the intention of the speaker shows a reason to the hearer in the process of communication. That suggests that the intentional utterances in the course of communication intention *activate* & the knowledge states [belief states] of both the speaker and the hearer. And thereby the consequent linguistic behaviour that follows from the communicative linguistic initiates a process of knowing or recognizing each other's intention. There is reason for providing 'belief states' as the ground of "truth supporting condition" of IBS. As Schiffer writes, "Let's call reasons which are held in this way "truth supporting" reasons. One's reason for believing *p* need not be truth supporting; one might have moral or prudential grounds for thinking that *p*. "[50] Thus, belief states are not only having psychological basis but also they are based on social grounds. The social ground constitutes the framework of communication intention.

Now, the question arises, what sort of moral or prudential grounds as the speaker's belief states pertaining to? Morality or prudentiality is considered as the *rational* precondition for the intentional communication. It's rational in the sense that the communication intention is not always necessary to merely trigger the recognition of the belief states and its effects. Rather, the rational criterion emphasizes the possible and desirable way of generating the linguistic behaviour. In this regard the utterances of the speaker are not taken as mere utterances but its basic structure involves certain norms or *values*. [51] As Schiffer puts it, "the meaning of utterance types in terms of a basic account of S-meaning that what S means by uttering x is not at all determined by what is uttered, i.e. by value of 'x'. This does not mean that one can do or say whatever one likes and mean thereby anything one pleases to mean. One must utter x with a relevant intentions, and not any value of 'x' will be appropriate to this end."[52] Hence, ascribing *value* to a particular utterance or sentence depends upon the whole of the belief setup. It is not simply the person's ascription of intention. Moreover, the regulation of linguistic behaviour, especially the intentional communication, must differentiate between the *affective attitudes* from the intentional attitude. Affective attitudes are entangled with the emotions, which sometimes influence the intentional behaviour. In the strict sense of *IBS*, for Schiffer, the intentional attitude with intending and believing as basic character must dissociate from the affective or emotional attitude. Intentional attitude, in the case of intentional linguistic behaviour, is associated with the notions like *deliberation* and *decision*. With regard to the intention of producing or activating the desirable responses in the hearer we need to possess a sort of intention exclusively pertaining to intentional attitude. In Gricean expression, the distinction is clear when he proposes that the agent must have *motive for* doing 'that' whereas in the case of emotional action we fail to distinguish such motives.

Schiffer's conception of utterance meaning includes both compositional and non-compositional semantics. But the primacy is given to the non-compositional types of meaning for two basic reasons; it is simple and historically prior. The question arises how is that the non-compositional meaning is determined? As we have discussed earlier, *intentional meaning* is mostly an exercise within the group which shares some mutual knowledge. In the 'surest communicating circumstance' the speaker's intention is not only a subjective factor in bringing out the effect in the audience, rather the circumstance itself is an important and unchangeable condition in bringing out the effect. This unchangability condition of a linguistic convention is not just a *practice* or *habit* prevailing amongst the members of the linguistic group, as Grice defines.[53] Schiffer, on the other hand, refutes Grice's analysis for certain unacceptable reasons: Firstly, 'For S, x may have some meaning other than "p"; so it cannot be S's policy to utter x only if he wants some A to think S thinks that p.' Secondly, 'S may have some other utterance type by which he also means that p; so it cannot be S's policy to utter x if he wants some A to think that p. '

There is no subjective imposition of meaning in the conventional means of communication. A group shares certain mutual knowledge and maintains a perfect coordination among its members. Though often the basic intention of members of a group is a complex and conflicting phenomenon insofar as the realization of the goals are concerned. In that state of affairs, Schiffer suggests that there is a 'strategic interdependence' maintained to regulate each agent's goal oriented behaviour. And, it results in equilibrium in such a prevailing context.[54] The equilibrium maintains a co-ordination among the agents who share the same convention. 'Agents in a co-ordination problem mutually expect one another to seek a coordination equilibrium that possesses certain feature(s) which makes the coordination equilibrium a rational choice.' Coordination equilibrium provides a universal basis for standardizing the goal-oriented behaviour of rational agents in a convention.

Furthermore, Schiffer does talk about the possibility of a conventional shift (change) within a group. The emergence of new convention within a particular period of time as a natural phenomenon is decided by the group consent. That, moreover, provides a mutual platform, "it is not difficult to see how a convention might arise and perpetuate itself amongst a group of people for whom a certain types of coordination problem is recurrent."[55] Even if the convention changes, the emergence of new convention in linguistic community will result in simultaneous change in community intention. So that the shifting or changing the convention will not be a hindrance to determining the meaning.

Schiffer, however, in his latter work, nullifies the conventional model of *IBS* analysis by promoting the "psychological model"[56] for explaining meaning. Psychological model strongly argues for the micro level structural components of sentential meaning. The conventional paradigm is considered as incomplete in its explanation of *IBS*. As he puts it, "A self perpetuating regularity of this sort would be a convention, their attractive features of IBS is the way it is so nicely meshes wishes, and exploits a notion of convention itself defined wholly psychological and non-semantic terms."[57] Insofar as the incompleteness of IBS is pointed out, the variables of intentional features, specifically intentionality, have to be determined by the propositional attitudes of the mental states, not by public language (macro-level structure) functions. Propositional attitude is taken as fundamental constituent of the sentential meaning. Moreover, the rationale of the denial of macro-level functionality of language for intentional semantics consequently denies the *compositional semantics.*[58]

The structural explication of sentence shows the semantic value embedded in the sentence. Sentence is constituted of some of the micro-level constituents, such as words, and the syntactical mechanism. Propositional attitudes (PA), as generating mechanism, have direct relational effect on the world. They are about the "relation of things believed, desired, feared, and so on'. PA being the intrinsic aspects of *language of thought,* talks about meaning as an exclusive feature of *mental representation*. For Schiffer, the mental representation involves the conceptual role of composite semantics as well as the truth-theoretic or referential semantics. Nevertheless, what has been so important for the Mentalese is the inner structure of language playing the conceptual role. The conceptual role of language of thought is the basic ground for producing innumerable sentential states and expressions. As Schiffer writes, "The conceptual role of inner sentences, we already know, is the counter factual property of that sentence, which property is specifiable independently of any semantic properties the sentence might have in a way that the details of the causal or transitional role of that sentence in the formation of perceptual beliefs and theoretical and practical reasoning."[59] Schiffer takes the Fodorian standpoint while explaining the fundamental feature of *LoT*, in which the belief contents of the sentential states are explained in terms of the meaning of inner formulae. And the inner formulae of language do not need any further sort of semantics. Hence, psychological model of semantics takes *LoT* as the bedrock for the explanation of the composite semantics, since the meaning of a sentence or expression is constituted and determined by the words and the syntax. Precisely in the sense that *LoT* does not presuppose a composite semantics. In this regard, it is important to discuss the understanding or the comprehending capacity of natural language. This capacity is considered logically prior to the comprehension of compositional semantics.

Understanding and knowing are correlated notions. To say that one knows the meaning of the sentence means one also understands the intention of the sentence. The understanding of simple and composite sentences which determine the total expression follows the understanding of complex sentence. Once we understand the constituents of the sentences then its syntax can also be comprehended. Syntactical components are the constituted properties of the sentences understood as the potential features of language which are semantically relevant.[60] The grammar of the sentence of language determines the meaning of sentences in that language. In the context of language function, there is a series of correlation among the sentences. And in some cases the meaning of sub-sentences is derived from more complex variety of sentences. For Schiffer, "These derived subsentential sequences may be called phrases of G, and the propositional determinants, thus correlated with them their *meanings in* G; once G determines L, sentences of L, may also be called sentences of G, their meanings in L is also called their meanings in G."[61] Here, G signifies the basic syntactical micro components of language as the substantial property having the capacity to generate linguistic representation. Therefore, these micro [syntactical] components determine the meaning of the expression.

More interestingly, Schiffer's later conception of semantics sounds contradictory in comparison to the earlier version, when he advocates the notion of *no-theory of meaning*. He writes, "The notion of 'no-theory of meaning' comprises two components; one no-theory of linguistic representation, that pertains to language and to meaning in a strict sense; and another, the no-theory of mental representation, that pertains to the intentionality, or content, of propositional attitudes."[62] We have already seen how he discards the compositional semantics while reducing meaning into language of thought or mental formulae. But, so far as his 'no-theory of mental representations' is concerned he rejects the notion of intentionality which plays a role in relation to description of the sentential states or belief states. Intentionality is not considered as an independent and defining feature of the mind as whole. And the belief states are formulated and directly connected with the neural networks of the brain organism, so far as their function and realization are concerned. Hence, it can be said that the structural correlation of the sentential states and their representational features are *derived from* the representational features of brain's constituent parts and structure. Furthermore, Schiffer makes it clear that LoT hypothesis does not amount to a stronger version of semantics. Rather, it is the hypothesis of propositional attitudes with relation to the mental representations which explains meaning. Meaning is ascribed to the mental representations: "To know the meaning of mental representation *s* is to know what one believes when s is stored in one as belief where one believes the content of one's belief, is conveyed by 'that'→clauses of belief-predicates true."[63] Thus, Schiffer's psychological model proposes a cognitive version of meaning, by associating semantic discourse with the structure or organization of the mental states.

Unlike Schiffer, Loar's interpretation of *IBS* also suggests *propositional attitude semantics* which rejects the Gricean notion of meaning. According to Loar, the complete account of IBS can only be given in terms of semantical properties like conventional regularities and communication intention. In brief, it has been a "false impression" that these two properties promote sound public language semantics. No doubt, intention based semantics comprises the *communication intention* and *conventional regularities*. But it does not focus much on the *central* role of language, i.e., neither compositionality of sentential meaning nor the conventional meaning.[64] The difficulties that Loar finds in the case of the above constituting factors of IBS is, "That the communication intentions don't presuppose anything semantic conflicts in no way with intentions about the extreme dependence of communication as conventional regularities. Instead, they provide a non-circular way of saying what those regularities are, and thereby a way of explaining the intention that conventional regularities are central to communication."[65] On the other hand, Loar says it is important to have (i) the linguistic characterization of mental states saying that mental states are linguistic states, and secondly, the "non-circular explication of the content of the concepts". And he advocates the functional description of the belief states for explicating the semantic content of utterances by only discussing the functional semantic properties and truth conditions. Moreover, he claims that this analysis can be done without bringing language into discourse and developing it within a naturalists framework.

Belief states are characterized as non-linguistic mental states. "A non-linguistic account of content provides an attractively flexible basis for sketching the manifold possible dependencies of thought upon language; the key point is that the ascription of content to propositional attitudes is at a more abstract level than ascription of meaning to the natural language. The point is, if my functional account of belief-individuation is correct, intentions are not required in the theory of propositional attitudes and their intentional properties."[66]

Loar emphasizes the functional correlation of the belief states for the determination of the semantic content. As he cites, "This [correlationship] allows for maximal plasticity in as writing: certain mental function can be switched from one neurological states to another. No neurological state type as reserved for certain mental role may be radically contingent for how it would interact with others may change for moment to moment."[67] Hence, the functional plasticity of the structure of mental states does not have fixed function, rather their function is interchangeable. However, Loar's functional semantics does not significantly entertain the role of neurophysiological processes, so far as the determination of the content of language is concerned. The functional characterization of belief states which constitutes 'structure' or structural network, are necessarily syntactically interconnected. In his words, "for beliefs to have a syntax is not required that some states be suitably isomorphic in physiological structure of English." In other words, Loar's description of the functional correlation of belief states and process can be called "information processing model" that abstracts from the neurophysiological structure.[68] As it has been pointed out, the sentential characterizations of the belief states are syntactically correlated. The "sentential indices" are sufficient enough to apprehend the interconnections of belief states which involve syntax. But there is no isomorphic relationship between the functional role of the structural network and the *indices*. It also goes against the conception that there is an *isomorphic* relationship between thought and speech. Moreover, Loar finds the notion of thinking in terms of language as trivial. In his view, the hypothesis of *thinking in terms of language* includes two difficulties. One, "the fact that Z's internal states are functionally organized in according with belief-desire theory does not entail that Z's belief exhibit linguistic structure. And another is, the fact that our belief exhibits linguistic structure, even isomorphic to that of our spoken language, does not entail that we think in language we speak."[69] In this regard, the functional analysis of the content does not accept the primacy of the psycho-functional approach of semantics. Rather it proposes a notion of meaning which involves certain complex phenomena called 'socio-psychological properties.' For Loar, 'semantic' [I mean] not only the referential truth condition level of description but also the functional; if linguistic structure is to be discerned in a functional system, it would seem there must be two parallel structures, syntactic and functional."[70] The socio-psychological model, precisely, maintains parallelism between the syntactic and functional aspects of meaning. It is psychological with reference to the very nature of understanding of the language or knowledge of language, and it signifies its internal processes for the formulation of propositional attitudes. This process not only deals with acquiring the language but also includes the capacity to think in language. This, in other words, is called *internal representation.*

This cognitive model of semantic analysis for the determination of content in its discourse discusses the functionality of the internal representational states as well as the capacity for generating the concepts. The capacity, as Loar points out, is something *genetic*. Hence, acquiring concepts is uniquely important for further understanding of reference and truth condition. This reference and truth condition is represented in the grammar of the language, and they substantiate the constituting conditions for meaning and truth.[71] Loar calls it a *holistic* fact about sentential meaning. The holism pertains to two basic levels: '(i) in the determination of propositional attitude content by its place in overall belief-desire functional organization, and (ii) in the implicit holistic considerations inevitably appealed to indetermining truth conditions of beliefs on the basis of reliability'.

The functional description of *propositional attitude semantics* of Loar and Schiffer is, found to be thoroughly naturalistic and reductionistic. Now, the question arises, whether Grice really advocated the naturalistic notion of meaning. Contrary to the interpretation of Schiffer and Loar Anita Avramides'[72] reveals a new dimension to Grice's *IBS* which comes closer to the notion of semantics of Austin's and Searle's. In brief, Gricean semantic notions like timeless meaning and conventional characterization of communication intention are purely non-natural in their character. According to Anita, "Griceans like Schiffer and Loar who wanted to vindicate a reductive interpretation of Grice's original analysis began to concentrate less on the explication of the propositional attitudes mentioned on the right side of analytic biconditional. Each in his own way believed that we would advance the program of intention based semantics by developing functionalists account of propositional attitudes."[73] They emphasize much on the cognitive as well as functional aspects of syntax where propositional attitude of mental states is part of physical feature of the brain. Moreover, to say that Gricean semantics is nonnatural having Austinean and Searlean outlook is to strongly claim that 'Gricean account of meaning does bring the philosophy of language within the scope of philosophy of mind and the theory of action' .

Avramides, however, makes two important remarks regarding the basis of reductive attitude of the Griceans. Firstly, they believe that Grice's notion of *timeless* meaning is exclusively related to the psychological states. And, secondly, there is an *asymmetrical* relationship between the semantic and the psychological. On the other hand, the Gricean notion of timeless meaning signifies the autonomy of meaning. The timeless meaning signifies the function of language both at the micro-level and at the macro-level. So far as the interrelationship of the belief states are concerned, it is apprehended in our linguistic representation or linguistic behaviour. As Avramides points out, "...the Gricean account of speaker meaning of an occasion and timeless meaning of an utterance are the foundation of a general account of language use..." She also suggests, "a distinction between what the speaker *said* (in a certain favoured, may be in some degree artificial, sense of 'said') and what he has 'implicated' taking into account the fact that what he has implicated may be either *conventionality* implicated... or *nonconventionality* implicated."[74] Though there is a conventional regularity maintained in the discourse of communication intention, speaker's intention is not bound by the conventional regularities. Rather it sometimes goes *beyond* the conven-tional meaning. The communication intention or *expectation* of the speaker is more often confined within the limits of other community member's mutual expectations and intentions which are in general connected with the utterances. To show the openness of the conceptual boundary of the mutual community intentions, the expectation or the intention allows two important things to happen: 'One, though some members of the community may never utter certain sentences, these sentences retain their meaning in the language of that community. Two, though a member of a community may employ an utterance in a way that goes against the expectations of other members, meaning of that utterance does not change in the community. (consider the cases of irony, sarcasm and jokes etc.) Such expectations also explain with the community not just any string of work or sounds can be used to mean a given position' . Meaning is thus retained in community intention even if some expressions or modes of expression are not used before. The deliberate or accidental changes that occur in particular language use in a linguistic community find their meaning within the intentional framework of the community.

Avramides' interpretation of the Gricean semantics gives a deeper analysis of the interrelationship of the semantic and the psychological. The interrelationship is *asymmetric*, according to both Loar and Schiffer. Psychological states or propositional attitudes being indispensable part of their programme involve a reductive analysis with the view that the whole conception of meaning is 'secondary to psychological concepts in our over all scheme of concepts'. However, there are two existing types of asymmetry relationships in the Gricean's semantics. As Avarmides points out, they are, (i) *ontological asymmetry* (OA) and (ii) *epistemological asymmetry* (EA).

OA. "... a creature need not possess thoughts to be

capable of language, although capable of language a creature must possess thoughts."

EA. "... for there to be knowledge of what other thinks one need not know what his words and sentences mean, although to know what another's words and sentences mean, one needs to make assumption about his propositional attitudes."[75]

Since human beings use language it logically entails that human beings have thought which is intrinsic to the mental life of human beings. Language processing in the case of machine's linguistic behaviour will not presuppose that machine possesses some thought. Secondly, the EA shows propositional attitude is essential for comprehending the meaning of the intention of linguistic representation.

Now question arises what sort of asymmetry relationship exists between the physical cognitive states and their linguistic counterparts. It could be answered with reference to the knowablity of the nature of mental or psychological states. In this regard, the notion of accessibility becomes a prime condition for the analysis of such asymmetry

The very notion of accessing the truth of the fundamental psychological states is through semantics, for Avramides, The asymmetry accessibility provides us with one possible understanding of the claim that there is an epistemological asymmetry between our psychological and semantic concepts. I shall label this asymmetry of accessibility 'surface epistemological asymmetry.' The asymmetry lies between the thought and its expression. At the surface level they are asymmetrical because of their structure. Moreover, the asymmetry relationship that Loar and Schiffer argue for is a *deep epistemological asymmetry* (DEA). In the case of DEA, "We can in principle know the belief and interpretations of language users prior to understanding their language. This possibility becomes apparent when we move from "ordinary" evidence to evidence on a 'new level' (a neurophysiological functional level)."[76] Loar and Schiffer advocate DEA because they hold a conceptual gap between the neural or syntactical states of the organism and the linguistic expression. Linguistic expression is composed with both syntactical and semantical contents, whereas the language of thought is purely syntactical. This is no doubt a naturalistic interpretation of the semantics which emphasizes the neurological functional states and structures of the mental states.

The accessing the mental life of other has twofold dimensions, i.e. accessing from *the first person perspective*, a subjective way of knowing other's mind and accessing from *the third person perspective* or the objective way of knowing. The former has been commonly understood as the Cartesian way of looking at the phenomena called the mental, whereas the latter seeks to provide an objective account of the mental. In this regard, obviously, there has been an asymmetry between the first person and third person perspective. Moreover, in the objective perspective accessibility always refers to knowing the mental life through behaviour. But, does behaviour really determine our experiences of others mind? The difficulty that Avramides observes is that 'the first person accessibility does not rely on the behaviour while the third person has no immediate perspective or experiential qualities attached to it.' With this assumption, she rejects the ordinary way of looking at the Cartesian as well as the physicalistic perspectives of knowing the mental. However, the most commonsensical approach she puts forward is that "Once we conceive mind as a reductive phenomenon, we are in a position to reject, our ordinary everyday perspective of the mind of another revealing of the true nature of the mind."[77] Since mental states embodies semantical properties it cannot be exclusively characterized as physical or syntactical, because the process of characterization will certainly result in reductionism. Moreover, the properties of the mental are something different from the physical properties so its analysis does not fall with the method of observation and experiment which is generally used for the analysis of physical phenomena.

Following Nagel's hypothesis[78] regarding the subjective or first person perspective of studying the mental, Avramides comes out with a new perspective of semantics where the ordinary way of looking at the interdependence between semantic and the psychological disappears. This new perspective questions the approach of the reductivists by advocating a *subjective model of accessibility* that results in the objective criterion of meaning. This perspective which is placed within the realm of linguistic behaviour shows an alternative method of accessibility to the mental life. ' From this new perspective one can argue that the semantic is not really important to our understanding of the psychological. It is only thought to be so if not in principle replaced by the other perspective'. Stating that linguistic behaviour is the starting point for accessing the mental life, she does not accept the view of Loar and Schiffer who claim that propositional attitudes are only contingently related to the linguistic behaviour. As she clarifies, '*any* theory that denies that mind is manifest in linguistic behaviour→that is, any theory that makes the relation between mind and linguistic behaviour merely contingent→embodies an objective conception of mind. And since, the Gricean is committed by his reductionism to holding that mind is only contingently related to linguistic behaviour, he is *ipso facto* committed to an objective conception of mind."[79] The conception of mind that has been studied from the *first person perspective* of linguistic behaviour has wider function. It includes the not only the representation or the expressions of something in language but also the grasp of the concepts as well as thoughts. Thus the functionality of linguistic behaviour is *infused* with the notion of mentality. And therefore this is not simply called linguistic behaviour, rather it is known as *behaviour proper*. We would like to call it *proper linguistic behaviour* (PLB). PLB is not physicalistic rather it has been characterized as mentalistic. PLB, for Avramides, "is the behaviour infused with mentality; behaviour mentalistically characterized. If we understand matter this way we are in the path of conceiving the mind as subjective phenomenon". To deny the mind's manifestation in the behaviour is in fact to deny its *essential subjectivity*.[80] Essential subjectivity talks about first person's knowablity or accessibility of his/her mental life, without performing any behaviour. Furthermore, since both first person and third person perspectives assert conception of mind, it would be mistaken to say that 'we conform properly subjective conception of mind, and still deny that mind is a manifestation of behaviour: There is, then a route from the reductive Gricean's denial that mind is manifested in behaviour to a commitment to an objective view of mind. In short, the objection holds that a properly subjective conception of mind is consistent with the mind is only consistently related to behaviour.'

Since PLB is intrinsic to the realm of the mental, now question arises whether we can ascribe the notion of intrinsic intentionality to the linguistic behaviour. There can be two interpretations of this view. Either one accepts the structural isomorphism between the conscious-thought-experience and their linguistic representations, where intentionality plays a connecting principle. Or, one denies the role of connecting principle and advocates an independent functional use of language. The latter is more important in two respects; firstly, it helps to explicate the conception of proper linguistic behaviour, and secondly, it recognizes the role of intentiona-lity. In this regard, we would like to refer to Millikan's inter-pretation of Grice's IBS, who advocates the proper function of language or normal language use. Normal language use implies that language as a device must have standard or stabilized functions. It emphasizes the role of literal use of language..Intention is derived from the proper function of language. The communication intention as a the part of the proper linguistic activity sustains, rather proliferates because of the perfect coordination among speakers and hearers. As Millikan writes, "the stabilizing function of imperatives is to produce compliance the stabilizing function of indicative mood is to convey information, i.e., to produce belief."[81] Moreover, she points that in the case of imperatives and indicatives there is no independent role of language. Rather, the literal use of language is fundamental because the individual's intention is being interpreted through community intention or existing rules to confirm the meaning of the proper function. Though there are alternative motivations of the speaker proposed but they don't assert stabilized function of language.

The notion of meaning operates in the framework of stabilized proper functions of language the stabilized version of language helps in sustaining meaning through its normal function. Sentential meaning is taken into consideration here. Though sentential meaning is determined through relational descriptions of other context related sentences, insofar as the basic unit of meaning is concerned, it not word but sentence that is in focus.[02] Another important function that is related to the determination of meaning is called 'mapping function'. Mapping condition determines the truth and falsity of sentences, specifically because there is an ontic relationship between the facts of the world and the mapping structure of the psychological states. 'The meaning of the sentence is its own special mapping functions→in accordance with which it 'should' or is 'supposed to' map onto the world'.

Intentionality is considered as a relative phenomenon attached to the sentences of the stabilized functions of the language use. Meaning and intentionality are relative to the 'propositional content'. Millikan's naturalistic conception of intentionality in particular and language function in general gives a coherent view which includes meaning, truth, inner representations, signs etc. However, intentional-ity is located within the normal function of language. Language as having a stabilized function, precisely with reference to *IBS*, is divided into two categories called indicative paradigms and imperative paradigms. Intentionality which operates within these paradigms does not have an independent status. Intentionality, in Millikan's naturalistic scheme, is characterized as a dependent intentionality. It is dependent on the sentential usage of language. As she mentions, "If it were not for the intentionality of the people's thoughts, which get communicated via sentences, sentences would not be intentional but would be quite ordinary objects..." "Briefly, sentences are intentional in a derivative sense, requiring reference to something other than that of intentional *per se*; so whatever is intentional *per* se cannot be understood on analogy with sentences. The essential conclusion is that basic intentionality is something had directly by beliefs and intentions. For proceeding further with regress could serve no purpose."[83] Millikan denies that there could be any basic intentionality independent of the language function. Intentionality is displayed within the mapping structure of stabilized functions of language. And it is derived not from the inner representational states of beliefs and intentions but from the sentences that are used in communication. Hence there is no intentionality condition involved in causing intentionality in the specific sense. 'Intentionality of public language sentence is not derived from the intentionality of inner representation, that it normally produces and expresses sentences are basic intentional items'.

External intentionality in contrast with internal intrinsic intentionality is ascribed to the language use, not to consciousness. Intentionality is treated as a basic feature of consciousness. It places intentionality in consciousness or conscious experiences. That further explains the person's being consciously aware of or about the facts of the external world. As Millikan remarks, "The position is that intentionality is grounded in external natural relations, normal and or

in the philosophical and linguistic literature sentences lead naturally to next conclusion: what I have said about literal meaning also applies to intentional states in general. A man who believes that the cat is on the mat or who expects they will bring him a medium rare humburberg has his belief and expectation only against a background of other inexplicit 'assumptions'."[87] He also states that "Just as literal meaning of sentence will determine different truth or obedience conditions relative to different state of assumptions, so as belief or expectation will have different condition of satisfaction relative to different sets of assumptions."(Ibid)

Thus precisely a parallelism persists between the literal meaning and the intentional states. The parallel structural movement is possible through intentionality. It is the intentionality which enables the speaker to represent the mental states in the public form of language use. What makes the representation possible? Or, whether there can be complete representation at all in the case of semantical discourse? Question such as theses can be raised only with reference to the Background assumptions. We have already discussed in the previous chapter that the Background conditions are responsible for representation of intentionality. However, our concern is 'can there be literal meaning without any reference to convention?' Searle's answer would be 'no'. For him, 'meaning is a matter of convention'. Referring back to the interrelationship of literal meaning, intentional representation and their association with convention, Searle maintains, "I don't know how to answer these questions expect by saying that literal meaning is dependent on context in the same way as the other nonconventional forms of intentionality are dependent on context. There is no way to eliminate these dependencies in the case of literal meaning which would not break the connection with other forms of intentionality and hence would eliminate the intentionality of literal meaning altogether."[88] This dependence results from the basic form of intentional states and experiences. Visual experiences are associated with the most basic forms of intentionality; when the experience is represented in language it not only carries the qualitative aspects but also gives rise to further intention or expectations for the condition of satisfaction.

It is difficult to say how much the Background condition is important to determine the literal meaning of the linguistic expression. But it can be at least said that literal meaning is Background dependent. It is because of the fact that literal meaning is interpreted according to the Background presuppositions or the Background capacities of the person. As Searle puts it, "each sentence is interpreted against a Background of human capacities (abilities to engage in certain practices, know how many ways of doing things, etc.) and those capacities will fix different interpretations, even though the literal meaning of expression remains constant."[89] Searle does not deny the significance of linguistic conventions. For him, the proper understanding of utterances and compositionality of language are absolutely important in order to give a coherent account of language. However, interpretation of the literal meaning of utterances needs the Background presuppositions precisely because of the additional content it brings forth. And understanding of the additional content attached to the utterance is always supported by the inductively based set of expectations.[90] The Background presuppositions are primary, in the sense that otherwise literal meanings by themselves are incomplete. As Searle writes, "Literal meaning determines the conditions absolutely in isolation. But literal meanings are vague and literal descriptions are always incomplete. Greater precision and completeness are added by supplementing literal meaning with collateral assumptions and expectations."[91]

Now, coming back to the second thesis that meaning is primarily an illocutionary act, Searle explicates the basic concepts that are involved in our linguistic activities. The very conception of recognizing the intention of the speaker in IBS or recognizing the knowledge states of others we try to understand what the speaker is intending. Gricean semantics rather emphasizes the speaker's intention in bringing out the notion of understanding. To say that recognition of intention is, an effect makes the meaning circular. Searle suggests that 'meaning and understanding are too closely tied for the latter to be basis for an analysis of the former'. One may also ask, what is the essential component to be understood in our 'representation-communication'?[92] To put it differently, what constitutes understanding of literal sentences? Since the notion of understanding sentence entails knowing its meaning, how this knowing does follow? For Searle 'The meaning of a sentence is followed by rules, and those rules specifically includes both condition of utterance and also what count to us'. Here, by condition of utterance and the recognition of utterance signify the two constitutive aspects of semantic rules. It is not simply that the process involves various concepts like speaker's being intention to specifically represent his her intention that the recognized by the audience. This state of affairs is rather regulated by certain rules—'intending to get him to recognize in virtue of his knowledge of rules of the sentence uttered.'

Let's talk about the concept of understanding the 'semantic rules'. Understanding the semantic rule entails how the concept is being applied in the language use. For example, to illustrate the concept of "greeting"; one may know different forms of greetings. But, in each form of greeting, a person greets the other person saying "hello" or "good morning". It is expected that the other person will subsequently acknowledge and respond accordingly by greeting him. Hence for the understanding of the semantic rule of greeting one must know how the greetings are being conventionally performed in the language use. It is obvious that these concepts are always linguistically expressed. Furthermore, the concepts are having typical function as we master the language if greeting. A child learns to greet others by observing his friends, relatives, parents and others (within the cultural environment in which s(he) grows. During the period of learning the child is not just picking up things, rather the child follows instruction from the elders how his greetings will be more appreciated by everybody. As Gillett writes, "Concept are developed in practices which determine other use and applications of the terms by which a child comes to pick out and think about those objects he is learning to perceive around him."[93] Therefore, for the very notion of developing concepts by understanding its typical role in the conventional use or linguistic-conventional use, one must observe that there is an epistemic gap between the emerging structural concepts and the new encounters that the person meets in his socio-linguistic set up. Gillett further illustrates, "Conceptual abilities have been analyzed as rule governed engagements with the world of objects and how we react to them, and thus the analysis fineness the role of internal/ subjective states which intervene to allow the use of the word "experience" other than a natural term to refer to what happens to sentient people."[94] We have already discussed how the sensitivity and flexibility are part of conscious features for the development of concepts. Searle also agrees on these notions and points out further regarding the development of linguistic categories as the basic functional features of biological and social backgrounds.[95]

Searle, however, maintains that intentionality is a part of the process of conceptual development. Intentionality is involved in the very act of representation or communication. In the speech act representations it is essential for the agent to recognize the psychological mode because the very act of formulating an intentional state and representing it results in the condition of satisfaction. In this case the directedness is from the world-to-mind. For instance, as a management trainee one is taught how to motivate and deal professionally with customers. But learning how to do the things is different from developing one's own skill.[96] Developing any sort of stance is again a part of the Background condition. This development is a process. As we have already mentioned that Searlean Background is an inevitable feature for representing the intentional states. For Searle, it is the linguistic categories[97] which are responsible for the experience of the world. Linguistic categories are involved in consciousness. Of course, Searle uses the notion of linguistic categories instead of using concepts. It is precisely because, he finds it unproblematic in the sense that linguistic categories function within the framework of the network of intentional states. And the intentional states are in principle linguistic Intentional states are part of the structure of consciousness. There are certain other features which are attached with the linguistic categories such as aspectuality of intentionality, the aspects of familiarity, etc. Hence, the whole idea of representation in terms of language is a notion derived from the structural Network of intentional states. Insofar as the semantic rule-following is concerned, Searle suggests whenever we apply any concept or use any word we necessarily follow certain rules. The rules are built into the very nature of linguistic rerpesentations. But learning a rule or 'concept word' in an intentional process, can be otherwise called intention-in-action. Though it seems to us that we follow a rule unconsciously, explaining of our linguistic behaviour is nothing but giving an intentional-causal explanation. This intentional-causal process in the case of our linguistic behaviour is rule-guided. Thus intentionality follows necessarily as an inseparable part of our linguistic behaviour.

(a) *Structure of Consciousness and Language: Reestablishing structural isomorphism*

By structure of consciousness, we mean that the phenomenon of consciousness involves certain composite properties; they are called *intentionality*, *phenomenality*, and *introspectibility*. These properties are not only interrelated with each other but and also intrinsic to our *conscious-thought-experiences.*[98] All our experiences, have a space for intentionality in it. My experience of seeing 'x stands in alert position' shows the directedness of my conscious representation of what I experience when 'I am watching x'. Similarly, the feature of phenomenality is associated in my experience. When I am asked, 'how did x stand like there in front of you?', then my immediate response is 'x was quite alert in his position'. That reveals the qualitative aspects of judging different postures. This qualitative difference of our experiences is defined as qualia. By introspectability here is meant the reflexivity of consciousness. It is otherwise known as self-consciousness or consciousness of something being conscious. The subtlety of the statement lies in not creating any gradation of consciousness as first order and second order consciousness. Neither does it create any metaphysical ambiguities.[99] Rather the logical possibility of embodying reflexivity as an essential feature of conscious-thought-experience shows the inward directedness of consciousness, i.e. the intentionality of mental reference which does not deny the biological form of consciousness. To deny the reflexivity of consciousness is to deny the intentionality of mental reference.

Now one may ask, what sort of structurality exists between consciousness and language. To bring forth the conception of structural isomorphism we would like to focus upon the Searlean perspective of consciousness and language. It provides a broader perspective for language and consciousness. The significance of 'conscious-thought-experience' is that the composite feature of consciousness is always entangled with representational states. The very nature of formulation and expression of representational states is a continuous *process* where the representational states are impregnated with the properties of consciousness or conscious-experiences. And thereby the 'intentional content' (which includes qualia and aboutness) is not only present in the representational states but also gets systematically structured for expressing it. This systematization as a normative process further entails that the syntactic component is also involved in the process of formulation. Moreover, the centrality of the isomorphism lies in the notion of the intentional content of the representational states and its semantic or linguistic representations. It is precisely the intentional content that holds the continuity intact. That is, the intentional content flows over from one conceptual field of function called *mental field* to another conceptual field of function called *linguistic field*. This flow is a parallel process, it reveals the *logico-isomorphic* view of structurality as a whole. Furthermore, the parallelism pertains to the mental representation as well as semantic representation where intentional content plays the key role in specifying the mental reference and linguistic reference. In the case of mental reference, for instance, when I play cricket, I think about my style of bowling; my desire is to give a delivery in such a way that the ball spins perfectly well and confuses the batsman at play. By having this desire, I too strongly believe that I can place the ball in right order. And this continuous process of thinking about my bowling procedure is nothing but the intentional content of my experience which has only an inward reference called intentionality of mental reference. On the other hand, when I perform an action or represent my states of belief, it discloses the outward directedness called the linguistic reference.

However, the question arises, what sort of transformation takes place in the case of semantic representations when representational states are formulated? For Searle, the whole conception of semantic representation is a linguistic exercise, and thereby, representation is always propositional in nature. There are two facets of representational states considered to be significant. They are, the representation of our visual experiences and the representation of mental states. In the case of visual experiences, we are not just seeing the object but rather experiencing it in the visual field. And, when we are reporting that particular experience, we usually say I *see* the object *as* it is presented to me, i.e. the *aspectual content* of my experience.[100] Thus, there is a sort of *transformation*[101] as a continuous process, from our visual representation to our linguistic representation. For Searle, "...the verb 'see' takes spatial modifiers that under the natural interpretation require us to postulate an entire proposition as content of visual experience." Whereas in the case of linguistic representation, "...verbs of 'desire' take temporal modifiers that require us to postulate entire propositions as content of desire."[102]

Rejecting the notion of syntax as core to the consciousness, Searle suggests that the representation of intentional states takes place in language and so the expression of content is just a formal entity in language. Moreover, he supports the view of generative semantics, "...the generative component of linguistic theory is not syntax... but semantics... the grammar starts with the description of meaning of a sentence and then generates the syntactical structures through the introduction of syntactical rules and indexical rules."[103]

Searle, however, remarks that intentional content as an intrinsic feature of the representational states brings out the compatible relationship between {mind→[language] intentional content}→ to the world and vice versa. This logical compatibility unfolds the two essential components of intentional states called the propositional content and the psychological mode. The propositional content relates to the object or the states of affairs in the world, whereas the psychological mode to the condition of satisfaction. Whenever someone is representing something (s)he also expects that there would be change in the state of affairs according to the representation of their belief. That shows the directedness of intentional content to the world. And if the changes occur favourably to their belief then the directedness is world-to-the-mind. Thus, the interrelationship between the mind and the world becomes more concrete. Of course, language as the basic part of representa-tion maintains the link between the mind and the world in general . More particularly, the intentional content or the semantic content as an essential component of representational states pertains to the *conscious-thought-experience*.

(b) Consciousness and Language: Towards unity

Structural isomorphism, as advocated by Searle, further unfolds the intrinsic relationship between consciousness and language in relation to the notion of life. That is, the function of language as conscious activity can be analyzed referring to the inner life or the mental as well as social life of human beings. In other words, these two facets of life can also be called the micro-level and macro-level functions of conscious-linguistic activities. As Wittgenstein rightly puts it, "Only from consciousness the uniqueness of life arises; religion, science, art,... consciousness is life itself."[104] To say that "consciousness is the life itself" is not to undermine language rather all the forms of life whether religious, scientific, or artistic will presuppose language to understand the phenomena of life in it. Moreover, consciousness here is to be understood as an *underlying principle* for a holistic view of life.

Within the naturalistic framework, biological naturalism provides a scope to understand such a holistic view of life focusing on the intrinsic relationship of consciousness and language. However, one might ask whether the intrinsic relationship of consciousness and language pertains to one ontology? Insofar as Searle's biological naturalism is concerned, the very nature of intentional states is such that they are not only linguistically structured but also in principle conscious. Thus, the ontology here refers to the structure of brain organism as the basis of consciousness. Insofar as the domain of mental life is concerned, it includes the neurological processes and representational states. Only representational states have features of the mental. As Searle remarks, "two states in me, my belief and my axon myelination: both have something to do with my brain, and neither is conscious. But only one is mental and we need to get clear about what makes it mental and connection between that feature—whatever it is—and consciousness."[105] To say that all representational states are not conscious states is not to make any logical division between conscious representational states and unconscious states. Rather unconscious states are potentially to consciousness. Moreover, the difference is that they are *two modes of consciousness*. Searle further suggests, this distinction arises because we are yet to make out the distinction between the state of *latency* and state of *manifestation*. He remarks, "The naïve picture of unconscious states confuses the causal capacity to cause a conscious intentional states with a conscious state itself, that is, it confuses the latency with manifestation... To repeat, the ontology of the unconscious is strictly the ontology of a neurophysiology capable of generating the consciousness."[106] However, he advocates the connective principle: "all unconscious states are in principle accessible to consciousness". And, all conscious and unconscious states are linguistically structured. Their linguistic structurality signifies the *intentional form* of consciousness which includes various forms of intentionality, aspectuality (modality), subjectivity, familiarity, etc.

The intentional form of consciousness includes the different modes of experiencing and representing the *intentional form* which specifically pertains to the inner life of human beings. Besides the objectivity in representing it or experiencing it, it is always from the *first-person point of view*. This inner life not only comprises consciousness and language but also floats in a conscious-linguistic *process*.[107] The inner life refers to the conscious occurrences of mental states of human beings; we do fantasize, we recite poetry without any lip movements, we do indulge in imagination,...

so on and so forth. These are precisely the "first-person episodes"[108] where the person is internally involved in conscious linguistic activities or we can say that the person is consciously engaged in experiencing his/her belief states. Moreover, this first-person intentional forms of representational states are not causally bound. Rather, their interrelationship is an intentional process both in the case of formulation and representation.

This subjective representational attitude of semantics of representation does not contradict the other objective exercises of linguistic activities such as meaning, truth etc. In short, the linguistic representation does involve a macro-level function of language. Because, human beings not only think inwardly but also do speak and communicate. The communication is just an exhibition or the manifestation of our thoughts. As Wittgenstein puts it, "A man's thinking goes on within his consciousness in a seclusion in comparison with any physical seclusion as an exhibition to public view."[109] Thus, consciousness continues to be reflected in the public life or in the macro-level linguistic activities. And we have innumberable language games to describe each form of life. As if we are living in the "sea of languages". This macro-level function of language shows how language holds the world in its multiple forms of uses. Insofar as communication is concerned we do engage in communica-tion through different language games. Each language game has its own form and thereby helps in representing a particular form of life. And these are continuous conscious activities. For Wittgenstein the term 'language-game' is meant to bring into the prominence of the fact that speaking of language is a part of an activity or "forms of life" (*PI*, #23). It is the forms of life which makes the language game meaningful. As Malcom illustrates the intrinsicness of language games and forms of life; "The language games are internally connected with human activities, forms of life [even if there are changes in forms of life and accordingly there will be change in language games.] The changes in modes of living create unforseeable uses of language. Language game and human life both are unforseeable and inexplicable. This is not actually a comparison of two separate things. For what would the life of ours be without the language games? Every perception, every striving, every emotion—seeks its expression in language. The observation and description of language games, if it is sensitive and detailed, is actually a study of human life."[110] Because, human beings not only speak or communicate with each other they do participate in various forms of life. The depth of consciousness becomes transparent by its inaction and manifestation in various forms of life. As Searle categorically suggests, "By consciousness I do not mean the passive subjectivity of Cartesian tradition but all the forms of our conscious life—from the forms 'four's' of fighting, feeling, feeding and fornicating to driving cars, writing books and scratching our itches."[111] Having a form of life or following a form of life shows how human beings are systematically engaged in the world or participating in the world. This further unfolds the very structure of forms of life which signifies the normative aspect of human life. That is to say, every form of life follows certain rules. Following a rule again, according to Searle, is an intentional activity. Because, the forms of life of human beings are not only rule *governed* but also the rules can be consciously *described* by human beings.[112]

Notes and References

1. John Searle, *Intentionality: An Essay in Philosophy of Mind*, p.160.
2. *Ibid.*
3. *Ibid.* pp. 160-61.
4. *Ibid.*
5. *Ibid.* p. 164.
6. *Ibid.*

7. *Ibid.*,p166
8. *Ibid.*,p172
9. *Ibid.*, p. 167
10. *Ibid.*,p166
11. *Ibid.*, pp. 176-77
12. *Ibid.*, p. 198
13. *Ibid.*, p. 192.
14. *Ibid.*, p. 211.
15. *Ibid.*,p. 213.
16. Noam Chomsky, *Rules and Representations,* Basil Blackwell, Oxford, 1980, p. 222.
17. Chomsky, "Language and Nature", *Mind*, vol. 104, no.416, 1995, p. 12.
18. Chomsky, "Linguistics and Philosophy", *Language and Philosophy*, ed. Sydney Hook, New York University Press, New York, p. 53.
19. Chomsky says that interaction with physical and social environment refines and articulates these systems as the mind matures in childhood and the less fundamental respects, throughout life.", *Rules and Representations*, p. 241.
20. *Ibid.*, "On the Biological Basis of Language Capacities", p. 197.
21. *Ibid.*, p. 233.
22. Fodor discusses the notion of "propositional attitudes" from the standpoints of both realism and anti-realism. He says, "I propose to say someone is a Realist about propositional attitudes iff (a) be holds the there are mental states whose occurrence and interactions cause behaviour and do so, moreover, in ways that respect (at least to an approximation) the generalization of commonsense belief/ desire psychology; and (b) these same causally efficacious mental states are also semantically evaluable. See, "Fodor's Guide to Mental Representation: The Intelligent Antie's Vade-Mecum", *Mind*, vol.94, January 1985, p. 78. Henceforth, FGMR.
23. For Fodor "representations" is always mental and thereby internal. But to make the distinction between *representation* and *internal representation* here signifies representation has both syntactic and semantic properties whereas internal representation is exclusively syntactical in its nature.
24. Fodor explains it in the chapter "Propositional Attitudes" *Representations*, The Harvester Press, Sussex, 1981, p. 200.

25. *Ibid.*, p. 137.
26. See Fodor's *Psychosemantics*, p. 138
27. The structure of cognitive states is causally connected and this causal connection is "fundamental", according to Fodor. *Ibid.*, pp. 135-36.
28. Fodor says since mental states are physical states their function falls in the domain of basic science. Physics being considered as basic science holds causal laws for the explanation of the phenomena. See, Fodor's "Making Mind Matter More", *Philosophy of Mind: Classical Problem/ Contemporary Issues*, eds. Brain Beakly and Peter Ludlow, The MIT Press, Massachusetts, 1992, pp. 152-153. (Henceforth, MMMM.)
29. Fodor maintains three criteria for "property" in order to be causally responsible. First the individual property must be "subsumed by the causal law." Secondly, the property is "projected by the causal law." And thirdly, the instantiation of which the occurrence of event is nomologically sufficient for the occurrence of another." See, *MMMM*, p. 155.
30. Fodor discusses about productivity and systematicity in Psychosemantics, whereas in his article "Fodor's Gudie to Mental Represenations" he uses the concept constituency instead of systmaticity. In both the cases they are simultaneously used in the sense that they are interrelated. See *Pyschosemantics*, pp. 148-50. And *FGMR*, pp. 89-90.
31. See, FGMR, p. 89.
32. See, *Psychosemantics*, p. 148.
33. See, Fodor, FGMR, p. 91.
34. *Ibid.*, p. 93.
35. Gillett calls it 'Formal Representational Theory of Meaning (FRTM)." See, Grant Gillett, "Representation and Cognitive Science", *Inquiry*, Vol. 32, No. 3, September 1989, pp. 261-62.(Henceforth, *RC*)
36. He also says "language, as a part of milleu in which behaviour takes shape, plays a large part in determining the map, its construction and what is mapped may be the elucidating our representational activity" *Ibid.*, p. 263.
37. Mostly these three criteria describe his analogy of "Parallel Distributing Processing", for explaining the complex function of the brain-processing networks. *Ibid.*, p. 265.
38. The *flexibility* character of the agent can be defined through agent's capacity of selectivity and attentional control. And

this according to him is a conscious activity of the agent. See, "Generality Constraint and Conscious Thought," *Analysis*, Vol. 47, 1987, p. 21. He also says that flexibility can also be defined as agent's "sensitivity towards the environment". See "Consciousness, Brain and What Matters," *Bioethics*, Vol. 4, No. 3, July 1990, p. 183.

39. See, *RC*, p. 271.
40. *Ibid.*, p. 272.
41. See, Gillett's "Leaning to Perceive", *Philosophy and Phenomenological Research*, Vol. 48, No. 4, June 1988, p. 603.
42. Op. cit., *RC*, p. 274.
43. Searle, *The Rediscovery of the Mind.*, p. 199.
44. Frank Liedtke discusses the notion of *intentional semantics* precisely with reference to Marty and Grice, and finds that they had similar conception of meaning. See, F. Leidtke, "Meaning and Expression: Marty and Grice on Intentional Semantics", *Mind, Meaning and Metaphysics: The Philosophy and Theory of Language of Anton Marty*, Kluwer Academic Publishers, Dordrecht, 1990, p. 29.
45. H. P. Grice maintains the distinction between natural and non-natural or conventional method of analyzing meaning referring to Stevenson. According to him Stevenson argues for the natural intention based semantics. See, Grice, "Meaning" *Philosophical Review*, Vol. 66, 1957, p. 379. (Henceforth, "Meaning").
46. Behaviourists explains meaning through notion of "psychological habits". And each habitual states then becomes a dispositional states. In the case of linguistic communication or linguistic behaviour the dispositional states get affected and brings forth certain responses. Hence behaviourists emphasize the speakers psychological states. Anita Avramides discusses it in her introductory chapter 'Approaches to Meaning', *Meaning and Mind: An Examination of a Gricean Account of Language*, A Bradford Book, The MIT Press, Massachusetts, 1989, p. 1.
47. For Grice, $meaning_{nn}$ signifies the nonnatural meaning. See, "Meaning", p. 384.
48. Grice, "Utterer's Meaning and Intentions", *Philosophical Review*, Vol. 78, 1969, p. 166.

49. *Ibid.*, p. 385.
50. Stepen Schiffer, *Meaning*, Oxford University Press, London, 1974, p. 57.
51. *Ibid.*, p. 64.
52. *Ibid.*
53. Schiffer summarizes Grice's definition "For S, (nc) means "p" iff it is S's policy (practice, habit) to utter x if, for some A, S stands (wants) A to think that S think that p. " See Schiffer, *Meaning*, p. 133.
54. *Ibid.*, pp. 138-140.
55. *Ibid.*, p. 148.
56. See Schiffer, *Remnants of Meaning*, The MIT Press, A Bradford Book, Massachusetts, 1989, p. 205. (Henceforth, RoM)
57. *Ibid.*, p. 242.
58. Schiffer falsifies the compositional semantics in the sense that "I have denied the natural language has compositional semantics, but I certainly don't wish all aspects of semantic compositionality. I especially don't wish to deny that language contain truth affecting interactive devices." See, *RoM*, p. 208.
59. *Ibid.*, p. 186.
60. *Ibid.*, p. 214.
61. *Ibid.*, p. 254.
62. *Ibid.*, p. 265 .
63. *Ibid.*, p. 75.
64. Brain Loar, *Mind and Meaning*, Cambridge University Press, Cambridge, 1981, pp. 238-241.
65. *Ibid.*
66. *Ibid.*, p. 203.
67. *Ibid.*, p. 45.
68. Cf. *Ibid.*, p206.
69. *Ibid.*, p. 208.
70. *Ibid.*, p. 205.
71. *Ibid.*, p. 222.
72. See, Anita Avramides, *Meaning and Mind: An Examination of a Gricean Account of Language*, A Bradford Book, The MIT Press, Massachusetts, 1989.
73. *Ibid.*, p. 35.
74. *Ibid.*, pp. 74-75.
75. *Ibid.*, p. 78.

76. Loar mainly acknowledges this pure naturalistic conception of describing the semantics with reference to the neurological structures. *Ibid.*, p. 107.
77. *Ibid.*, p136.
78. Nagel's hypothesis, "1. Subjective experience is part of the world. 2. An objective view tells us nothing about the subjective point of view. 3. \ The objective view is an incomplete view of reality. Comparing this — — — puts her own hypothesis, 1 Particular belief, intentions, and the like are part of the world[a]; 2.[b] knowledge of the physical realms does not suffice for knowledge of these propositional attitudes, 3 \knowledge of the physical realm is incomplete knowledge of[a] the world. *Ibid.*, p. 101.
79. Objective study of the mind is pure scientific and that scientific tendency advocates, there is only the method of knowing the mental life. This she finds goes against the commonsense notion of knowing the mental. *Ibid.*, p. 146.
80. *Ibid.*, p. 159.
81. Millikan's proper function of language category includes two moods, (I) imperative and (ii) other is indicative mood. She further states, "we are looking for a focused function that is value both to speakers and hearers's that might explain the survival and proliferation of both of speaker's utterances and hearers responses to imperative and indicative." See, Ruth Garret Millikan, *Language, Thought and other Biological Categories*, The Bradford Book, The MIT Press, Massachusetts, 1984, pp. 53-54.
82. *Ibid.*, p. 80.
83. *Ibid.*, p. 89.
84. *Ibid.*, p. 93.
85. John R. Searle, *Speech Acts: An Essay in the Philosophy of Language*, Cambridge University Press, Cambridge, 1970, p. 44. (Henceforth, SA.)
86. *Ibid.*, p. 45.
87. See Searle, *Expression and Meaning: Studies in the Theories of Speech Acts*, Cambridge University Press, Cambridge, 1979, p. 130.
88. *Ibid.*, p. 135.
89. John Searle, *The Rediscovery of the Mind*, The Bradford Book, The MIT Press, Massachusetts, 1992, p. 179.

90. See RDM, pp. 181-182. "Inductively based set of expectations" refers to the structured desire states or the belief states.
91. *Ibid.*, p. 183.
92. For Searle both representation and communication involve intentionality. In the latter work, *Intentionality*, he talks about the logical priority of representations as intention of expressing mental states whereas communication follows later.
93. See, Gillett's "Learning to Perceive," p. 616.
94. *Ibid.*,p. 614.
95. See the chapter on Background in *Intentionality*.
96. I have described it in the *discussion* paper "Intentionality of Mental Reference", *Journal of Indian Council of Philosophical Research*, Vol. XV, No. 1, Sept-Dec., 1997, p. 96.
97. See Brain Magee, *Men of Ideas*, Oxford University Press, London, 1987 p. 156.
98. I have discussed about the *structure of consciousness* in the Chapter-II.
99. In response to G.P. Ramachandra's paper on "Is There Such Thing called as Self-consciousness, " Pradhan remarks that self-consciousness should not be understood as a mystical notion rather it is very much part of our conscious forms of life. See, R.C. Pradhan, "Is There Such Thing as Self Consciousness? A Response," *Journal of Indian Council of Philosophical Research*, Vol. XV, No. 1, Sept-Dec., 1997, p. 87.
100. The aspectual content of experience is always subjectivity, in the sense that one's experience of the world is always 'perspectival' from the subject's point's of view. We have already discussed in the Chapter-II that subjectivity is a feature of consciousness. Searle, *RDM*, p. 95.
101. Since transformation is a process, it is called "transforming", i.e., providing the direct descriptions of sense experiences. L. Wittgenstein, *Zettel*, G.E.M. Anscombe, and G.H. von Wright, (eds.) Basil Blackwell, Oxford, 1967, sects. 433-44.
102. From this "it does not imply that visual experience is itself verbal." See Searle, *Intentionality*, p. 41.
103. See Searle's remark on Chomsky's theory of Generative Syntax, "Chomsky's Revolution in Linguistics", *The New York Review of Books*, 1972, This paper is later on published in Noam *Chomsky: Critical Assessment*, Vol. II, ed. C.P. Otero, Routledge, London, 1994, p. 19.

104. L. Wittgenstein, *Notebooks: 1914-1916*, G.H. von Wright, and G.E.M. Anscombe, tans. Anscombe, Basil Blackwell, Oxford, 1979, p. 82.

105. Searle, *RDM*, p. 154.

106. *Ibid.*, p. 172.

107. This process does not signify mechanical brain processes of the organism, but to agent's conscious feeling about his/ her intentional states. See, Wittgenstein, *Zettel*, #236. The process is of digestion can also be studied as a chemical process, independently of whether it takes place in a living being. We want to say "Meaning is surely a mental process, a process of conscious life, not of dead matter."

108. Backer acknowledges Searle's epistemological status of first-person point of view bring the conscious activities of inner life. See, the section "Consciousness and language," in Lynne Rudder Backer, *Explaining Attitudes: A Practical Approach to the Mind*, Cambridge University Press, Cambridge, 1995, pp. 187-188.

109. See, Wittgenstein's *Philosophical Investigations*, ed. G.E.M. Anscombe & Rush Rhees, trans. Anscombe, Basil Blackwell, Oxford, 1953, p. 200e.

110. See, Norman Malcom, *Wittgenstein: A Religious Point of View*, Coronell University Press, Ithaca , 1994, p. 77.

111. See, *RDM*, p. 227.

112. There are seven features, as Searle summarizes, in the case of intentionality explaining the rules: "First, the intentional content of rules must function, causally; second, rules have special shape and rule explanation are intentional-with-an-s. Third, the rules must be either conscious or accessible to consciousness. Fourth, rules must have semantic contents in the cognitive repertoire of the agent. Fifth, the rule-governed behaviour is voluntary, so the rule-explanation does not give any causally sufficient conditions. Sixth, rules are subject to interpretation and inference by other conditions. Seventh, rules must operate in real time. [My personal correspondence with Searle, dated 17th Sept. 1996.] He illustrates it in his unpublished paper "Explanation of Cognition".

Chapter - V

SEARLE'S BIOLOGICAL NATURALISM : A CRITIQUE

In preceding chapters, an attempt has been made to give an expository account of Searle's theory of mind, called biological naturalism. The discussion has been mainly focused on the key concepts like consciousness, intentionality and language. In this chapter, I shall develop a critical approach to biological naturalism in order to evaluate Searle's philosophical theory of mind. I shall examine whether Searle's biological naturalism is a viable response to the Cartesian dualism.

I. Searle's Cartesian Legacy : Dualism Persists

The seventeenth century Cartesian science entails a dualism insofar as the explanation of the mental phenomena is concerned. The mental is characterized as *res cogitans* having some specific features like consciousness, thoughts, sensations, etc. which are not extended in the spatial world and cannot be explained by the causal laws. Whereas, the *res extensa* includes the whole of the physical phenomena extended in space and time. Dualism divides the mental and the physical into two separate realms of explanation. The mental and the physical are considered as to separate or unique substances. Substances are independent and irreducible phenomena according to Descartes.

Searle has questioned the very foundations of the Cartesian dualism. He says, "We have an inherited resistance to treating the conscious mind as a biological phenomenon like any other. This goes back to Descartes of seventeenth century. Descartes divided the world into two kinds of substances. Physical substances were the proper domain of science and the mental substances were the property of religion. Something of an acceptance of this division exists even to the present day."[1] In Searlean sense dualism persists in philosophy of mind because of our Cartesian hangover and our unwillingness to accept mind as a part of nature. The mental life including consciousness, subjectivity (thought, feelings and experiences etc.) has not been accepted as a suitable topic for scientific study. Searle acknowledges these difficulties writes, "There are four features of mental phenomena (consciousness, subjectivity, intentionality, mental causation) which have made them seem impossible to fit into our 'scientific' conception of the world as made up of material things. And it is these four features that have made the mind-body problem really difficult and they are so embarrassing that they have led many thinkers in philosophy, psychology and artificial intelligence to say strange implausible things about the mind to incorporate consciousness in the nature and at the same time to demolish the Cartesian structure of dualism I think the existence of consciousness ought to seem amazing to us. It is easy enough to imagine a universe without it, but if you do you will see that you have imagined a universe that is truly meaningless."[2] In this connection, Searle's basic thrust is to incorporate the mind in the natural world and hence he accepts the interaction between mind and the body. He, besides, admits that mind evolves within the biological nature of man. Hence his theory is called biological naturalism.

The question now is: Is there any Cartesian legacy in Searle's Biological Naturalism? Of course, Searle would seriously object to this question as his whole endevour is to get rid of Cartesianism and reductionism. Because, for him dualism and materialism cannot be treated as healthy theses in philosophy of mind. Dualism divides the reality into two separate independent realms and materialism or physicalism eliminates the autonomy of mind. That is, the mental phenomena are reduced systematically to the physiological or neuro-physiological functions of the brain. In Searle's theory of mind, consciousness and intentionality stand as irreducible phenomena. Mind as an evolutionary phenomenon is to be understood as part of the biological worldview. However, the mental is not causally determined, rather its function reveals its own determining features. Moreover, these features are irreducible to the neuro-physciological states and processes of the brain.

Dualism that results from the Searlean theory of mind is *naïve dualism*; a naïve distinction between body and mind. Searle is ready to accept the commonsensical distinction between the mental and the physical. There is a gap between the physical and the mental because, according to Searle, the physical causes the mental states. The mental phenomena, which are, in principle, *conscious phenomena* are logically irreducible to the microstructure of the physical organism, which *causes* them. It is because, so far as the explanation of the mind is concerned, there is a strong conception of *causal asymmetry* between mind and body. The asymmetry relationship reveals the causal function of the brain processes and the intentional functions of the Network of mental states. Furthermore, the Network is autonomous having its own function and the function in principle pertains to the realm of consciousness. Consciousness is intrinsic to the mental states which possess other features like phenomenality, subjectivity, intentionality, etc. These phenomena can be said to constitute the mental realm. The mental is purely non physical because it embodies certain nonphysical properties which are irreducible to the nonphysical functions.

Moreover, for Searle, the mental states emerge in an evolutionary process and thus are real. In this regard his notion of irreducibility of the mental states parallel to the Cartesian notion of irreducibility. Moreover, the Searlean notion of irreducibility of the mental should not be interpreted in the sense of Cartesian notion of substance. It is because the Cartesian theory leads to Substance-dualism. In this sense Searlean dualism differs from the Cartesian substance-dualism.

The non-Cartesian dualism that follows from Searle's thesis of biological naturalism is a consequence of his evolutionary theory of mind. According to this theory, mind can be explained with reference to the neurophysiological compositional structure of the human body. As Heil illustrates it, "The composition relation holds among substances. Several substances compose or make up a complex substance when they are grouped together appropriately, what constitutes an appropriate grouping will depend upon the character of the collection."[3] For Searle the human body has a compositional structure with multiple neurobiological structures.

The human body is a complex biological organism. So far as the mind is concerned it has evolved out of the complexity involved the neurophysiological structure of the body. The mind emerges out of the neurophysiological structures. In this connection Searle would also accept the view that the mental is dependent on the brain (the most vital part of the body). Because the mental phenomena are caused by the brain. But there is no causal law operating in the realm of the mental. On the other hand, the physical behaviour (actions) are intentionally defined. Intentionality is one of the basic features of the conscious mind. Thus the relationship between the mental and the physical is one of asymmetrical dependency. Asymmetrical dependency shows that both the mental is dependent on the physical but is not reduced to the latter.

Now the question arises, how far the notion of asymmetrical dependency could be acceptable. The asymmetrical dependency in Searle shows mental is dependent on the physical in the sense that the former is caused by the later. And, at the same time, they have their own specific functions, so one cannot fully be reduced to other. Moreover, for Searle, the physical actions at their macro level description are intentional. It is because the mental states which are in principle conscious and intentional. And at the micro level the mental is caused by the neuro-physiological states. However, once the mental is caused, it acquires its own functions and characteristics, which are purely naturalistic. Thus Searle makes room for the irreducibility of the mental to the physical states and processes of the brain. Thereby he concedes autonomy to the mental.

However, in order to clarify this the functional autonomy of the metnal, one has to understand it with reference to the notion of *metaphysical dependency*. As Heil elaborates "The notion of dependence, or metaphysical dependence, is the notion of existence of one thing absolutely requiring the existence of some other things. '*A*' metaphysically depends on '*B*' when '*A*' could not exist unless '*B*' exists. Metaphysical dependence is to be distinguished from the causal dependence. You could not exist in the absence of oxygen, so your existence depends on the existence of oxygen. The dependence here is causal, however, not metaphysical. You might have existed (if only for brief period) in the absence of oxygen. Compare dependence of this sort with a metaphysical dependence with a whole (the wooden boat, for instance) on its parts at a given time. Although we can imagine the boat's continuing to exist when none of its part exist." [4]

Thus, the metaphysical dependence reveals the fact that existence (reality) of the mind can be distinctly conceived from that of the body. That is, mind exists autonomously in spite of its causal dependence on the body. The unique feature of mind is that it is a complete *unit* having its own faculties, like imagination, memory, (thinking as whole), etc. And the function of the mind can be conceived without giving much importance to the bodily function. What we mean the possibility of mind functioning independently along with its own features cannot be logically ruled out.

It is important to note here that, we are not denying the fact that brain is causally sufficient to produce the mind. Mind as something non-physical, its properties emerge out the physical natural order of the universe. Mind in this regard is part of nature. But being a part of nature does not allow that mind be completely reduced to the physical universe. Searle repudiates reductionism of all sorts. According to the biological naturalism, material *world is causally self-contained*[5]. This proves that mind as biological unit can exist own its own. That fact that neurophysioligical function of the human body produce consciousness or mental phenomena underlies only one thing that the former is causally sufficient to produce the latter. But it does not prove that mind cannot exist own its own. As Heil clarifies it referring to Kant, "The self affects the material world, although not by initiating the causal chain. Indeed, in one important respect (and excluding uncaused events), nothing in the world initiates the causal chain. Rather to put it somewhat (and perhaps unavoidably) mysteriously, the self makes it the case that the world contains a pattern of causal sequences issuing in a particular bodily motion."[6] Searle's conception of intentional causation clarifies further the point which Heil is making regarding the self. According to Searle brain function may cause the consciousness. But consciousness itself is not a part of the physical world. Consciousness is purely intentional. In this regard, intentionality is logically presupposed as the ground of all conscious states. Thus brain and consciousness are logically distinct, in spite of the causal relations. That is to say, consciousness is the product of brain processes but not identified with brain processes.

Searle is aware that the relation between brain and consciousness cannot be truly exhausted by the causal categories. As Searle puts it "there are enormous empirical mysteries about how brain works in detail, there are no logical, or philosophical or metaphysical obstacles to accounting for the relation between the mind and the brain in terms that they are quit familiar to us from the rest of nature."[7] The brain-mind relationship, however, has to be empirically explained. This is the task of neurophysiology. Neuro-physiologists believe in the scientific study of each aspect of the brain processes in order to eliminate the mystery of consciousness. Most of the Cartesian like Hartfield try to bring out the causal interactionism between mind and body. Hertfeild writes, " he [Descartes] generally treated mind and body relation as mystery. When he explained the relation between bodily state and its mental effect (or vice-versa), he appealed to the 'Institution of the nature' which in effect is a relationship established by God and such as to account for the fact that an 'appropriate' mental occurs on occasion of a given bodily configuration".[8] Searle follows Descartes in not denying that there is a deep mystery in the mind-body relation. However, we may try we cannot finally resolve the mystery.

Searle's Cartesian legacy consists in that though biological naturalism rejects the Cartesian dualism, still it holds that consciousness is something independent of the brain processes and irreducible to the neurological processes. Like Descartes, Searle also shares the view that consciousness pertains to the realm of the mental. Searle maintains that, consciousness involves features like intentionality, rationality, freewill, subjectivity, etc. Thus Searle's biological naturalism sounds very much Cartesianism.

II. Searle's Functionalism and Description of Consciousness

As we have already discussed in the second chapter, Searle gives a functional description of the structure of consciousness. The functional description of consciousness is important from the two reasons. It shows how consciousness is caused or how the conscious mental states emerge out of the brain process. It also shows how consciousness is manifested in our behaviour. The former is known as micro-level function whereas the latter is known as macro-level function of consciousness. Now the question arises, are these two levels of functions independent of one another or are they interrelated? If they are interrelated, then Searle is offering a functionalist explanation of the mental phenomena. But, obviously, Searle does not accept this conception of the mind. Though the mental phenomena are caused by the neural configurations and realized by the same neurological structure, there is no identity as such between the physical level and the mental level. Thus, the mental is not just an emergent property but is something real.

Let's begin with the micro-level function of consciousness. The significance of the micro-level structure is that it constitutes the causal source of consciousness or conscious mental states. Moreover, the whole of mental life, including intentionality, subjectivity, free will etc. is caused by the neural or micro-structure of the brain. As Searle says, "All mental phenomena, whether conscious or unconscious, visual or auditory, pains, tickles, itches, thoughts, indeed all our mental life, are caused by the processes going on in the brain."[9] Searle also includes the function of the central nervous system as an important aspect of the brain processes for causing mental phenomena. There are hierarchies in the lattice structure of the brain which cause the mental phenomena. Because, the micro level focuses upon what goes inside the core of the brain, but not on the external peripheral stimulie. Sometimes it so happens that 'events occur outside the central nervous system, but of nothing happened to the brain there would be no mental events.' Whereas, 'if right things happen in the brain, then the mental events occur even if there is not external stimulus'. For instance, when a patient is given anesthesia for operation of the body, no doubt some vital part of the body functions but the nerves system does not carry any external stimuli to the brain and the mental life does not get disturbed. What Searle wants to mean here is that though the body is sensitive enough to carry the stimuli the brain possesses vital capacity to produce mental life. Thus Searle distingushes between the physiological structure of the brain and its functions.

The micro-structure causes the macro structure or the brain processes cause the mind, but the mind cannot be reduced to the same brain processes. Then one must need to know the role of causation involved in the process of the emergence of the mental. As Searle puts it, "When you have a thought, brain activity is actually going on. Brain activity caused bodily movements by physiological processes. Now, because mental states are features of the brain, they have two levels of description, – the higher level in mental terms. The very same causal powers of the system can be described at either level."[10] At the micro level the brain processes cause the mental states. On the other hand, the same causality is not applicable to explicate the mental properties. Because those properties are higher order phenomena, and significantly differ from the physical phenomena. Searle writes, "there is a cause and effect relationship but at the same time the surface features are just higher level features of the very system whose behaviour at micro level causes these features."[11] At the higher level or mental level the role of causality is different in the sense that causality is being intentionalized. This we have already discussed in the Chapter III. To be brief, when a person is acting or behaving, his/her behaviour is explained by the intentional states of the person. And intentionality is manifested in the various representations of mental or intentional states. Thus, behaviour needs intentional description rather than strictly causal explanation.

Critics like Freeman and Skarda question Searle's micro

level function in relation to the macro-level. According to them there are two main difficulties: first, the causal relationship of global neural activities with the mental level is not explained by Searle. Second, though Searle argues against dualism, still the division between the physiological function of and the mental level remains unbridged.[12] As the critics argue that he neural function of the each single neuron as an unit of information functions with relation to the whole network of brain functions. That is to say, the content of information embodied in the single neuron neither can be determined by itself nor the embodiment of content can be seen there. Rather, content of the information is functionally determined with reference to the neural network. This process of determination is a continuous process. So far as establishing the link of the neuron with other neurons are concerned each is autonomous. Searle does ignore the distinct function of the neurons, but talks about the micro level function of the neurons. He only says micro level neural function causes conscious mental states.

The second difficulties according to them, is that Searle's physiological explanation of behaviour lacks biological sense. In the case of any biologically evolved organism, it is found that the organisms are sensitive to their environment. And the organism has the capacity to face the new difficulties it encounters in the process of living or surviving. Hence sustainability is a 'self-organizing capacity' which is a part of the dynamic behaviour of the internal neural structure of the organism. In the case of human behaviour, self-organized dynamism is a process. The pattern that is made available to the rest of the brain and behavioural relevant for the kind of relation that we usually associate with learning and memory are internally generated neural process for explaining the coordination as well as integration of the stimulus and the reflexive behaviour. This whole model of explanation is known as reflexive model. Hence, as far as the over all suggestion of Freeman and Skarda goes, the brain as a self-organizing system develops its own structural mechanism to explain its various forms of behaviour, whether it is perceptual or olfactory. Searle cannot deny the biological capacity of the brain. Because all the capacities of the human organism including the brain system producing various features like consciousness, intentionlity, free will etc. are biologically evolved. His denial of this may cause the collapse of his whole thesis called biological naturalism. At the same time, he cannot also deny the role of intentionality which occurs prior to biological sense of defining the behaviour. Intentionality that is involved in the first person attitude of seeing or experiencing determines the *intentional content* of the perceptual behaviour. Thus the role of consciousness or intentinality is recognized prior to the neurological capacity of the brain process. Thus either his biological naturalism entails Cartesianism or lacks the foundational biological sense.

Searle's response to the above criticism sounds a mere repetition of his old thesis. As he writes, "My views about intentionality and mind-body problem do not commit me to any particular theory about how the brain works at the neurological level, but my views if true, would make it seem most unlikely that the only appropriate level for discussing how the brain produces cognition were that of individual neuron. In any case nothing I say is inconsistent that appropriate explanatory for cognition is that of 'mass neurons'."[13] In his view, both pertain to different levels of description. Perception is a matter of interaction between the organism and environment. On the other hand, perception as having a sort of *intentional content* is related to the subjectiveity and aspectuality of consciousness. And Searle does not find any inconsistency between these two levels of explanation. We may not infer strictly the causal relation from the neurological function causing behaviour but that does not deny the cause-effect relationship insofar as the mental phenomena are concerned. He answers, "my present states of consciousness are caused by a series of neurophysiological events in my brain, and this fact is perfectly consistent with the claim that there are no strict laws under any description correlating the former with the latter. The absence of even the possibility of strict inference does not show the absence of causation."[14]

However, critics like Alistar Hanny asks whether there can be causal relationship between the bottom level neural structure and the conscious properties, such as intentionality, free will, rationality, etc. which arises contradiction if one accommodates conscious features within the natural framework. Firstly, if the causal relationship is explained from the bottom level neural function, then consciousness as an effect must be explained by the molecular and sub-atomic structure of the brain processes. Consciousness including its other co-features can be determined by the functions of the molecular and sub-atomic particles of the brain. Thus there is a bottom up causal relation between the lower order functions of the brain and the higher order conscious states.

Because, the higher level function of the state of the brain can be always explained by its lower level or bottom level structure.[15] Secondly, if the causal explanation is given from the top-down order, i.e. from the level of mental to the physical structure of the brain processes, then a contradiction also arises. Freedom of will as one of the co-features of consciousness is always realized in the intention-in-action. Suppose, for instance, my hitting the ball is caused by my intentional state to put it in the hole. My decision to hit the ball there must be acquired by occurring in the neural configurations of my brain. But the question here is what is the neural function for my taking the decision to hit the ball? Is it that every case of my choosing or deciding to act in my own way is a result of pre-functional neural state? If not, then the decision making feature as part of consciousness stands distinctly independent from the brain processes. Moreover, the demerits of the top-down order in explaining the conscious events through the brain processes is that our every step of proceeding to lower level analysis will make us depart from consciousness. Then one may reach the point where the question obviously arises whether consciousness exists at all. Because in the process of analysis we reach at the micro level physical structure which is not controlled by consciousness.[16]

However, Hanny finds an advantage in the higher order explanation. According to him, whatever scope there may be for alternative description at the phenomenological level, one advantage of hierarchical view outlined here is that it at least encourages to seek ways of combining our intuition of freedom with conception of consciousness which predisposes us to think of it as having some significant directive function. So that if there is indeed an essential link between our sense of freedom and consciousness, we might then conceive it in a way which ties the former with the determination of the behaviour of the states. Freedom is realized in the various activities which engages in. In this regard, Searle's association of *freedom of will* with conscious-ness can only be phenomenological in its description. The description must include only the macro level functions of the human beings.

As we have already pointed out in the previous section Searle maintains two different notions of causal relationship insofar as the micro-level and macro-level functions of mental states and their relationship with neural structure is concerned. Searle writes, "Brain produces the conscious states that are occurring in you and me right now, and it has the capacity to produce many others which are not now occurring. There is brute, blind neurological processes and there is consciousness, but nothing else."[17] Thus there are the brute physical processes of the brain and the concurrent states of consciousness simultaneously happening. But one is puzzled with very notion of function of consciousness and the function of brain processes. Which of the two are logically prior? Searle's answer is that the brain process are empirically prior. But can they be logically prior to consciousness? Searle does not have any answer to this notion of logical question. He provides only a causal explanation. So far as the formulation of causal model goes it includes both causal as well as the intentional level of analysis. Searle calls it "original-intentionalistic-explanation". It differs from the reductionistic explanation which omits intentionality from explanation, e.g., explanation of plant behaviour. For Searle, "The original intentinalistic explanation of plants behaviour turned out to be false, but it was not just false. If we get rid of intentionality and invert the order of explanation, the intentionalist claim emerges as trying to say something true."[18] In the case of explanation by brain processes intentionality is also missing. It is because 'brain processes in principle inaccessible to consciousness have no intentiona-lity because they do not meet the condition of having intentionality.' Furthermore, "The brain has an intrinsically mental level of description because at any given point it is causing actual conscious events and it is capable of causing further conscious events. Because, the brain has both conscious and unconscious mental states, we are also inclined to suppose that in the brain there are mental states that are intrinsically inaccessible to consciousness."[19] Though Searle gives primacy to the 'original intetionalistic explanation' for explaining the behaviour of an organism yet supposes that intentionality is inaccessible to the brain processes. However, one must note that the brain has twofold functions: one of causing consciousness and preserving it, and the other of having unconscious brain functions. There are two simultaneous processes: there is conscious intentionality acting through out and there is unconscious physiological activity going on in the brain. Searle describes this as follows: 'We have conscious intention: keep our visual intention on the road and at another level; deep unconscious level makes the eyeball movements in relation to the eye sokets that are equal to and opposite by the head movements to keep the rational image stable.

On the other hand functionalists' like Dennett's interpretation stands quite opposite to the view of Searle. He emphasizes the unconscious process or the sub-personal level of analysis of the mental phenomena. Because mostly the function of generating conscious features depends upon the bottom level or micro-level. His sub-personal level or hardware conditions for explaining the mental needs special attention. We would discuss the point separately in the following section. The response of Searle regarding this is quite closer to Cartesianism. As he writes, "In this case the result is conscious, though the means of achieving it are unconscious. But the unconscious aspect has all the earmarks of intelligent behaviour. It is complex, flexible, goal directed, and it involves information of processing and has potentiality of infinite generative capacity."[20] One may ask what is the *status* of that brain capacity which Searle is always talking about? Is that completely physical or completely mental. It is certainly not mental the way consciousness and other features are. Because, this unconscious, non representational and non-intentional capacity signifies his notion of the Background. Background, for Searle, is mental which satisfies all the above conditions. The Background is an important concept in Searle's philosophy which needs to be investigated further.

III. Does the Background Condition meet Hardware Explanation?

The Hardware level of explanation is a technical name similar to the micro-level analysis of the mental. That is, it basically deals with the function of the whole sub-systems or the sub-organisms that the brain is constituted of. The brain has been taken here as an instrument functionary for generating intelligent or national behaviour. We have already discussed this notion of Dennett in our Chapter II with reference to the *SPL* model and *MDM* model. *MDM* is a latter version of *SPL* which explains rational behaviour. This well *designed* hardware system is based on the analogy of a mechanical system. The brain is taken as physical organism to explain both goal directed and goal discriminated behaviour. Our focus will be on the *SPL* model to the mechanical theory of mind. In this regard, it is important to compare Dennett's mechanistic model with that of Searle's. Dennett denies the reality of consciousness while Searle affirms it.

Dennett's deep structure analysis is important because it the controlling conditions for all our personal level activities. It is the arrangement of the various subsystems in perfect coordination for making intelligent behaviour. Dennett suggests, "Deep structure controls the personal level function of conscious activities. Content of the speech acts is being controlled with relation to the sub-personal function of the neural process."[21] Hence, the importance lies in the extensional description of the different sub-systems. A person as a conscious being is nothing but an organization of sub-systems. As he says, "Subpersonal theory proceeds by analyzing a person into an organization of sub-systems (organs, routines, nerves, faculties, components—even atoms) and attempting to explain the behaviour of whole person as the outcome of the interaction of the sub-systems."[22] The sub-systems are arranged in such a way that the person has the capacity of self-generating cognitive states. And the person is also capable of interpreting these states. For Dennett, brain as a cognitive organism can be called the *intentional system*. The system is having belief and desire as cognitive states. It is rather the largest cognitive systems organized in such a way that the constituent subsystem "could itself be viewed as an intentional system (with its own specialized belief and desires) "[23] Intentional system theory has the method and technicalities involved in interpreting the cognitive states. It maintains the parallel process which the system undergoes while functioning and generating intentional behaviour. It deals with the notion of internal structural networking, the visual capacity and the Background (genetic). The capacity as a whole justifies the system as intentional. In response to the evolutionary biology, Dennett suggests, "It is not only the intentional predicate that is projectible predicate in evolutionary theory; since it is more general than its species-specific counter part predicates (which characterizes the successful mutation just in birds, or in bats), it is preferable. So from the point of view of evolutionary biology, we would not want to 'reduce' all intentional characterizations even if we knew particular instances what psychological implementation was."[24] Thus, to build up an intentional system quite parallel to the brain mechanism we need to emphasize more on *design stance*. Design stance refers to the different physical components that are arranged in systematic order for the goal directed behaviour or goal discriminated behaviour. More or less, the function is called purposive-relative. As Dennett cites, the instance, the capacitor, the register, the transmitor are well connected with each other—"each with a task to perform—and he can give a design stance prediction generated by assuming each functional part will functional property."[25]

Moreover, the function of *SPL* model emphasizes the internal structure of the brain processing for any sort of intelligent behaviour. In the case of information processing, the brain process is important to be taken into account, because it directly shows how the impulses are stimulated through nerve fibers. The role of nerve fibers is independently determined however the complexity of its structure. For instance 'c-fiber' carries out the pain sensation to the brain. The internal structure can be explained through the electro-chemical or cyrptological input sequences. Rather the functional structure of the whole organism is such that there is plasticity involved in the organism to encounter the new inputs. Thus the brain has the capacity to produce functional structure within its pre-wired mechanism. The function of the various sub-cortexes of brain's organism are interrelated in such a way that in the case of afferent-efferent conditions the brain has the capability to "discriminate significance and store and use the information significantly."[26]

Then one is curious to know how the neurological functions of the brain structure produce the appropriate cognitive states. The cognitive states are emerging out the processes involved in various patterns of brain activities. Dennett says, "the organism and the environment determine the input and output surface of the nerves system. At the peripheries there are sensory transducers and the motor effectors. The transducer respond to the pattern of physical energy impinging on them by producing syntactic object—'signals' with certain properties. The effectors on the other hand will respond to the syntactic objects—'commands" by producing muscular reflexive actions of certain sort."[27]

However, deep structure analysis shows the emergence of neural states and the determination of content. The content as the intrinsic part of the neural states needs special focus for its determination. That we would discuss separately. The analysis of Dennett's *SPL* model shows its close proximity with Searle's Background condition. The Network, according to Searle, is formed by both conscious and unconscious mental states. And mental states emerge out of the brain processes and are realized in them. For Searle, once the conscious states emerge out of the brain functions they have their own life. But Searle denies the independent operation of the Network. The Network function is relation to the functional capacities of the Background. As Searle says, "The Network of unconscious intentionality is the part of the Background. The occurrent ontology of is the part of the network that are unconscious is that of those part of neurophysiological capacity, but the Background consists entirely such capacities."[28] He also says,

"Background consists of mental capacities, dispositions, stances, ways of behaving, know-how, only manifest only when there are some intentional phenomena, such as intentional action, perception or a thought, etc."[29] Thus, for Searle, the Backgraound is a neurophysiological capacity of with the capacity for generating mental states.

According to Searle, the Background is an unconscious, nonrepresentational, nonintentional *mental* capacity whereas the Network is mental and has a structure of both conscious and unconscious mental states. But how the unconscious mental states become intentional and then the intentional states are represented depends upon the capacity of the Background. But, for Searle, that is a physical neurological capacity. So how can the unconscious nature of the mental Background cause consciousness? For Searle, these capacities and disposition are not physical, but unconscious. The unconscious mental states are potentially or in principle conscious.

We must now investigate how the capacities of the brain are responsible for the emergence of consciousness? For Searle, 'some capacities of the brain do not generate consciousness, but rather function for the fix application of conscious states'. They unable me to walk, run, write, and speak, etc'. There are different aspects of brain working together; one is causing consciousness another is making potentially unconscious states conscious or intentional and subsequently some other is helping the same intentional states in their manifestation. Thus one may find out how consciousness is generated. The various sub-systems of the brain are involved in the process of causing consciousness. Furthermore, if the 'Network is the Network of Intentionality' then intentionality is either determined by the background conditions or by the neurophysiological structure of the brain processes. If one looks at the basic hypothesis of Searle that consciousness is caused by the brain processes and realized in the brain processes, then no doubt his claim resembles the Dennetian

SPL model of analysis. But certainly Searle is not making the same point about consciousness as Dennett does. Dennett *explains away* the whole notion of consciousness. On the other hand, Searle categorically talks about the irreducibility of consciousness or the ontology of *subjectivity*. The first person consciousness is important in the sense that my walking, writing and speaking are not only intentional actions but they are also determined by *conscious subjectivity*. Hence, according to Searle, there is consciousness on and above the mechanical functions of the brain. That is, consciousness is ontologically real. All our conscious activities involve intentionality as fundamental presupposition of doing or willing to do certain actions. In this regard my will to do is not dependent on the causal links with the brain. Will as the intrinsic feature of consciousness remains above the physical functions of the brain. That is the way to realize the conscious subjectivity. Thus, Searle concedes the Cartesian demand that the mental is real. If that is the case, then the background is latter development of our conscious activities. Whenever a person tries to develop *skill* or *stance* it shows how a person is consciously involved in making it possible. Because intending to acquire is a part of the conscious-intentional activities of the mind not the brain. Of course, brain possess the biological capacity to cause consciousness. So, the background is both biological and mental.

Moreover, as Stroud says, "It could perhaps be argued what disqualifies ability being apart of the "Background" that Searle insists must consists of "mental phenomena" is that an ability not a mental phenomenon, and it is not itself something mental even if it has the ability to do something mental."[30] There are so many activities going on in the realm of the mental; we calculate, we imagine, we do divisions. They are exclusively mental activities. However, the abilities to do these activities may not be purely mental in the sense that they do not carry intentionality. Stroud's point is that even in the case of walking, writing, any other physical or mental capacities (acquiring certain skill or stance) the capacity is a prerequisite. But whether it is a part of the background condition and whether it pertains to the realm of mental or the physical is difficult to determine. There are certain abilities and capacities, which we may or may not acquire in life. But will that ability be considered as part of the background or not?[31] Searle's response in this regard is that the Background is mental. He says, "I am claiming that the Background is mental. Many people find it uncomfortable to describe such things as my ability to swim or ski as mental capacities. I share reluctance and, in fact, I am unsatisfied altogether with the traditional vocabulary of 'mental' and 'physical'. Nonetheless, it is important to emphasize that the Background abilities are not dependent on how things in fact work in the world. All of my Background capacities are 'in the head', in that sense I use the word **mental** to describe them. In short, when I say the Background is mental without being intentional there is no inconsistency implied or presupposed. I am simply saying that the Background is not itself a feature of the world independent of the mind."[32] There are many things *in our head;* the neural physiological structure [neurons, cells, synapses and axons, chemical flow] and of course the emerging mental states. If they are all mental then Searle's vocabulary is wide enough to include both the physical and the mental.

IV. Is Searle a Property Dualist?

For Searle, the mental states are having certain specific properties. They are conscious, possess intentionality, they can cause action, and moreover, they are of person's mental life. In brief, these features are called; consciousness, intentionality, mental causation, subjectivity, etc. The mental properties, according to Searle, are real and intrinsic to consciousness. They are intrinsic to consciousness because consciousness has been treated as the most fundamental feature mind. These are intrinsic to the mind as they constitute consciousness. If consciousness is reduced to certain physical process, consciousness becomes external to the brain. In that case they become second order properties. Therefore, they cannot have first order intentionality. Now, one may also ask, does their irreducibility result in property dualism? Or, if they are so intrinsic to the consciousness do they lead to substantial dualism? Searle's biological naturalism rejects any form of dualism. But it does talk about naïve mentalism and naïve physicalism. Both mental and physical are real and co-exist in nature. The mental is the part of the physical and thus consciousness, along with its co-features are caused by the brain processes. As Searle says, "One way to characterize this position is to see it as an assertion of both physicalism and mentalism. Suppose we define 'naïve physicalism' to be the view that all that exists in the world are physical particles with their properties and relations. 'naïve mentalism' to be the view that mental phenomena really exist. They really are mental states; some of them are conscious, many have intentionality; they all have subjectivity, and many of them function causally in determining physical events in the world Naïve mentalism and naïve physicalism are perfectly consistent with each other. Indeed, as far as we know anything about how world works, they are not only consistent, they are true."[33] Thus Searle does not deny the dual nature of the reality; it being physical and mental at the same time naïve mentalism, however is not a strong form of dualism. It does not solve the problem of Cartesian dualism. To say that mental is realized in the brain process is to say that mental is dependent on the physical. On the other hand, the irreducibility of the mental leads to ontology of consciousness. The conscious mental phenomena are the emergent properties of the neurological processes of the brain and so cannot be identical with the brain processes. Searle writes, "The existence of consciousness can be ex-plained by the causal interaction between the elements of the brain at the micro-level, but consciousness cannot itself be deduced or calculated from the sheer physical structure of the neurons without some additional account of causal relation between them.If consciousness were *emergent*$_2$, then consciousness could cause things that could not be explained by the causal behaviour of the neurons. The naïve idea here is that consciousness gets squirted out by the behaviour of the neurons in the brain, but once it has been squirted out then it has a life of its own."[34] We have been repeatedly insisting on this point in our earlier sections that according to Searle, consciousness has its independent function though it is caused by the neural processes. Therefore, for him, the cause-effect relationship is significant. Searle is aware of the danger that causal reductionism will result in the ontological reductionism. However, Searle is in a dilemma: either biological naturalism will fall in the same stream of reduction or his defense of first person ontology will result in some sort of Cartesian dualism. Searle is opposed to both.

However, the claim of Searle is that the perfect scientific explanation of the mind does not lead to ontological reductionism. Causality is not rejected fully by the scientific explanation of the mind. Rather the analysis that he tries to project clubs both scientific and pre-scientific experience with of phenomena. The pre-scientific experience here refers to the common experience of things in the world. Our experience of water as liquid that quenches thirst is not scientific explanation. The real scientific explanation tell us what causes water as a liquid, i.e. its combination of two hydrogen molecules and one oxygen molecule. In that case can we discard the pre-scientific understanding of the water. Similarly, in the case of pain, there is a physiological process involved in it. And the mental aspectuality is also not denied. By aspectuality here we mean the subjective experiences of pain or the first person feeling of pain. The question before us is not only to include the real causal analysis or scientific analysis of the pain behaviour or experiences of water etc., but to include our pre-scientific experiences with the phenomena as well. And this can be applied to the notion of consciousness. It has both pre-scientific as well as scientific explanation. For Searle, "Part of the point of reduction was to curve off the subjective experiences and exclude them from the redefinition of the real phenomena, which are now defined in terms of the features that interest us most. But where the phenomena that interest us most are the subjective experiences themselves, there is no way to curve anything off indeed it is a general feature of such reductions that the phenomenon is defined in terms of 'reality' and not in terms of 'appearance'. But we cannot make that sort of appearance-reality distinction of consciousness because consciousness consists in appearances themselves. *Where appearances are concerned we cannot make the appearance reality distinction because appearance is the reality.*"[35] The appearance of consciousness are the various conscious activities. These are the macro level function of consciousness. All our macro level activities carry features of consciousness and other properties of it. On the other hand, consciousness refers to the macro-level physical reality of the brain because it is caused by the nerurological structure of the brain organism. This, however, is not the appearance-reality distinction. In the case of consciousness, no such distinction arises.

Dennett questions the Searlean way of analyzing the mental states and the properties. He questions the *ontological status* of the mental phenomenon. As he says , "When are elements of the pattern real and merely apparent? Answering this question will help us resolve the misconceptions that have led to the proliferation of 'ontological positions' about beliefs, the different grades or kinds of realism."[36] To get into the ontological status of the mental states the method of study must be *objective*. Once we understand the designing pattern of the organism or the system as assembled of, we could then well detect the phenomena and their intrinsic value. The objective features of the mental states are referred to by the micro level structure of the brain organism. Because that is the root and the center of controlling the behaviour as far as Dennett's analysis is concerned. Dennett says: "We can adopt the physical stance toward a configuration of Life world, our powers of predictions are perfect: there is no noise, no uncertainity, no probability less than one. Moreover, there is no back stage hidden variables; the unfolding of the physics of life world is directly and completely visible."[37] The physical stance signifies the neurological structure of the brain organism causing neural states and operating them further to cause different behviour. Dennetts' sub-system analysis explains clearly the operations of the sub-organism involved in the function of neural states. Brain as a biological organism is part of the life world and is accessible to the 'physics of life'. The entire physics of life world is such that it is completely explained by the 'single unexceptional law, which .is the 'foundational law of physics.' The physical laws could explain the various features that occur in the biological system. The real pattern that exists in reality must be amenable to description by the physical laws. However, it is difficult to locate the 'intentional order' in the life world. He writes: "If you "look at" the world in the right way, the patterns are obvious. If you 'look at' (describe) the world in any other way, they are, in general, invisible."[38] Furthermore, he maintains that "A pattern exists in some data—is real—if there is a description of the data then there is more efficient than the bit of map, whether or not alone can concoct it".[39]

Dennett mentions that the Searlean model always insists upon the deeper structure analysis of the mental states but the search has been *forlorn*.[40] Once we go into the deeper fact analysis we proceed through the structural configurations of the organisms for causing such features. And the consequence may prove that there is nothing called original intentionality or real intentionality. Because real intentionality not only has a subjective appearance but needs to have the micro-fact or deeper fact. Dennett's complain is that their supposition fails to *identify* such fact.[41] Dennett's analogy of human behaviour and the behaviour of intelligent robot nullifie the Searlean notion of intrinsic features. Rather their function show that mental states carry *as if* intentionality. To say that the micro-level structure is real in the sense of causing the subjective appearances reveals the whole designing of the system or the organism as purely unconscious stuff. And the designed is the source. Then this notion of original intentionality is also a phenomenon derived directly from the body structure and indirectly from the whole of natural selection.[42]

However, Searle treats the intentional properties as real and basic to the very notion of our conscious activities. The conscious activities of human beings reveal the structure of consciousness. The structure of consciousness further reveals its constituents as intrinsic to the very notion of consciousness. Since our *subjective* attitude is a part of the constitutive features of consciousness, it has been treated as an irreducible ontological feature. Searle tries to naturalize this *subjective ontology* in his theory of biological naturalism. That is, he treats the subjective attitude as part of the biological capacity of the neural processes of the brain. It has a neurological basis. Thus the subjective ontology has a special status with reference to its *independent* function throughout its *intentional* interaction with the world. The intentional interaction is basic to the conscious participation or interaction because it is the cause of bringing out further intentional states and *realization* of those emerging states. Since Searle's emphasis is always on the commonsensical understanding of the mind, he is not able to deny the subjectivity as the prime feature of consciousness. It is because, everybody has his or her way of looking at the phenomena and their experience differ accordingly. And insofar as the ontology of subjectivity is concerned it remains always the first-person ontology. My awareness of my mental states and attitudes is certainly distinct from that of others as their attitudes differ from mine.

As Searle says, "This subjectivity is marked by such fact that I can feel my pains, and you cannot. I see the world from my point of view; you see it from your point of view. I am aware of myself and my internal mental states as quite distinct from the selves and mental states of other people." [43] Thus for him, subjectivity is an objective phenomenon. Dennett questions this notion of Searle's "subjective ontology." He writes, "it is highly idiosyncratic: what is special about consciousness is it subjective ontology along side (not within) otherwise science can accommodate subjective ontology alongside (not within) otherwise objective ontology. Once we clear away some widespread confusions about what science requires, and dismisses the misbegotten fluid of cognitive science that has been engendered by those confusions the subjective ontology of the mind, be claims, will loss its aura of unacceptable mystery."[44] Since Dennett's methodology is completely *hetrophenomenological* he denies the very notion of *central meaner* or the subjectivity as the core point of seeing and experiencing the phenomena. By positing subjectivity as a central or irreducible factor Searle brings in Cartesianism. But the Cartesian subjectivity is the notion that both Searle and Dennett reject. Dennett's heterophenomenological analysis explains away the very notion of consciousness and thereby the notion of subjectivity.

Searle's aim in rejecting the Cartesian subjectivity is to naturalize the very concept of subjectivity in the intentional framework of bioloigical naturalism. That is the reason, Searle posits, a specific notion of mental causation which retains subjectivity. According to Searle, there are three mistakes the Cartesians commit. They are,

1. "All consciousness are self conscious.
2. Consciousness is known by the special feature of introspection.
3. Knowledge of our conscious states are incorrigible."[45]

First we would like to analyze the first two mistakes together, by taking self consciousness. Introspection is otherwise known as self-reflection. Consciousness is always reflexive in its nature. It is reflexive in the sense it is aware of its contents. That is, consciousness is directed towards itself. Reflexive significance of consciousness thus lies in subject's being aware of or conscious of own its mental states. Consciousness is not only about the world but also about the various mental lives. We are aware of our background capacities. We are simultaneously aware of our rules and regulation whenever we are actively engaged in doing something. Hence there is a series of mental processes involved when one is imagining something or expecting something to happen. The consciousness reflects over itself in all our mental activities. This sort of conscious experience is called as reflexive feature of consciousness. For Searle, this sort of reflexive consciousness cannot be denied. He says "In short, if by 'introspection' we mean simply thinking about our own mental states, then there is no objection to introspection. It happens all the time, and is crucial for any form of knowledge. But if by introspection we mean, special capacity, just vision only less colourful, that we have to *spect intro* then it seems to me there is no such capacity. There could not be model of specting intro requires the distinction between the object *spected* and the *specting* of it, and we cannot make this distinction of conscious states."[46] The Cartesian notion of 'introspection' refers to the analysis of thought and thought processes as an exclusive feature of mental activity. Therefore in the *Meditations* Descartes emphasizes the *reflexive act* of the thought processes. It is the reflexive feature of consciousness which is a property of thinking. Moreover, reflexivity is a kind of *thinking about thinking.* As Descartes while clarifying the unique feature of consciousness says, "it is not sufficient for it to think: it is further required that it should think that it is thinking, by means of a reflexive act, or that it should have awareness of its own thought."[47] Descartes in this basic sense does not differ from Searle. The disagreement is not on whether there self consciousness or not, but on the fact that it is another *special faulty* of consciousness. As Descartes mentions, 'we can direct our mental state at another; we can think about our thoughts and feelings; and we can have feelings about our thoughts; but none of these involves a special faculty of introspection.' Reflexivity in Descartes however, is not attached with a special faculty, rather it is the special feature of consciousness. As he maintains, "But it must be noted that, although we are always actually aware of the acts or operations of our mind, we are not always aware of minds faculties or powers, except potentially. By this, I mean that when we concentrate on the employment are of our faculties then immediately, if the faculty in question resides in our mind, we become actually aware of it, hence we may deny that it is in the mind if we are not capable of being aware of it."[48] This self-awareness is about the inner capacities of the mental life. Hence it has been treated as special feature of intentionality of consciousness. For Searle, the change of intentional reference implies the *shifting* of consciousness. Shifting is special feature of consciousness in having inner directedness. In this regard Searle defends the self-awareness.

And all our conscious activities are the part of this self-consciousness. All the conscious representations together constitute the notion of self-consciousness. Searle is not defenitely talking about discrete consciousness. Rather consciousness for him is having *unity*. Searle talks about two sorts of unity the vertical and horizontal unity. The vertical unity describes the assembling features of all conscious experiences. As Searle writes, "Vertical unity is matter of simultaneous awareness of all diverse features of any conscious states we have little understanding how brain achieves this unity. In neurophysiology it is called "binding problem" and Kant calls the same phenomenon the transcendental unity of perception."[49] This simultaneous awareness is a part of the subject's conscious activity. And our ordinary notion of conscious experience and the reflexive consciousness are related to the notion of self-consciousness. It is because they all together constitute self-consciousness. Consciousness is the foundation of this self-consciousness. Searle does not deny fully the notion of self consciousness. He remarks, "To know consciousness with certainty, we must know it by a special faculty that gives us direct access to it. Hence, the doctrine of introspection. And though I am less confident about historical diagnosis—if self is the source of all knowledge and meaning, and therefore to be based on its own consciousness, then it is natural to think that there is a necessary connection between consciousness and self-consciousness; hence the doctrine of self-consciousness."[50] Thus, the subjective nature of consciousness entails the self conscoiusness. Searle accepts unity of consciousness which is unfolded in self-consciousness. Hence, self-consciousness is the root of these underlying features of all our conscious activities. The Conscious mental states have subjective ontology". In this regard the mistakes that Searle finds in the Cartesian tradition does not seem to be a mistake at all.

V. Why Cognitivism is not a Theory of Mind?

There has been much talk about cognitivism in the recent time. Cognitivism as theory of mind advocates that the whole function of the mental phenomena can be explained within the model of Artificial Intelligence. The ground of cognitivism is basically based on two theories of mind; cognitive psychology and neuroscience. The artificial intelligence model as an approach of cognitivism talks about the intelligent behaviour in terms of machine function. That is, the functions of the machine quite resembles to the intelligent behaviour of the human beings. In brief, intelligence or rationality is an effect of certain sophisticated mechanical functions of the system. The digital computers and the robots are the prime instances of intelligent behaviour. According to Searle, there has been two version of artificial intelligence; the weak AI and the strong AI. The weak AI proposes the notion of computer being a powerful tool for formulating and testing hypothesis more rigorously. According to strong AI, "the computer is not merely a tool in the study of the mind rather, the appropriately programmed computer really is a mind, in the sense that computer given right programs can be literally said to understand and have other cognitive states, the programs are not merely tools that enable us to test psychological explanations; rather the programs are themselves the explanation."[51]

Searle strongly opposes the view of strong AI and cognitivism in general. According to him the theories of cognitivism does not really resolve the issue of dualism. Rather it maintains a *gap* between the mind the brain. It appeals to the notion of program of the brain. The *program* is an independent phenomenon in the brain processes. Because the computational process of the writing or running the program is no way connected to the brain. As Searle points out, "If mental operation consists in computational operations in formal symbols, then it follows that they have no interesting connection with the brain; the brain just happens to be one of the indefinitely many types of machine capable of instantiating program. This form of dualism is not traditional Cartesian variety that claims there are two sorts of *substances*, but it is Cartesian in the sense that it insists that what is specifically mental about the mind has no intrinsic connection with the actual properties of the brain. This underlying dualism is masked from us by the fact that AI literature contains frequent fulmination against 'dualism'; what the authors seem to be unaware of that thesis position proposes strong version of dualism."[52] The whole of computational processes is analogous to thinking. And thinking is a part of information processing. But in the case of information processing the machine only does the manipulation of the symbols. The symbols are the inputs which get processed by the algorithm or the program. As Searle puts it, "On this view, then, the talk of cognitive science is to characterize the brain, not at the level of cells, not at the level of conscious mental states, but rather at the level of its functioning as an information system. And there where the gap gets filled."[53] Thus, the program is implemented for processing information some where in between these two levels.[54]

According to cognitive science the information processing in any artificial system depicts the process of thinking of the living organism. Information processing is causally linked with the hardware functions. That is, thoughts that emerge are caused by the neurobiological process of brain are realized in the brain processes. Thus thoughts are causally linked with the micro-level structure of the brain. Thought processing, according to Searle, is a mental activity at macro level. Therefore, it is not a mere physical activity as the functionalists believe.

According to the critics, like David Cole, William Paraport and Dale Jacquette, Searlean conception of *thought experiment* [55] entails materialism. Searele describes the conception of thought experiment in his Chinese Room Experiment (CRE). *CRE* maintains three phases for unfolding the very process of thought experiment. In the *CRE* context the person who is totally ignorant about Chinese language is kept inside closed room. In the first phase, the person is given some Chinese script and Japanese scripts but he is unable to distinguish the differences of the scripts. At the second phase, the person is offered with a set of *rules* stated in English and instructed to correlate the Chinese scripts with Japanese scripts. At the third phase, the person correlates two scripts with the help of the rules. According to Searle, though the person kept in the closed room is not a native Chinese speaker but perfectly answers the questions asked from the outside. In that case, can we say that the person follows or understands Chinese? For Searle, the answer is 'no'. Because during the period of information processing, the machine is simulated and the operation is formally carried out by the program or rules in it. There is no question of *following the rule* as the way human beings do. As Cole summarizes Searle's position: "(a) This behaviour cannot conclusively demonstrate understanding (weakest); (b) behaviour shows something but not enough attribution to the mental predicate; (c) gross behaviour by itself shows nothing but understanding; and (d) behaviour, even coupled with an explanation of the generation of the behaviour in the form of program shows nothing about whether there was understanding (stongest)."[56]

Thinking in the case of human being entails understanding whereas the machine simulation does not entail understanding. Understanding is a process that must be ascribed to the very function of algorithm. Because it is the running process of the algorithm produces and not the algorithm as such. According to Paraport, "Searle concedes it".[57] Machine simulating processes are causally linked. The program which itself is a synthetic structure defines the various linkages and the steps and sequences followed during the time of operation. Thus there are two types of understanding; the *syntactic understanding* and the *semantic understanding*. For instance, in the case of solving any equations the algorithm is simulated in sequential order to get result. Following this sequential order to reach at the goal is called syntactic understanding. On the other hand, operating the algorithm with interpretation in terms of concepts is called semantic understanding. Paraport describes the procedure of sorting the equation 2x+1=3 in the following steps :

"1. Remove a 1-unit weight from each pan, leaving weights of 2x units and 2 units on each pan.

2. Halve the weights on each pan, leaving weights of x units and 1 unit on each pan.

3. The solution to the equation is thus X=1."[58]

This step by step solution involves semantic understanding.

According to Searle, understanding or following the rule depends upon the semantic content. Semantic content is not intrinsic to the mental state; it is added through interpretation. In that case, the algorithm's following the rule or functioning in accord with the rule is extrinsic. Human beings are, however, guided by the actual content of the rule. That is, following the rule is a part of human behaviour. But in the case of a machine, performing certain activities will not imply that the machine is following the rule *literally*. Rather, it will not as if it is following the rules. Hence, for Searle, there are two types of information processing. One is the *psychological* information processing and actually thinking, and the other is *as if* information processing.[59] The psychologi-cal information processing is part of real thinking whereas, *as if* information processing deals with computational information processing. The program is designed in such a way that it shows the psychological aspects of it. As Searle describes the psychological information processing, "It is an obvious fact that brain has level of real psychological information processing. To repeat, people actually think, and thinking goes on in their brains. Furthermore, there are all sorts of things going on in the brain at the neurophysiological level that actually cause our thought processes."[60] Searle is not opposing the micro-level structure of the brain and its interrelationship with the thought process. But he denies the information processing as an additional feature of the neural network.

The pattern of Searle's thought experiment involves two basic levels of description; the description at the physical level and the description at the mental level. The physical level description of the information processing has been an important aspect of functionalism. The neurological structure is treated fundamental for the information processing. The emphasis given on hardware is a part of the sustaining capacity for the implemented software. In the information processing the program is not the only thing running and controlling simultaneous functions, but there is collective function involved in the hardware to carry out the functions. Searle rejects the functionalists approach of information processing. Though the brain has *intrinsic causal capacity* to generate thought, the real description of thought processes could be given at the realm of the mental. Searle's conception of the intrinsic causal capacity of the brain has been criticized. Critics like Cole and Rapaport interpret him as materialist. According to Cole, Searle is a materialist, because he emphasizes the micro-level structure of the brain process which is the root of information processing. The conscious thought process is logically a part of the neurological manifestation of the causal capacity, which is physical. According to Rapaport, the Searlean materialism has two forms; the *narrow form* and the *wide form*. "It is narrow in that minds are not material, but a particular *kinds* of material; yet it is wide in that Searle accepts part of the functionalists claim that mental phenomena are algorithmic, insisting only that algorithm will only exhibit intentionality when running in the right kind of material, namely on having the requisite causal powers to produce intentionality."[61] There are two main points both Cole and Rapaport are highlighting: the causal powers of the system and the ontological status of the program for describing intentionality. For Searle the program does not have the real causal power for explaining intentionality. The real causal power lies in neurophysiology. Other than the neurophysiology the implemented program has no ontological status. "The implemented program has no causal powers other than those of the implemented medium because the program has no real existence, no ontology, beyond that of the implementing medium." Searle says "My own view is that only machine could think, and indeed only a very special kinds of machines, namely brains and machines that had the same causal powers of the brains."[62] He also says, "Any other system capable of causing minds would have causal powers (at least) equivalent to those of brains."[63] It implies that thinking is a specific causal capacity of the biological structure of the brain. The causal, for Searle is intrinsic to the brain. Machine can think only when they have the some causal power. According to Searle, intending is an innate capacity of the brain. And machine programming is not sufficient enough to fulfill the condition of intentionality. It is therefore wrong to say that there can be a machine having equivalent causal powers for generating intentionality or thoughts that the machines can simulate the brain activity. Therefore it is not real and causally sufficient to produce intentionality. Cam says, "This is an error. Certain brain processes may be sufficient for intentionality, but *what* [Any mechanism capable of producing intentionality (strong AI) could not succeed just by designing programs but would have to duplicate the causal powers of the human brain.] implies is that, they—or rather their causal 'powers' or equivalent thereof—are necessary for intentionality."[64] The reason for the error is, x may be a sufficient condition for causing y but it may not be necessary condition for causing y. Thus, according to Cam, Searle's conception of causal capacity is quite puzzling and is not a sufficient condition for explaining thought processes. It only provides a physical condition for the emergence of mental activity.

However, Searle's thesis cannot be characterized as materialism especially with reference to the thought experiment. Thought experiment remains exclusively a mental act. Searle emphasizes this point in his thesis regarding the realization of the mental states. The realization of the intentional states depends upon the intentional representations of the intentional states. The whole of the Network functions consciously and intentionally. There is no direct physiological link with the operation of intentional states. The realization or the condition of satisfaction is mostly related to the Background. The Background as we have discussed earlier is a part of the mind and not necessarily a part of the neurological structure of the brain processes. Hence, the *real* cognitive explanation needs the description of the mental level. Though neurological features cause intentional states and the very function depends indirectly upon the structure of neural network, thought processes have an independent existence. The mechanical function of any program of information processing will not be self-sufficient. So its function is always relative to semantic interpretation. Searle writes, "Now in addition to that there will be also a mental level of description, we know, for example, perception in function of expectation. If you expect you see something, you will see it much more readily. We know furthermore that perception can be affected by various mental phenomena. We know that mood and emotion can affect how and what one perceives. And again within the mental level, there will be different levels of description. We can talk not only about how perception is affected by individual beliefs and desires, but also how it is affected by such global mental phenomena as the person's background abilities, or his global world look. But in addition to the level of neurophysiology and level of intentionality we don't need to suppose there is another level, a level of digital computa-tional processes."[65] The passage indicates the independent function of the mind or the subjectivity. Not that thought processes are accessible to consciousness, but the conscious self and all the subjective attitude function above the neurological structure of the biological brain. But *reality* of thought processes is completely an independent of neurological processes. This entails a dualism of some sort.

VI. Mind-Body Problem Naturalism and Beyond

In the naturalistic schema of Searle, dualism persists in spite of his biological explanation of consciousness in particular and the mental life in general. Dualism persists both at the micro level and the macro level. We would like to discuss his micro and macro distinction little more. At the micro level function the brain causes conscious mental life. And at the macro level the consciousness is expressed in language, i.e. conscious states are manifested in the linguistic behaviour. There is an isomorphism between the structure of mental states and that of the linguistic expressions. It is thus the nature of the consciousness which is the underlying metaphysical principle in Searle. As Nagel writes, "This is a radical thesis, consciousness is physical property of the brain in spite of his subjectivity, and that it is irreducible to any other physical properties, is the metaphysical heart of Searlean position."[66] That is, the internal mental is the root of the conscious subjectivity. This conscious subjectivity is a higher order feature of consciousness. Thus, Searle accepts not only the reality of the physical process of the brain to show the *objectivity* of consciousness but also accepts that consciousness is ontologically subjective. From this it is obvious that dualism persists between the micro level of physical properties of the brain and the whole of the functions of conscious mental life including the conscious subjectivity.

Now the question before us is whether there can be a link between the micro level physical and a macro-level mental. This is the old mind-body problem expressed in a way. Searle explains the mind-body relation in a biological framework. According to him, consciousness along with its other co-features evolves in a biological way. Searle says, "This may sound mysterious, the hunk of matter, gray and white out mill textured substance of the brain should be conscious than it seems mysterious that his other hunk of matter, this collection of neucleo-protein molecules stuck onto calcium frame should be alive. The way in short, to dispel the mystery is to understand the processes. We do not fully understand that process, but we understand the general *character*, we understand that there are some specific electro-chemical activities going on among the neurons or neuron-modules and perhaps other feature of the brain and there processes cause consciousness."[67] Thus the brain as whole is taken as the case of consciousness. Dualism between brain and consciousness arises in Searle's framework. Searle unlike the functionalists like Dennett and Churchland, tries to explain consciousness and account for its reality.

Searle's entire theory goes to reestablish the reality of consciousness and its ontological subjectivity. Though the mental life is realized in the physical, the intentionality of the mental states signifies the importance of the mental network. Here lies the mystery of consciousness that it emerges out of the physical matrix of the brain. "In our present situation no one has a plausible answer to the mind-body problem, all we can really do is to try to develop various alternatives one which may prove in long run an ancestor of credible solution."[68]

Like Searle, Nagel, also admits the reality of consciousness. Subjectivity is the hallmark of consciousness according to him. The subject qualifies our own understanding of conscious experience. As Nagel writes, "This bear directly the mind-body problem. For if the facts about experience—facts about what is it like *for* the experiencing organism—are accessible from one point of view, then it is a mystery how a true character of experience is revealed in the physical operation of the organism."[69] Subjectivity as the root of conscious experience is independent of the physical organism. The body equally plays a significant role in causing consciousness. Thus Nagel holds a *dual aspect theory* that claims, "Our bodies and in particular our central nervous system belong to the physical world, as do the bodies of all other organisms capable of mental activity. We have seen to think that connection between mental life and the body is very close, and that no mental event can occur without a physical change in the body—in vibrates the brain—of its subject."[70] The vibratory function of the brain process causing consciousness or any other change in the physical behaviour on the body depends of the compositional structure of the body. The scientific account of the functional aspect of the body is not sufficient enough to determine the relationship between the mental and the physical. Science in that respect plays a limited role. Nagel writes, "Consciousness should be recognized as a conceptually irreducible aspect of reality that is necessity connected with other irreducible aspectbut the task of conceiving how the necessary connection might hold between the subjective view and the physical cannot be accompanied by applying analogy from within physical science."[71]

Nagel, however, is quite apprehensive about the new conceptual device to tackle the problem of interaction. The device must be founded upon the principle of 'objective phenomenology'. The objective phenomenological character of a concept designates its real properties. The real property is inexhaustible in its explication. Consciousness as such is independent of a particular point of view, since it belongs to the category of objective phenomenology. It is objective, because the very explanation of the phenomenon remains unexhaustive. For example, the objective feature of lightening is not exhausted by the visual appearances. Therefore he holds: "The ordinary concept of water is unsaturated so to speak, since it contains a blank space to be filled in the discovery of the real, and essential, chemical composition of water. Thus we make a room for possibility of such discovery by denying that the manifest properties of experience exhaust its nature'. Similarly, there is something specific to the concept of consciousness which cannot be revealed in its causal history. No introspective consciousness can comprehend the real nature of consciousness.

Searle denies Nagel's thesis that causal explanation is inadequate to determine the interaction between the mind and body. For Searle, an adequate science of the brain and the necessary causal explanation would certainly solve many of the conceptual mistakes. The *inconcevability* thesis of

Nagel is wrongly formulated: 'explanation in science implies causal necessity and necessity implies inconceivability of the opposite.' As Searle clarifies this remark of Nagel, 'If adequate scientific explanation implies necessity and necessity implies inconceivability of the opposite, then by contraposition the conceivability of the opposite that we do not have any explanation'. Where Nagel sees mystery, Searle finds a play for scientific explanation. Particularly consciousness looks mysterious to us because the molecular biology is yet to completely explain the nature of our biological organism. But that does not deny our over all understanding of the brain processes which are responsible for the emergence of consciousness. Then where does the notion of *inconceivability* stand? Moreover, it would be difficult to formulate the inconceivability thesis from the standpoint of *conscious subjectivity*. Because, the focus is on the subjectivity of experience and therefore the relationship is to be seen as a part of subjective experience. Though we form the necessary causal relationship within from our conscious experiences, the problem with Nagel is that we cannot get out of the subjectivity of our consciousness. And the formulation of such necessary causal relation needs to be pictured from the outside. The subjectivity of a consciousness is always presupposed by our scientific discourse. It is because subjectivity is an objective phenomenon, for Searle.

McGinn puts forward a similar argument in favour of the *mystery* of consciousness. It is a miracle that mind and body are interacting. The mystery persists because we are yet to determine the exact nature of interaction. His whole endeavour is to identify the *link* between the mind and the body to eliminate the deep mystery. McGinn advocates the theory of realistic naturalism that talks about both consciousness as an emergent property of the brain processes and consciousness as having its own independent function. Hence, for McGinn, there are two axes of explaining the link between the mind and the brain. They are called *axis of embodiment* and *axis of intentionality;* the former signifies the relationship of consciousness with brain whereas the latter signifies the intentional relationship of mental states with the world.[72] The axis of embodiment is the major theme of scientific naturalism. Naturalism, especially the emergentism variety focuses on the causal capacity of the brain process causing consciousness and thereby it tries to naturalize consciousness. This, according to McGinn, remains a problem because naturalization must emphasize the naturalization of the embodiment. For him, 'the problem of embodiment is essentially the same as the problem of emergence, seen the other way on. To ask how consciousness can be embodied in the brain is another way of asking how consciousness can emerge out of the brain'. In this regard, our understanding of both bottom-up inquiry fails because we are not able to identify the real causal properties of the brain. That is, the empirical investigation into the neural function is not sufficient. And similarly the top-down method of looking at the function with the help of introspection does not fully reveal the *real* nature of consciousness. As he writes, "the brain is not a potential object of introspection and consciousness is not (as such) a potential object of perception. Perhaps if we would do these impossible things we would be in a better position to bridge the gulf that separates our conception of oneside from our conception of other: we could juxtapose one perception based conception with another, or one intropspection based conception with another, instead of having to compare conceptions derived from different faculties. But since we cannot so we have to live with the conception we can obtain, however inadequate and incomplete they may be".[73]

Hence, McGinn is not skeptical about the solution of such a mystery. The mystery lingers because the conceptual problem lies in the very discourse of formulating such a conception, called *cognitive closure*. In any case of theorization of consciousness, 'mind is cognitively closed with its property *P* if and only if the concept forming procedures at M's disposal cannot extend to grasp of *P* (or and understanding of T)'. The property cannot be grasped fully because it possesses the double action principle. The property such that it is a part of the brain as well as a part of conscious-ness. The very feature of property is such that "what enables consciousness to emerge from the brain is the same as what allows consciousness to be embodied by the brain. Consciousness would have a protomental hidden structure—that constituted by the particular configuration or protomental properties instantiated by the brain from which it emerges. The property *p* has to face both direction; it cannot be the property of the brain and not the property of consciousness."[74] This property cannot be properly investigated by neurobiology. It remains beyond all scientific explanation. For McGinn, the cognitive closure does not establish the irrealism about the property itself. On the other hand, it only facilitates the method of *conceiving* such property. In brief, the property remains a noumenal property. That is, the characterization of property as noumena shows that the property exits but is not cognitively accessible to mind.

McGinn adovates that there is something hidden in the very nature of consciousness and that it is to be conceived, that is, it can be made intelligible though it is a noumenal property. By locating the noumenal feature in the hidden structure of consciousness, he does not subscribe to any Cartesian assumption that the mental is completely private. Rather the hiddenness of the property of consciousness reveals the *depth* of consciousness. The *depth* of consciousness is analogous to the depth of life, mind, matter, language, etc. McGinn writes: "When the stream of consciousness ripples with thoughts there are patterns beneath the surface—patterns that are imperfetly mirrored by the disturbances at the surface.... Consciousness, like language, disguises its underlying logical structure, and in so doing it tempts us into philosophical error. We avoid such error by declining to be fascinated exclusively by the surface of langague or consciousness. We must peer beyond this surface". This surface level function of consciousness makes the hidden structure transparent but it does not really reveal the whole of the *reality* of consciousness. The hidden structure is the mediation between the surface and the inner configurations which are being revealed at the surface level. Since consciousness is an emergent property of the physical brain processes the surface level of consciousness is not enough to point out its necessary connection with the physical fact. On the other hand, the surface level instead of demonstrating the connection rather *conceals* the relationship. In this regard, the hidden structure of consciousness pertains to the physical aspects of reality. Moreover, the connecting principle from the hidden structure to the surface level is a subject matter of logic. That is to say the logical analysis can capture the link between the surface level and the depth level.

As McGinn suggests, "We do not say that I have these experiences and there is some *other* causal source at work inside me. Attributing the experience to me is sufficient to capture the causal powers being exercized."[75] This can be elaborated with reference to the *conscious thoughts*. Conscious thoughts have both *logical forms* at the deeper level and the *grammatical structure* of the thoughts at the surface level. The grammatical structure is accessible to introspection and thereby to consciousness whereas its logical form is revealed by the logical analysis. The logical forms of the thoughts are causally efficacious. Their causally efficacious feature has the power of discriminating feature that seems to be working at the surface level. McGinn remarks: "There is hidden causality in respect of the logical features of conscious thougts. We saw that thoughts have a hidden logical strcuture; now we see that this structure plays a causal role."[76] Of course, the causally efficacious feature has divided consciousness into two levels but these levels; deep and the surface, function simultaneously in the case of conscious behaviour. Moreover, this does to solve the problem of determining the linkage.

There must be a linkage from the emergent conscious states to there cause and then realization in the brain states. In that way we can intelligibly formulate the causal law. What seems to be puzzling, for McGinn, is that both psychophysical operation and the formulation of causation 'require the knowledge of hidden structure of consciousness. Without this knowledge we shall not be able to progress much beyond crude physical correlation'. To avoid this puzzle, McGinn adovcates, *noumenalism* about the psychophysical link. Noumenalism talks about conceiving the relationship. As he says, "Our perceptual access to material things, including the brain, sets limits on the way we can conceive these things; and our introspective access to consciousness sets limits on the way we conceive of it. We need a manner of conception that abstracts radically from these two fundamental ways of apprehending the world, we simply have no such manner at our cognitive disposal Thus I am prepared to embrace a kind of noumenalism about the psychophysical link; since this link hinges upon the hidden structure of consciousness, I am ready to accept noumenalism about the structure. There can be nothing delving down into it."[77]

Searle is very much critical of McGinn's conception of the *impossible principle* of determining the psychophysical link. The realistic naturalism of McGinn treates conscoiusness as stuff which is given to the faculty of introspection. Searle remarks, "the solution is a Cartesian style solution (with the added disadvantage that the hidden structure of consciousness is unknowable in principle. At least the pineal gland was accessible!) However, the pineal gland solution is no solution. If we need a link between consciousness and the brain, we need a link between the hidden structure of consciousness and the brain. The postulation of hidden structure even if it were intelligible—gets nowhere."[78] McGinn, of course, admits the metaphysical reality of consciousness. He therefore needs a linkage between the psychological and the physical. Searle is also presoppose the same linkage. Biological naturalism does not cover all aspects of the mental life. It only shows how the life of consciousness has emerged in the evolutionary processes. Searle's bottom-up causal explanation fails to describe how the emergence takes place. Hence to know the operation of the mental life of the conscious thought process one has to see through the various features of consciousness. As we have already seen, Searle does not deny that. But the reflexivity of consciousness along with other co-features does not reveal how consciousness is caused by the brain process. He has only the general commonsensical assumption that brain is causing consciousness. In this regard, Searle's scientific inquiry does not take us very far from the standpoint of *mystery* that has been often cited by Nagel and McGinn.

One of the interesting common notions shared by Searle, McGinn and Nagel is the concept of *conscious subjectivity*. The subject is in principle conscious. And it is irreducible to any thing physical. Science whether it is biology or physics can only give a bottom level explanation of the emergence of these conscious features. Because the top level explanation deals with different properties which are completely mental and non-physical. These features have their own function in relation to consciousness. Consciousness embodies intentionality, free will, subjectivity, etc. Subjective representation remains a unique feature to the realm of the mental. Subjectivity is taken as an objective fact for any sort of theorization. But the problem is whether biological naturalism can really explain conscious subjectivity.

VI. When Searlean Subjectivity Meets Transcendental Subjectivity

One may find it difficult to entertain such an idea that Searlean subjectivity meets transcendental subjectivity.

Naturalism in general advocates causal explanation of consciousness whereas the phenomenology advocates transcendental explanation of the structure of consciousness. Thus they stand quite opposed to each other in their explanation of reality. Insofar as biological naturalism of Searle intentionalizes causation and advocates a non-causal description of consciousness there seems to be a similarity with *constitutive phenomenology*. Constitutive phenomenology (*CP*) is Mohanty's reconstruction of Husserl's transcendental phenomenology. As Mohanty says, "Contitutive phenomenology is really tracing the gensis of meaning (of being) to their last origin. Such an origin can be in the domain that is: (1) amenable to pure refelctive glance without losing its 'originary' characters, (2) in that sense can be brought to *refelctive self evidence* (as constrasted with merely prereflective transparence), and (3) can be exhibited as a self-complete autonomus origin."[79] CP represents three phases of description of subjectivity. They are all correlated within the framework of phenomenological description of consciousness. It includes, first the physical aspect of the *body* as the primary discourse of the subjectivity. Secondly, it shows that the embodied consciousness is not really part of the body but having a unique function called reflexivity. And thirdly, apart from the reflexive nature of consciousness, the subjectivity maintains its autonomy in its function. Before going to discuss the details of the *CP's* conception of subjectivity one must need to know why the Searlean subjectivity needs to be correlated with the phenomenological notion of subjectivity.

For Searle, conscious subjectivity refers to the first-person ontology. The uniqueness of the conscious subjectivity is constituted of the person's attitude, feelings and points of view. Searle says, "All of my conscious forms of intentionality that give me information about the world independent of myself are always from a special point of view. That world itself has no point of view, but my access to the world through my conscious states is always from my point of view."[80] This is the uniqueness about every conscious being. Each conscious being has access to the world in its unique way. This intentional participation of conscious subject is what Searle calls state of "impingement". Impingement is revealed in the intentional behaviour of the conscious beings. Intentional behaviour involves person's representation of intentional states and his realization of the intentional representations by manipulating consciously within the domain of interaction. This gives a macro level description of the consciousness subjectivity. The problem with Searlean subjectivity is that it does not go beyond the macro description of subjectivity. Searle stops at that point without giving any further description, about the very function of the conscious subjectivity. Subjectivity, according to him, is not a part of the micro level reality. He says, "There is, in short, no way for us to picture the subjectivity as a part of the world view, because, so to speak, the subjectivity in question is the picturing. The solution is not to try a special mode of picturing, a kind of *superintrospection,* but rather stop picturing altogether at this point and just acknowledge the facts. The facts are the biological process that produces conscious mental phenomena, and these are irreducibly subjective."[81] Thus, subjectivity emerge from the biological processes.

Conscious subjectivity represents the *self* or self-consciousness. That is, it talks about both person's *consciousness of* the world and *consciousness about* person's own conscious states. This self-representation includes self-understanding. The emergence of subjectivity, however, involves both the cognitive processes as well as its interactions with the environment. It includes social naturalism as well. As Flanagan puts it, "the capacity of self-conscious in the first sense, the self is not something we are born with. Maturation, living in the world, being socialized in a life form acquiring certain ways of thinking are required before one can start to build the complex set of representations, that taken together come to constitute the narrative self."[82] Self represents the person and thereby establishes personal identity in the society. And the ermergence of passes through the socialization processes which include "language, time, maturity, autonomy and elaborate multifarious interaction with others'. Flanagan further says, 'The self emerges from, and is subsequently controlled by, a complex of interacting forces. These include the social environment, the entire system that the model self serves, and the reflexive action of self-construction and narration'. Hence, in this regard it would be more logical to give the description of conscious subjectivity in the framework of social function or the macro level function of consciousness.

Mohanty's constitutive phenomenology (*C P*) tries to solve the problem of dualism by explicating the phenomenological notion of *body*. The phenomenological conception of *body* discloses the *natural unity* of mind and body or brain and consciousness through the help of the concept of a living-body. It does not discard the naturalistic view of consciousness as an phenomenon out of very constitution of the physical organism. Rather it tries to show the role of consciousness involved in the living organism. Body mediates in the function of consciousness. The natural unity between the physical organism and its embodiment of consciousness shows the intrinsic corporeality of consciousness. The being as living body embodies consciousness and thus is a part of the *intersubjective* world. Thereby consciousness is linked with nature. Mohanty says: "It is so called 'realisation of consciousness', its 'linking-on' to the corporeal—which gives rise to the peculiar type of 'apperception'—or rather apperceptive interweavings. This linking on does not effect the essential nature of consciousness."[83] The realization of consciousness shows its involvement in the various strata of the body. The strata include the body as a physical object, body as living organism; body an expressive object and the body as cultural object.[84] These strata show the very function of consciousness in them. The first step demonstrate the causal capacity of the physical organism to produce consciousness, the second, shows how the body has consciousness which is pre-reflexive and pre-objective. The third stratum shows the subject as thinking or linguistic being. The being is not just conscious of the world around but s(he) expresses experiences, desires, intentions, willing, etc. Consciousness has certain amount of reflexive feature in this stage. And this reflexive feature further establishes the logical separation of consciousness from the physical aspect of the body. Reflexivity pertains completely to the mental behaviour. Fourthly, the cultural body is being identified as the "being-in-the-world" or the person as a part of the society. The self or life is treated as a form of behaviour. The apperceptive feature is completely realized in the last two strata of the body but the *link* of the body and consciousness continues.

Consciousness, according to Mohanty, is life worldly in the sense that consciousness is linked with the body. However, life worldly conscious experience is prescientific. It only shows its primitive link with the world. Therefore, it only possesses the rudimentary sense of the reflexive feature of consciousness. But the life world consciousness is defined as "a mode of givenness that does not presuppose any other or any methodological operations This is not to neglect other and more founded modes of giveness that are made possible either at of reflection or higher order idealizing acts—all of which refer back life worldly experience". Hence "its original naivity cannot continue as it is under the gaze of reflection." As Mohanty writes, "Life world does not include within its scope reflexive thought. However, transcendental consciousness by its very conception, is reached in reflexive thought after the epoche and through static and genetic constitutional analysis. It is exhibited by self-grounding, and even include life-worldly experience as but its pre-reflexive operative functioning."[85]

The study of conscious subjectivity, thus, remains as the macro-level for both Searle and Mohanty. Macro level signifies its exclusive reference to the realm of conscious mental activities. Though Mohanty talks about the importance of transcendental consciousness having a unique form of conscious subjectivity, he never denies the existential import of it. That is, the existential import of subjectivity lies in its analysis of the phenomenological notion of body with relation to the life world. The interaction of the 'being-in-the-world' discloses the two forms of phenomenological intentionalities; the psychic intentionality and the life-world intentionality. And these two forms are sufficient to define the *act of experience* and the *intention of experience* in the Husserlian sense. The Searlean conception of subjectivity also entertains these phenomenological notions. Searle does not distinguish the psychic form of intentionality from its life world form, but he does talk about the intentionality of mental reference and the ordinary form of intentionality, viz., the visual experiences. Intentionality of mental reference is basically the form of intentionality that deals with thought experience. Thus consciousness is not only directed towards the world it also involves directedness towards the mental life. In that sense, Searle also entertains the notion of reflexivity of consciousness.

Furthermore, both Searle and Mohanty focuses not only on the *being's act of experiencing* the world but also *act of realizing* and understanding it. That brings the Searlean conception of conscious subjectivity closer to Mohanty's transcendental subjectivity. The very act of experiencing and realization are completely linguistic activities of *being*. Linguistic activity is grounded on the notion of *intentional content*. Intentional content is intrinsic to consciousness and thus it discloses the notion of being as "language-centric-conscious-being." The intrinsicness of being language centric is revealed in the being's feature of expressibility. Expressibility makes the being transparent by expressing the inner mental states. In this connection both Searle and Mohanty move away from the Cartesian sense of the inner.[86] The intrinsicness of language to the human being or human life reveals the autonomy of human existence with relation to the world. The linguistic being has two important dimensions. As Pradhan suggests, "Life, seen in the empirical way, is positioned state of human existence; it is conditioned, limited and finite. It has verbal dimension and its is thoroughly structured with rules of the symbolic organization. Yet, it has a dimension of giveness which is not dictated by a priori logical machinery."[87] The verbal dimension of the conscious being signifies the necessary link between consciousness-language and the world. The link is established not because of the being's inherent consciousness but because of its inherent linguistic feature. It is due to the fact that intentional content is present in the very act of expression and realisation. And it is also extended to the realm of the functional domain of language. Our use of language with reference to the exercise of meaning and truth is embedded in language games and forms of life. According to Mohanty, this notion of meaning or language use in general shows the external bond between language and the world. Because language use for Husserl as well as for Mohanty is conscious activity. As Mohanty writes about Husserl, "But speech act is not merely a rule-governed behaviour of a certain sort. It is an intentional act. Speaking is a mode of consciousness. Not only is speaking an act of consciousness, but it has a universality that does not belong to any other sort of act. This is what is implied by the Husserl's thesis that the *noema* or *sinn* of any act is expressible."[88] Thus, Mohanty shows that phenomeno-logical notion of content or sense is embedded in consciousness. For Searle, intentional content is also not only intrinsic to the representational states but also part of conscious activity. The very act of representation shows the intentionality in it. And all representational states are in principle conscious.

However, within the functional domain of language the being represents the world and thereby participates in forms of life from a first-person point of view. For Searle, the first person subjective experiences are the unique way of experiencing or knowing the world. The 'experiences' can be reprsented. As Kent Baldner remarks, "My awareness of representation as fully 'conscious activity' necessarily belongs to me as a particular unitary subject".[89] It is not the case that s(he) is always a first person unitary subject, rather the *subject* also acts as the third-person. And meaning is confirmed, as Searle says, "from third-person point of view."[90] It does not deny the first-person experience of intentional content. Rather the act of representation brings out the compatibility between *my* point of view and *our* point of view. And there is no reduction possible because subjectivity for Searle is an ontological category. Thus each human being is an autonomous being and simultaneously all the human beings act within forms of life. Thus every one is *aware of* 'oneself' and thereby there is at all no question of *opacity*[91] among the human subjects. In order to know the subject or being we have to know the various modes of existence, i.e, the way s(he) participates in the world. As Blender rightly says, "I am aware of myself, just as I am aware of everything else, only as I appear to myself, and so my knowledge that this representation is mine cannot consist in any knowledge that it "belongs" to some unitary enduring self-in-itself. The unity or identity of self necessary for the possibility of experience is not to be found in some "noumenal self" that *transcends* experience, but in what is immanent within experiences: it is none other than identity of the rule or function by which we recognise representation into experiences of objects."[92]

Thus the Searlean subjectivity comes closer to

Mohanty's transcendental subjectivity if one looks at it from the broader prospective of *language* in general and intentional content in particular. The Searlean subject is not a mere experiencing being but is also one participating in the normatively structured forms of life. Thus *experiencing subject* has a transcendental status in both Mohanty and Searle.[93] This study of conscious subjectivity will not only eliminate the paradox that Searle assumes but also have a proper ground for the macro level explanation of the mental phenomena. That will also consequently help us in resolving the form of dualism that Searle apprehends in his biological naturalism. If Searle thinks that both naïve physicalism and naive mentalism are inevitable, then his solution to the problem of dualism fails. It is precisely because the very explanation of physical phenomena has to be comprehended through the reality of consciousness. And if one says consciousness is dependent on the neurobiological processes of the brain, then it has certainly a causal dependency. This causal dependency may not put consciousness at the centre of the discussion on mind. Consciousness as the defining feature of the mental needs an independent status. And that autonomy has be accepted in order to solve the mind-body problem.

To conclude herewith, the present study is broadly a study of consciousness. And the study of consciousness is the study of life. The metaphysics of evolution shows the relationship of consciousness with the phenomenon of life. The evolutionary dimension of life shows how mind and consciousness have affected in the evolutionary process. Consciousness, in this case of human beings, is being regarded as one of the specific properties, which characterizes all human activities. Human beings as conscious beings are not only just part of the evolutionary aspect of reality, but they also describe the reality, i.e., they try to know what is there in the reality. This essay has addressed the question as to how consciousness is related to the world through language and the intentional states of mind.

Searle's specific contribution to philosophy of mind is his theory of evolution of mind from biological sense of the word. For him mind is an emergent reality. However, according to him, the emergence of consciousness from the neurophysiological process of the brain shows that its ontology is dependent on the ontology of neurophysiology of the brain. The Searlean biological naturalism finds it difficult to deny that mind is real. And the acceptance of ontology of mind makes the Searlean hypothesis a dualistic one. It denies neither the ontology of the brain processes nor the independent and irreducible nature of consciousness. According to this hypothesis consciousness, however, is *caused* by the brain processes and *realized in* the brain processes. Even then, consciousness is an independent reality.

The emergence of consciousness in the human mental life is an irreducible property. Therefore, consciousness is an independent and autonomous realm of function. It is independent of the neurophysiological processes of the brain of human organism. It is autonomous because once consciousness is produced it has a life of its own. And it functions over and above the function of the neurophysiological processes of the brains. From these two claims of Searle, it follows that consciousness persists to function independently. Searle emphasizes two more points. They are; firstly, consciousness is by definition unified. Secondly, consciousness has the potency to make unconscious mental states conscious. It is because unconscious mental states are just minus consciousness or minus intentionality, but they are potentially conscious. They pertain to the realm of mental. In other words, consciousness binds the mental states together and makes the unconscious mental states conscious. On the other hand, he accepts that brain is the system which as a whole causes consciousness or has the capacity to cause consciousness. Such a potentiality is inherent in the structure of the brain. And the structure of brain maintains a hierarchy of functions at different levels.

The present study has further focused on the subjectivity of consciousness. The autonomy of mind is linked with ontology of subjectivity. Each subject is an autonomous *conscious being*. The ontology of mind has two basic aspects; they are *subjectivity* and *subjecticity*. Subjectivity represents a unified state of consciousness whereas subjecticity is a state of thinking or experiencing. They are interrelated with each other. The ontology of subjectivity entails the experiencing feature of the conscious being. Experiencing is a process considered as a part of the conscious thought processing or thinking. Subjectivity constitutes the first person experiences and representations of the reality. The first person accessibility to the conscious experience cannot be reduced to third persons' objectivity. If we leave out the first person experience then mind would be reduced to a certain mechanical function of the brain organism. So, in this regard, the ontology of subjectivity is significant since subjectivity is irreducible to the brain states and processes. However, it is important to note that the person is *conscious of* or is aware of his own *subjecticity*. In Searlean terms, we are unconsciously aware of our thinking because of the background conditions.

A conscious mind can well distinguish the hierarchy of conscious and unconscious notion of subjecticity. For instance, a conscious mind can distinguish the state of dreaming from the state of hallucination, the state of elation of joy from sudden fear of death. Since they do not have intentional *direction of fit* they are not considered as consciousness proper. However, they have some sense of mental reference, i.e., called intentionality of mental reference. It is precisely because the mind *construes* the phenomena, which generates mental reference. Feelings are also generated in the mind-to-world intentional relationship. In the case of intentionality of mental reference the object is only having the mental referent, not a referent in the world. Feelings are part of consciousness or conscious experience in particular. Hence, intentionality of conscious thought processes has a mental reference. And there could not be any experience without mental reference.

Searle's main thesis is that language use is an intentional activity. Intentionality embedded in the linguistic representations or language use is derived from the real or intrinsic intentional property of mental states. That holds an identity between the mental representations and linguistic representations. The identity is intentional in the sense that there is an *isomorphism* between the structure of intentional states and their linguistic representations. The structural isomorphism is intentionally defined. The intentional characterization of structural isomorphism shows the *flow* of intentionality from the mental to *social* or the world. It is because language use is a social phenomenon and it persists in the world. Such flow of intentionality which reveals that content is not distorted in the process of *transformation* of thought processes. Besides, for Searle, the intentional content is not purely syntactical but semantic.

The Searlean notion of *flow* of intentionality is important to explain the notion of meaning and truth in the discourse of intention based semantics. That is, language use or speech acts are not only intentional in nature but they reveal the intentionality in language. Intentional force is imposed in each and very performance of linguistic activities. That intentional force precisely *creates* the meaning and defines its *limitations*. Creating a meaning by imposing intentionality implies the intervention of subjectivity in the social conventional force. The conventional force or the meaning of language use concerns the literal meaning of language use. And language use in general is defined by the certain *constitutive rules*, which are followed in every linguistic discourse. Now the question arises, how are the rules of language constituted? The very form of language use, for Searle, is rooted in the intentional feature of consciousness. Language use is a later development in the evolutionary process of biology. Contents embedded in the discourse of language use originate from the very intentional feature of the mind. Intentional content is characterized as linguistic in the sense that *linguistic categories* are essentially related to consciousness. In other words, since the content is intentional the conventional language use embodies *conventional force.* This is what is known as social intentionality. Searle calls it *we*-intentionality. *We*-intentionality is a shareable *form* of intentionality which defines the constitutive rules of language use. Constitutive rules are shared by each linguistic being in general and linguistic community in particular. It helps in maintaining a normal semantic discourse. The discourse results in epistemic objectivity for meaning and truth. That is to say the objectivity of meaning and truth is neither distorted nor reduced to any subjectivity form of intentionality or to the mind. Rather such a subjective form of intentionality constitutes the objective form *meaning* intentionality. In other words, *I* intentionalities are the micro level constituents of *we* intentionality. Moreover, each linguistic representation unfolds the *psychological mode* and the *direction of fit,* which result in the *self-referentiality* of intentionality from the mind to the intentionality of language use. That is, the directedness of *I* or subjective form of intentionality towards *we* or objective form of intentionality. It reveals the fact that in the semantic discourse, the flow of intentionality is not only from mind-to-the world but also from world- to-the mind. Consequently, it entails that *intentional field* exists in the semantic discourse about the world.

The present work thus offers the conclusion that the mental is an autonomous reality. So ultimately there are two interdependent levels of reality, namely, mental and the physical. Searle himself has offered this mode of dualism between the brain states and the conscious processes. Searle categorically denies the notion of identity of the mental and the physical. He is aware of that such a supposition will consequently eliminate the very reality of mind. For him, that would be a sure logical impossibility as mind is also fundamental to human life. To deny the reality of consciousness is to deny life itself. However, the very conception of explaining away the conscious mind will definitely presuppose the metaphysics of mind.

Notes and References

1. Searle, *Minds, Brains, and Science,* p. 10
2. *Ibid.,* pp. 14-15.
3. John Heil, *Philosophy of Mind: A Contemporary Introduction,* Routledge London, 1998, p. 42.
4. *Ibid.* p. 42
5. *Ibid.,* p. 44.
6. *Ibid.* p. 46.
7. Cf. Searle, *Minds, Brains and Science,* "Mind-Body Problem", p. 22.
8. Garry Hearteild, "Descartes Physiology and its relation to Physchology", in *Cambridge Companion to Descartes,* ed. John Cotingham, p. 350.
9. J. Searle, *Minds, Brains, and Science,* p. 18.
10. *Ibid.,*p. 26
11. *Ibid.,*p. 21
12. See, Freeman and Skarda, in *John Searle and His Critics,* p. 121.
13. Searle's Response to Freeman and Skarda, *Ibid.,* p. 143.
14. *Ibid.,*p. 144.
15. See, Hanny, *John Searle and His Critics,* p. 132.
16. *Ibid.,* p. 135.
17. Searle, *The Rediscovery of the Mind,* p. 228.
18. *Ibid.,* p. 229.
19. *Ibid.,* p. 233.
20. *Ibid.,* p. 235
21. See, Dennett, *Brainstorms,* p. 157.
22. See Dennett, *Consciousness Explained,* p. 153.

23. Dennett mentions that each subsystems in a cognitive organism are interrelated there is no homunculus as an interpreter or used beyond the system. At the level of interaction they do interact with each other by passing simulation that is executed. See, *Brainstorms*, p. 123.
24. See Dennett's *Intentional Stance*, "Three kinds of Intentional Psychology", p. 59.
25. Dennett also mentions about two more other stances, i.e. the physical stance and algorithmic stance for the complete description of the intentional system. Since the emphasis is given more on the sub-personal level of discussion, we are more inclined to deal with the apscets which are directly refer to the hardware explanation of the brain organism or intentional system. See, , *Brainstorms*, "Intentional System", p. 4.
26. See, the Chapter-III, "Evolution in the Brain," in Dennett's *Content and Consciousness*, pp. 44-57.
27. Dennett, *Intentional Stance*, p. 25.
28. See, Searle, *The Rediscovery of the Mind*, p. 188.
29. *Ibid.*, p. 196.
30. Bary Stroud, "The Backgound of Thought", *John Searle and His Critics*, p. 250.
31. *Ibid.*, pp. 251-57.
32. See, Searle's Response to Bary Stroud, *John Searle and His Critics*, p. 291.
33. Searle, *Minds, Brains, and Science*, p. 27
34. Searle mentions about two varieties of emergence. The emergen1 would talk about the causal process where the effect as a product of the process can be reduced to the cause again. Whereas, in the case of emergence2 the effect is an independent feature though it is caused but must be treated as different and distinct in is existence and function. See, Searle, *The Rediscovery of the Mind*, p. 112.
35. *Ibid.*, pp. 121-122.
36. Dennett, "Real Patterns", *The Journal of Philosophy*, Vol. 88, 1991, p. 30. In this paper he exclusively discusses about the belief states and their ontology. He rejects the notion that belief states are grounded in consciousness or *centers of gravity*. There is no such thing so far as the mental states are concerned. The ultimate analysis leads to the denial of both consciousness and intrinsic

properties of the mental states. Since belief is the paradigm case of knowledge states for all our activities, the ontology may be the neural or the physical structure of the organism.

37. *Ibid.*, p. 38.
38. This is a clarification Dennett gives to Anscombe. According to Dennett, Anscombe is not able to detect the root of "an order which is there whenever actions are done with intention." But did not say where in the world this order has to be discussed. In the brain? In the behaviour? See, Dennett, "Real Patterns, Deeper Facts, and Empty Questions", in *Intentional Stance*, p. 39.
39. *Ibid.*, p. 34.
40. Dennett says it referring to Searle, Dretske, Fordor and other, "all are tempted to search for this deeper act, and how their search is forlorn." See, *Intentional Stance*, p. 42.
41. See, Dennett's *Intnetional Stance*, p. 249.
42. *Ibid.*, p. 318.
43. Searle, *Minds, Brains and Science*, p. 16.
44. Dennett in his review of Searle's *The Rediscovery of the Mind*. See Daniel C. Denntt, *Journal of Philosophy*, Vol. 90, 1993, p. 193.
45. Searle, *The Rediscovery of the Mind*, p. 141.
46. *Ibid.*, p. 144.
47. Refelexivity as a feature of consciousness is natural to the very nature of consciousness. One need not always reflect on this skill in order to establish it. He says, "refelxivity is not required in order for a thinking substance to be superior to matter. The initial thought by means of which we became aware of something does not differ from the second thought by means of which we become aware that we are aware of it, any more than this second thought differ from third thought by means of which we become aware that we are aware that we were are aware." See Descartes' [Seventh Replies: *CSM* II 382] "The Nature of Thought" Rene Descartes, *Meditations on First Philosophy with Selection from the Objections and Replies*, ed. John Cottingham, Cambrid University Press, Cambridge, 1986, pp-75-76.
48. See the "Fourth Replies," *Ibid.*, p. 76.
49. *Ibid.*, p. 130.
50. *Ibid.*,p. 149
51. Searle makes the distinction between strong AI and weak AI. See, "Minds, Brains and Programs" *The Mind's I: Fantasies and*

Reflections on Self and Soul, composed and arranged by Douglas R. Hofstadter and Daniel C. Dennett, Basic Books, INC, Publishers, New York, 1981, p. 353.

52. *Ibid.,* p. 372.
53. See the Chapter "Cognitive Science", in Sealre, *Minds, Brains, and Science,* p. 43.
54. Consciousness and brain processes are not necessary aspects of discussion in cognitive science. The basic function information processing takes place in the in the middle of these two functions. See, Searle, *The Rediscovery of the Mind,* p. 197.
55. See, David Cole, "Thought and Thought Experiment", *Philosophical Studies,* Vol. 45, 1989. William J. Rapaport's 'Discussion' on Cole's argument, "Sealre's Experiment with Thought", *Philosophy of Science,* Vol. 53, 1986. Dale Jacquette, "Adventures in Chinese Room", *Philosophy and Phenomenological Research,* Vol. XLIX, No. 4, June 1989.
56. See, Cole, *Ibid.,*p. 434.
57. See, Rapaport, p. 272.
58. *Ibid.,*pp. 272-273.
59. Searle, *Minds, Brains and Science,* pp. 48-50.
60. *Ibid.,* p. 50.
61. See, Rapaport, p. 276.
62. See Jacquette quotes Searle, p. 708.
63. Searle writes it in *Scientific American,* 1990. See, David Cole quotes Searle in his Discussion, "Artificial Mind: Cam and Searle", *Australasian Journal of Philosophy,* Vol. 69, No. 3, September 1991, p. 330.
64. Philip Cam, "Searle on Strong AI, *Australasian Journal of Philosophy,* Vol. 68, 1990, p. 104.
65. Searle, *Minds, Brains, and Science,* p. 54.
66. Nagel reviews, Searle's *The Rediscovery of the Mind.* Thomas Nagel, "Searle: Why We Are Not Computers", in Reprinted *in Other Minds and Critical Essays,* Oxford University Press, Oxford, 1995, p. 103.
67. See, Searle, *Minds, Brains, and Science,* pp. 23-24.
68. Nagel, "Conceiving the Impossible and the Mind-Body Problem," *Philosophy,* Vol. 73,1998, p. 338.

69. Nagel, "What Is It Like To Be A Bat?" *Philosophical Review*, 1974, p. 442.
70. For Nagel, the intimacy between the physical properties of the brain and the mental properties continues though we are yet to explore the possible interacting point. One of the consequences "One unsettling consequence of such a theory is that it appears to lead to a form of panpsychism – since the mental properties of the complex organism must result from some properties of its basic components suitably combined: and these cannot be merely physical properties." (p. 49) In Nagel, "Mind and the Body", *The View From Nowhere*, Oxford University Press, Oxford, 1986, p28.
71. Nagel, "Conceiving the Impossible and the Mind-Body Problem", p. 338.
72. Colin McGinn, *The Problem of Consciousness*, Basil Blackwell, Oxford, 1991, p. 47.
73. *Ibid.*, p. 61.
74. *Ibid.*, p. 68
75. *Ibid.*, p. 99
76. *Ibid.*, p. 112.
77. *Ibid.*, p. 114.
78. SeeSearle, *RDM*, p. 105.
79. J.N. Mohanty, *The Possibility of Transcendental Philosophy*, Martinus Nijhoof Publishers, Dordrecht, 1985, p. 149.
80. Searle, *RDM*, p. 95
81. *Ibid.*, p. 98
82. See, Owen Flanagan, "Consciousnes and the Self", *Consciousness Reconsidered*, p. 195.
83. Mohanty, *The Possibility of Transcendental Philosophy*, p. 128.
84. *Ibid.*, p. 136.
85. *Ibid.*, p. 150
86. *Ibid.*, p. 131.
87. R. C. Pradhan, "Life, Will and the World: Some Reflection on *Notebooks 1914-1916*," *Journal of Indian Council of Philosophical Research*, Vol. XI, No. 3, 1993, pp. 42-43.
88. Mohanty, *PTP*, p. 204.
89. Kent Blender, "Subjectivity and the Unity of the World," *The Philosophical Quarterly*, Vol. 46, No. 184, July 1996, p. 336.
90. Searle, *Intentionality*, p. 63.

91. Mohanty, *Transcendental Phenomenology*, Basil Blackwell, Oxford, 1991, p. 104.
92. Blender, op. cit, pp. 336-337
93. I have discussed the notion of Subejctivity with reference to the notion of *intentional content*. See, my "The Notion of 'Intentional Content': Mohanty and Searle, *JICPR*, Vol. XVI, No. 1, September-December 1998. p. 62

BIBLIOGRAPHY

Agar, N., *"Biocentrism and the Concept of Life"*, Ethics, No. 108, October 1997.

Anscombe, G.E.M., *Metaphysics and the Philosophy of Mind,* Basil Blackwell, Oxford, 1981.

Armstrong, D. M., *A Materialist Theory of Mind,* Routledge and Kegan Paul, London, 1968.

________, "The Nature of Mind", *Mind-Brain Identity Theory,* ed. C.V. Broost, Mcmillian, St. Martins Press, London, 1970.

Akins, K., "Of the Sensory Systems and the 'Aboutness' of Mental States" *The Journal of Philosophy,* Vol. XCIII, No. 7, July 1996.

Avramides, *Anita, Meaning and Mind: An Examination of a Graicean Account of Language,* A Bradford Book, The MIT Press, Massachusetts, 1989.

Backer, L. R., *Explaining Attitudes: A Practical Approach to the Mind,* Cambridge University Press, Cambridge, 1995.

Baldner, K., "Subjectivity and the Unity of the World," *The Philosophical Quarterly,* Vol. 46, No. 184, July 1996.

Beakkly, Brain and Peter Ludlow, (ed.) *Philosophy of Mind: Classical Problem/ Contemporary Issues,* The MIT Press, Massachusetts, 1992.

Bishop, John, "Searle on Natural Agency," *The Australasian Journal of Philosophy,* Vol. 68, No. 3, 1990.

Blackmore, Colin and Susan Greenfield, (ed.) *Mindwaves*, Basil Blackwell, Oxford, 1987.

Block, N., (ed.) *Readings in Philosophy of Psychology*, Vol. II, Harvard University Press, Cambridge, 1981.

Block, N. & Jerry Fodor, "What Psychological States are Not?" *The Philosophical Review*, Vol. 81, 1972. Reprinted in Fodor's *Representations*.

Broome, John, "Desire, Belief and Expectation," *Mind*, Vol. 100, 1991.

Broost, C.V., (ed.) *Mind-Brain Identity Theory*, Mcmillian, St. Martins Press, London, 1970.

Burge, T., "Philosophy of Language and Mind," *The Philosophical Review*, Vol. 101, 1992.

Canfield, J.V., "The Concept of Function in Biology", *Philosophical Topics*, Vol. 18, No. 2 Fall 1990.

Cam, Philip, "Searle on Strong AI", *The Australasian Journal of Philosophy*, Vol. , 68, No. 1, 1990.

________, "Consciousness and Content Formation, *Inquiry*, Vol. 27, 1987.

Carnap, Rudlof, "The Logical Foundation of Unity of Science," *Essential Readings in Logical Positivism*, ed. Oswald Hanfling.

Chomsky, N., "Linguistic and Philosophy," *Language and Philosophy*, (ed.) Sydney Hook, New York University Press, New York, 1969.

________, *Rules and Representations*, Basil Blackwell, Oxford, 1980.

________, Language and Nature of Mind, *Mind*, Vol. 104, No. 416, 1995.

Chrodinger, E. S., *What is Life?* Cambridge University Press, Cambridge, 1967.

Churchland, Paul M., "Eliminative Materialism and

Propositional Attitude", *The Journal of Philosophy*, Vol. 78, No. 2, 1981.

________, "Reduction, Qualia, and the Direct Introspection of Brain States", *The Journal of Philosophy*, Vol. LXXXII, No. 1, 1985.

________, "Some Reductive Strategies in Cognitive Neurobiology", *Mind*, Vol. 95, No. 379, 1986.

________, *Matter and Consciousness*, The MIT Press, A Bradford Book, Massachusetts, 1989.

________, "The Rediscovery of the Light", *The Journal of Philosophy*, Vol. XCII, No. 5, May 1996.

Clarke, P., "Explanation in Physical Theory, *Philosophy*, Supplement: *Explanation and Its Limits*, Vol. 27, 1990.

Clarke, D. M., "Descartes Philosophy of Science, *Cambridge Companion to Descartes*, Cambridge University Press, Cambridge, 1992..

Cole, D., "Thought and Thought Experiment, *The Philosophical Studies*, Vol. 45, 1989.

________, "Artificial Mind: Cam and Searle" *The Australasian Journal of Philosophy*, Vol. 69, No. 3, September1991.

Davidson, D., "Actions, Reasons and Causes", *Causal Theories of Mind*, (ed.) Steven Davis, Walter de Gruyeter, Holland, 1983.

Dennett, Daniel. C., *Content and Consciousness*, Routledge and Kegan Paul, London, 1969.

________, *Brainstorms*, The MIT Press, Massachusetts, 1986.

________, *Intentional Stance*, The MIT Press, Massachusetts, 1987.

________, "Quining Qualia", Mind and Cognition: A Reader, ed. William G. Lycan, Basil Blackwell, Cambridge, 1990.

________, *Consciousness Explained*, Little Brown and Company, Boston, 1991.

________, "Real Patterns", *The Journal of Philosophy*, Vol. 88, 1991.

Descartes, R., *The Philosophical Writings of Descartes*, Vol. I , trans. John Cottingham, Robert Stoothoff, Dugal Murdoch, Cambridge University Press, Cambridge, 1985.

________, *Meditations on First Philosophy: with selections from the Objections and Replies*, trans. John Cottingham, Cambridge University Press, Cambridge, 1986.

Dreyfus, Hubert, L., *What Computers Can't Do?*, Harper and Raw, New York, 1972.

________, (ed.) *Husserl, Intentionality and Cognitive Science*, The MIT Press, A Bradford Book, Massachusetts, 1982.

Fodor, Jerry, A., *Representations: A Philosophical Foundation to Cognitive Science*, The Harvester Press, Sussex, 1981.

________, "Fodor's Guide to Mental Representation: The Intelligent Antie's Vade-Mecum", *Mind*, Vol. 94, January 1985.

________, *Modularity of Mind: An Essay on Faculty Psychology*, The MIT Press, Massachusetts, 1983.

________, *Psychosemantics: The Problem of Meaning in the Philosophy of Mind*, The Bradford Book, TheMIT Press, Massachusetts, 1987.

________, "Why Should the Mind be Modular?" *Reflections on Chomsky*, ed. Alexander Gerorge, Basil Blackwell, Oxford, 1989.

Fodor, J. & Lepore, E., "What is the Connection Principle? *Philosophy and Phenomenological Research*, Vol. LIV, No. 4, 1994.

Foss, J., "On the Logic of What It Is Like To Be A Conscious Subject?" *The Australasian Journal of Philosophy*, Vol. 67, 1989.

________, "Materialism, Reductionism, Replacement and the Place of Consciousness in Science," *The Journal of Philosophy*, Vol. 92, No. 8, August 1995.

Flanagan, O., *Consciousness Reconsidered*, The MIT Press, Massachusetts, 1993.

Freeman G. and Skarda, *Searle and His Critics*, ed. Lepore, E. & Robert van Gulick.

Grice, H.P., "Meaning", *Philosophical Review*, Vol. 66, 1957.

________, "Utterer's Meaning and Intention", *Philosophical Review*, Vol. 78, 1969.

Gillett, Grant, "Learning to Perceive", *Philosophy and Phenomenological Research*, vol.48, no.4, June 1988.

________, "Representation and Cognitive Science", *Inquiry*, vol.32, no.3, September 1989.

________, "Consciousness, Brain and What Matters" *Bioethics*, vol.4, no.3, July 1990.

________, *Representation, Meaning and Thought*, Clarendon Press, Oxford, 1992.

________, "Generality Constraint and Conscious Thought", *Analysis*, vol.47, 1987.

Grimm, R. H. & Merril, Daniel D., (ed.) *Content of Thoughts*, The Arizona University Press, Tucson, 1988.

Hanfling, O., (ed.) *Essential Readings in Logical Positivism*, Basil Blackwell, Oxford, 1981.

Harman, G., *Thought*, Princeton University Press, Princeton, 1973.

Haugeland, J., "Understanding Natural Language", *The Journal of Philosophy*, Vol. 76, 1979.

________, (ed.) *Mind Design*, The MIT Press, Massachusetts, 1981.

Hartfield, Garrry, "Descartes Physiology and its Relation to Psychology" *Cambridge Companion to Descartes*, ed. John Cottingham, Cambridge University Press, New York, 1986.

Heil, J., *Philosophy of Mind: A Contemporary Introduction*, Routledge, London, 1998.

Hopkins, John, *Intentionality in Husserl and Heidegger*, Kluwer Academic Publishers, London, 1993.

Humberstone, I. L., "Direction of Fit", *Mind*, Vol. 101, No. 401, 1992.

Husserl, E., ***IDEAS** Pertaining to A Pure Phenomenology and Phenomenological Philosophy*, First Book, *General Introduction to Pure Phenomenology*, trans.Kersten, F., Martinus Nijhoff Publishers, The Hague, 1982.

Jacquette, Dale, "Adventures in Chinese Room, *Philosophy and Phenomenological Research*, Vol. XLIX, No. 4, June 1989.

Johnsen, Bredo, "Dennett on Qualia and Conscious-ness: A Critique" *The Canadian Journal of Philosophy*, Vol. 27, No. 1, March 1997.

Jolly, K. Dean, and Michael Watkins, "What Is It Like to Be a Phenomenologist?" *The Philosophical Quarterly*, Vol. 48, No. 91, April 1998.

Leidtke, F., *Mind, Meaning and Metaphysics: The Philosophy and Theory of Language of Anton Marty*, Kluwer Academic Publishers, Dordrecht, 1990.

Lepore, E. & Van Gulick R., *John Searle and His Critics*, Basil Blackwell, Oxford, 1991.

Loar, Brain, *Mind and Meaning*, Cambridge University Press, Cambridge, 1981.

Lowe, E.J.L., "The Causal Autonomy of the Mental", *Mind*, Vol. 102, No. 407, July 1993.

Lyons, William, *Approaches to Intentionality*, Clarendon Press, Oxford, 1995.

MacIntyre, R., "Searle on Intentionality", *Inquiry*, Vol. , 1984.

MacIntyre, R. and David W. Smith, *Husserl and Intentionality*, D. Rediel Publishing Company, Holland, 1982.

Magee, Brain, *Men of Ideas*, Oxford University Press, London, 1978.

McGinn, C., "The Structure of Content" *Thought and Object* (ed.) Woodfield, A., Clarendon Press, Oxford, 1984.

________, *The Problems of Consciousness*, Basil Blackwell, Oxford, 1991.

Miles, T.R., "On the Difference between Men and Machines, *The British Journal of Philosophy of Science*, Vol. VII, No. 28, February 1954.

Millikan, Ruth, G., *Language, Thought and Other Biological Categories*, The MIT Press, A Bradford Book, Massachusetts, 1984.

________, "Thought without Laws and Cognitive Science with Content," *The Philosophical Review*, Vol. XCV, No. 1, January 1986.

Mohanty, J.N., "Intentionality and Noema", *The Journal of Philosophy*, Vol. 28, 1981.

________, "Intentionality, Causality and Holism," *Synthese*, Vol. 61, 1984.

________, *The Possibility of Transcendental Phenomeno-logy*, Martinus Nijhoff Publishers, The Hague, 1985.

________, *The Transcendental Phenomenology*, Basil Blackwell, Oxford, 1991.

Mulhall, S., *On Being in the World: Wittgenstein and Heidegger on Seeing Aspects*, Routledge, London, 1990.

Nagel, E., "Are Naturalists Materialists? *The Journal of Philosophy*, Vol. 42,

Nagel, Thomas, "Physicalism" *The Philosophical Review*, Vol. LXXIV, 1965.

________, "What Is It Like To Be A Bat?" *The Philosophical Review*, Vol. 83,1974.

________, *A View form Nowhere*, Oxford University Press, Oxford, 1986.

________, "Searle: Why we are not Computers?" Reprinted in his *Other Minds and Critical Essays*, Oxford University Press, Oxford, 1995.

________, "Conceiving the Impossible and the Mind-Body Problem", *Philosophy*, Vol. 73, 1998.

Nelkin, N., "How Sensations Get Their Names", *Philosophical Studies*, Vol. 51, 1987.

________, "What is Consciousness?" *Philosophy of Science*, Vol. 60, 1993.

________, *Consciousness and the Origin of Thought*, Cambridge University Press, Cambridge, 1994.

Nemirow, Lwarence, E., "Understanding Rules", *The Journal of Philosophy*, Vol. 92, January 1995.

Owens, David, "Levels of Explanation," *Mind*, Vol. 98, No. 389, 1989.

Place, U.T., "Is Consciousness a Brain Process?" *The British Journal of Psychologoy*, Vol. XLVII, 1956. Reprinted in *Mind-Body Identity Theory*, C.V. Broost.

________, "Thirty Years on - Is consciousness still a Brain Process?", *Australasian Journal of Philosophy*, Vol. 66, No. 2, June 1988.

Poland, J., *Physicalism: The Philosophical Foundations*, Clarendon Press, Oxford, 1994.

Pradhan, R.C., *Meaning and Representations*, D.K. Printworld, New Delhi, 1996.

________, "Life, Will and the World: Some Reflections on the *NoteBooks 1914-1916*," *JICPR*, Vol. XI, No. 3, 1993.

________, "Is There Such Thing as Self Consciousness? A Response," *JICPR*, Vol. XV, No. 1, September-December 1997.

Putnam, H.,"Philosophy and Our Mental Life," *Mind, Language and Reality*, Philosophical Papers 2, Cambridge University Press, Cambridge, 1976.

________, "The Nature of Mental States," *Philosophy of Mind: Classical Problem/ Contemporary Issues*, (ed.) Beakkly, Brain and Peter Ludlow, The MIT Press, Massachusetts, 1992.

________, "Mind and Machine", *Dimensions of Mind*, ed. Sydney Hook, Collier Books, New York, 1960.

________, *Reason, Truth and History*, Cambridge University Press, Cambridge, 1981.

________, *Representation and Reality*, The MIT Press, Massachusetts, 1989.

Radner, Daisie, "Heterophenomenology: Learning about the Birds and Bees", *The Journal of Philosophy*, Vol. XCI, No. 8, August 1994.

Rapaport, William J., "Searle's Thought Experiment" *Philosophy of Science*, Vol. 53, 1986.

Rorty, R., "Contemporary Philosophy of Mind," *Synsthese*, Vol. 53, 1982.

Rosenthal, D., "Two Types of Consciousness", *Philosophical Studies*, Vol. 49, 1986.

Rowlands, M., "Teleological Semantics," *Mind*, Vol. 106, No. 422, April 1997.

Ryle, G., *The Concept of Mind*, Barnes and Noble, New York, 1949.

Scheer, R. K., "What I will Do What I intend to Do" *Philosophy*, Vol. 71, No. 278, October 1996.

Schmidtz, D., "Rationality with Reason," *The Journal of Philosophy*, Vol. LXXIV, September 1992.

Searle, John, R., *Speech Acts: An Essay in the Philosophy of Language*, Cambridge University Press, Cambridge, 1970.

________, *Expression and Meaning: Studies in the Theories of Speech Acts*, Cambridge University Press, Cambridge, 1979.

_______, "Intentionality and Method", *Synthese*, Vol. 78, 1981.

_______, "Intentionality and Its Place in Nature" *Synthese*, Vol. , 61,1984.

_______, "What is an Intentional State?" *Husserl, Intentionality and Cognitive Science*, (ed.) H. L. Dreyfus.

_______, "Meaning Communication and Representation", *Philosophical Ground of Rationality*, (ed.) Richard E. Grant & Richard Warner, Clarendon Press, Oxford, 1986.

_______, *Intentionality: An Essay in the Philosophy of Mind*, Cambridge University Press, Cambridge, 1983.

_______, "Minds, Brains with Programs", *Minds' I: Fantasies and Reflections of Self and Soul*, ed. Douglas R. Hofstadter & Daniel C. Dennett, Basic Books, INC, New York, 1981.

_______,"Mind, Brains without Programs," *Mind-waves: Thoughts on Intelligence, Identity and Conscious-ness*, (ed.) Collin Blackmore & Susan Greenfield.

_______, *Minds, Brains, and Science*, The Harvard University Press, Cambridge, 1984.

_______, *The Rediscovery of the Mind*, The MIT Press, A Bradford Book, Massachusetts, 1992.

_______, "Connection Principle and the Ontology of Unconscious: A Reply to Fodor and Lepore", *Philosophy and Phenomenological Research*, Vol. LIV, No. 4, 1994.

_______, "The Explanation of Cognition" (Unpub-lished) My Personal Correspondence, September 1996.

_______, "Consciousness and the Philosophers" *The New York Review of Books*. Vol. XLIV, No. 4, 1997.

_______, *The Construction of Social Reality*, Allen Lane and Penguin, London, 1995.

________, *Mind, Language and Society*, Phoenix, London, 1999.

Shiffer, Stephen, *Meaning*, Oxford University Press, London, 1974.

________, *The Remnants of Meaning*, The MIT Press, A Bradford Book, Massachusetts, 1989.

Shoemaker, S., "Qualities and Qualia: What is in the Mind?" *Philosophy and Phenomenological Research*, Vol. 50, 1990.

________, "Qualia and Consciousness", *Mind*, Vol. C, No. 4, 1991.

________, "Inverted Spectrum" *The Journal of Philosophy*, Vol. 79, no.7, July 1992.

Sintonen, Matti, "How Evolutionary Theory Faces the Reality," *Synthese*, Vol. 89, 1991.

Slors, M., "Why Dennett Cannot Explain the Inten-tional Stance?" *The Philosophical Quarterly*, Vol. 46, No. 182, January 1996.

Smart, J.C.C., "Sensations and Brain Process" *Mind-Body Identity Theory*, ed. C.V. Broost.

________, *Essays on Metaphysical and Moral*, Basil and Blackwell, Oxford, 1987.

Staz, Debra, & John FereJohn, "Rational Choice and Social Theory", *The Journal of Philosophy*, Vol. 91, February 1994.

Stone, Jime, "Why Potentiality Still Matters?", *The Canadian Journal of Philosophy*, Vol. 24, No. 2, June 1994.

Stich, S., "What is a Theory of Mental Representation?," *Mind*, Vol. 101, No. 402, April 1992.

Stroud, B., "The Background of Thought" in *John Searle and His Critics*.

Sturgeon, Scott, "The Epistemic view of Subjectivity", *The Journal of Philosophy,* Vol. XCI, No. 5, 1994.

Teichmen, J., *Philosophy and the Mind,* Basil Blackwell, Oxford, 1988.

Tye, Michael, "Naturalism and the Mental" *Mind,* Vol. 101, No. 403, July 1992.

Velleman, D. J., "Self to Self", *The Philosophical Review,* Vol. 105, No. 1, January 1996.

Voss, S., (ed.) *Essays on Philosophy and Science of Rene Descartes,* Oxford University Press, Oxford, 1993.

Wagner, S. I., "Mind-Body Interaction in Descartes", *Essays on Philosophy and Science of Rene Descartes,* ed. Stephen Voss.

Wilkes , V. K., "Brain States", *The Philosophical Quarterly,* Vol. 61, Nos.1-2, January-April 1980.

Wittgenstein, L., *Philosophical Investigations,* ed. G.E.M., Anscombe & Rush Rhees, trans. Anscombe, Basil Blackwell, Oxford, 1953.

_________, *Zettel,* ed. G.E.M., Anscombe & von Wright, Basil Blackwell, Oxford, 1967.

_________, *Remarks on Philosophical Psychology,* Vol. I, ed. G.E.M. Anscombe and Von Wright, Basil Black-well, Oxford, 1982.

_________, *Remarks on Philosophical Psychology,* Vol. II, ed. Von Wright & Hekki Nyma, Basil Blackwell, Oxford, 1982.

PHILOSOPHERS INDEX

Armstrong, D. M. 17 - 19, 23, 29
Avramedes, Anita, 170,195, 207, 208, 210 - 212
Blender, K. 288
Cam, Philip, 155 - 158, 271.
Carnap, R. 30, 31, 33
Chomsky, Noam, 170, 181 - 183, 189, 215,
Churchland, P.M. 15, 28, 29, 41, 274
Cole, D. 267, 270,
Dennett, Daniel, C. xvi, 23, 27, 54, 55, 63 - 75, 78, 83 - 86, 89-91, 94, 95, 97, 100 - 105, 123, 124, 135 - 140, 150, 155, 164, 250, 251 - 255, 259 - 262, 273, 274,
Descartes, R. 236, 9 - 14, 62, 93, 237, 242, 263, 264
Flanagan, O. 283,
Fodor, Jerry, xviii, 23, 31, 32, 125 - 135, 141, 153, 155, 170, 184, 185, 187 - 189, 201, 215,
Freeman and Skarda, 244, 245
Gillett, Grant, 170, 189 - 192, 220,
Grice, Paul, 170, 194-197, 99, 206, 207, 212, 216, 219,
Hampel, 34
Hanny, A. 247, 248
Heil, John, 241,
Hopkins, John, 143,
Husserl E. 141, 142, 145, 146, 287
Jacquette, D. 267,
Johnsen, 86
Johnston, Paul, 55
Jolley, 88, 89
Loar, D. xviii, 170, 203 - 207, 211, 215,
Malcom, N. 227
Marty, Anton, 194,
McGinn, C. 276 - 281
McIntyre, Ronald, 145, 146, 147,
Millikan, Ruth, G. 35 - 37, 170, 212 - 215.
Mohanty, J. N. 145, 147 - 149, 282, 284 - 287, 289
Nagel, Thomas, xvi, 76, 211, 273-276, 281
Nelkin, N. 76 - 78
Nemirow, 159
Paraport, W. 267, 268, 270,
Pradhan, R. C. 287
Schiffer, Stephen, xviii, 170, 195, 197 - 203, 206, 209, 211, 215,
Schmidtz, 152
Searle, John, R. xi, xii, xiv - 8, 38 - 49, 54 - 62, 68 - 79, 90 - 100, 110 - 123, 141,145 - 147, 150-

154, 158- 163, 165, 170-180, 193, 195, 207, 215 - 228, 236 - 243, 245, 246, 248 - 250, 253 - 259, 261, 262, 264 - 269, 273, 274, 281 - 283, 286, 288 - 290, 292 - 294
Shoemaker, S. xvi, 55, 78, 79, 81, 82
Smart, J.C.C. 17, 22, 23, 31, 39, 82
Staz & Ferejohn, 152
Stroud, B. 255
Sturgeon, S. 101, 102
Tye, M. 29
Watkins, W. B 88, 89
Wittgenstein, Ludwig, 55, 225, 227
Wood, 11

✧✧✧

SUBJECT INDEX

A

Act of Experience: 286
Affective Attitude: 198
Afferent-efferent connections: 66, 253
Alternative Metaphysics: xiv, xv
Animal life: 76
Animal Spirit: 12,
Anti-reductionism: 7- 8
Appearance: 259
Apperception: 284
Apperceptual Awareness: 78
Appropriate Idealization: 183
Artificial Intelligence: 26, 27, 41, 237, 265, 266
As-if Intentionality: 100, 110, 261
Aspectuality: 94, 97, 98, 116, 122, 258
Aspectual content: 224,
Asymmetrical Dependency: 239, 240
Asymmetrical: 207-209
Atomic theory: 44
Attributive theory of Mind: 18,
Autonomy of the Mental: 18
Auto-Phenomenological: 75
Axis of Embodiment and Axis of Intentionality: 277

B

Background: 59, 146, 160-163, 178, 216, 217, 218, 221, 250, 252-256, 272, 291,
Behaviourism: xv, 15, 16, 17
Being to the World/ Being-in-the-world: 100, 285, 286
Belief Fixation: 152
Biological Categories: 35- 36
Biological Explanation: 37, 38, 272
Biological Function;
Biological Naturalism: xiii, xiv, xv, xviii, 1, 2, 6 - 8, 27, 31, 34 - 37, 42, 45, 54, 55, 90, 93, 94, 103, 104, 136, 161, 164, 191, 225, 236, 237, 240, 242, 255, 257, 260, 262, 281, 289, 290
Biological Phenomena: 45
Biological Sciences: 43 - 45
Biological World View; 2, 44,
Biology: xiii, 30, 35, 36, 43, 49
Body: 284, 285, 286,
Bodily Movement: 15, 118, 120
Bottom-up and Top down: 277
Boundary Condition: 60
Bracketing: 145
Brain-State identity theory: 23, 24

Bridge Law: 31, 32

C

Canonical Connection: 101, 102,
Cartesian Categories: 74
Cartesian Dualism (Substance Dualism): xi, xii, xiv, xviii, 1, 7-9, 14, 38-40, 43, 49, 54, 63, 74, 90, 92, 228, 236-239, 242, 257, 258, 260, 274
Cartesian Legacy: 237, 242
Cartesian Metaphysics/Cartesian Worldview: xiv, 90
Cartesian Myth: 73
Cartesian Subjectivity: 262
Cartesian/ Cartesianism: 1, 8, 93, 94, 242, 250, 262
Category Mistake: 162
Causal Asymmetry: 238
Causal Dependency: 240, 289
Causal Efficacy: 2, 130, 279
Causal Explanation; xv, 38, 45, 101, 134, 244, 274, 275
Causal force: 121
Causal Power: 126, 129, 130, 135, 270, 271
Causal Property: 5, 9
Causality/ law of causality: 30, 32, 37, 119, 125, 148, 236, 258
Causally Sufficient: 2, 3, 98, 187
Caused by: xiv, 1, 5, 33
Central Gravity; 71
Central Meaner: 72, 74
Central State Identity theory: 17, 18, 19
Chinese Room Experiment: 267, 279
Cogito: 11
Cognitive Architecture: 186
Cognitive Closure: 277, 278
Cognitive Psychology: 27, 265
Cognitive Science; 267
Cognitivism; 265-266
Compositional Semantics: 201, 202, 203
Computational Process: 131
Communicative Intention: 175, 176, 179, 194, 195, 196, 203, 208, 213
Concept: 220
Conceptual Connection: 58, 68
Conceptual Dualism: 8, 9
Conceptual Dualism: 9
Condition of Satisfaction: 61, 62, 111, 112, 116 - 118, 120, 122, 123, 125, 160, 173, 175, 176, 178, 180, 220, 224, 271, 272
Conscious life: 3
Consciousness: xi - xiv, xvi, xvii, 2-6, 9, 11-14, 20-24, 28, 38, 44 - 49, 54, 62, 63, 65, 72 - 79, 82, 90, 91, 93, 95, 96, 98, 99, 100, 103, 104, 109, 115, 123, 142, 149, 157, 169, 170, 171, 193, 214, 222, 226, 236, 241, 242, 246, 248, 249, 254, 255, 265, 257, 258, 259, 262, 263, 273, 274, 275, 276, 277, 278, 279, 280, 281, 282, 283, 284, 285, 287, 289, 290, 291, 292, 294
Conscious (thought) experience: 23, 65, 67, 71, 76, 77, 78, 79, 88, 94, 96, 98, 101, 102, 115, 143, 222, 274
Conscious Subjectivity: 281 - 283, 286, 289
Constitutive Phenomenology: 282, 284
Constitutive Rule: 178, 292 - 293

Content Formation: 113, 114, 155-157, 192
Content of Action: 117
Content of Consciousness: 144
Content of Meaning: xviii
Content: xvii, xviii, 62, 109, 110, 117, 127, 155, 156, 172, 253
Contingent Identity: 19, 22
Conventional Force: 175, 207, 292, 293
Conventional Regularity: 203, 204
Coordination Equilibrium; 200
Creativity: 104, 193
Creative Thinking: 77, 193

D
Decision Making Strategy: 133
Deconstruct: 74,
Deep Structure: 182
Depth of Consciousness: 278
Derived from: xiii, 203
Designed Stance: 36, 136, 137, 139, 252
Determinism: 34
Direction of fit: 61, 111, 112, 115, 160, 177, 291, 293
Dispositional capacity: 16, 98
Dispositional: 16, 17, 24, 30, 31, 35, 39, 101
Dualism: 8, 38, 266, 272, 274, 293

E
Economics: 33
Electromagnetic process: 27
Eliminative materialism: 28, 29, 34, 41, 42
Emergent Property: 4, 35, 47
Empirical Reduction: 24
Epiphenomenon: 19, 86, 98
Epistemic gap: 10
Epistemic level: 97, 98
Epistemological Asymmetry: 208, 209
Essential Subjectivity: 212
Existential Explanation: 67
Epistemic [Connection]: 7, 8, 101, 102
Epoche: 145, 148
Emergence: xiii, 3 - 6, 94, 97, 98, 104, 105, 163, 173, 179, 183, 184, 189, 252, 258, 271, 277, 283, 290
Evolutionary Biology: 44, 45, 170
Extensional Explanation: 66

F
Familiarity: 59, 69
Field of Consciousness: 60
Fixation of Belief: 102, 126, 132, 152
First Person point of View: xv, 8, 48, 56, 66, 75, 82, 83, 86, 87, 181, 210, 211, 226, 227, 258, 288
First Person objectivity: 98
First Person Ontology: 261, 282,
Finite Modalities: 56
Flexibility: 104
Folk Psychology: 28, 82, 83
Forms of life: 227, 228, 286, 287
Freedom of will/Free will: 38, 152, 248, 281
Functional Economy: 24
Functional Identity: 23, 26
Functionalism: xv, 15, 24, 25, 27, 40, 41
Feeling: 7, 8, 11, 22, 40, 79, 94, 100, 158, 264, 291

G
Generality Constraints: 191
Generative Grammar/ Syntax: 182, 189
Gestalt psychology: 56
Grammatical Structure: 279
Grammatical Transformation: 182
Gricean Semantics: 219

H
Happy (iness): 47, 62
Heterophenomenology (ical): 75, 85, 86, 87, 262
Higher order consciousness: 104
Holism/ Holistic: 25, 42, 156, 206, 225
Homunculus; 72, 74
Horizontal Unity: 57
Human life: xi, 27, 35, 228, 294
Hypothesis: 20
Hypothetical Model: 9

I
Illocutionary Act: 177, 178, 216, 218
Illocutionary Force: 113
Imagination: 10, 11, 56, 58, 71
Inconceivability: 275, 276
Indexical Rules: 224
Information Processing: 69, 138, 267, 269, 271, 272
Innate: 16, 182-183
Inner Agent: 72, 73
Instrumentalism: 136
Instrumentalism: 136
Intention Based Semantics: 174
Intention of Experience: 286
Intentional Act: 77, 99, 111, 196, 287
Intentional Attitude: 198
Intentional Communication: 198
Intentional Causation: 118, 128, 151, 241
Intentional Content: 81, 115, 116, 119, 120, 122, 147, 175, 177, 179, 184, 194, 197, 222, 223, 224, 246, 286, 287, 289, 292, 293
Intentional Explanation: 66, 67, 178, 244
Intentional Field: 293
Intentional Form: 226
Intentional Meaning: 199
Intentional Property: xii, 113, 292
Intentional Similarity: 81
Intentional Stance: 136, 138, 139, 152
Intentional System: 251, 252
Intentional: 56, 61, 65, 99
Intentional: xi, xvii, 56, 57, 94, 99 151
Intentionality: ix, xii - xviii, 6, 27, 45, 47, 54, 57, 58, 75, 77, 78 - 81, 93, 97, 99, 102, 109, 110, 113 - 115, 120, 122 - 124, 126, 130, 135, 137, 139 - 144, 145, 149 - 153, 155, 156, 158 - 161, 163, 171 - 175, 177 - 179, 191, 203, 213 - 215, 217, 221, 223, 236, 238, 239, 244, 246, 249, 254, 256, 270, 271, 272, 286, 288, 290, 293
Intention-in-Action: 117 - 119, 123, 147, 221
Intersubjective: 284
Intersubjective realizablity: 56,
Intrinsic intentionality: 124, 130, 158
Intrinsic: xi, xvi, 4, 7, 46, 47, 49,

54, 84, 85, 94, 103, 126, 151, 161
Introspection: 56, 63, 93, 100, 102, 262, 263, 264, 277
Introspective certainty: 65
Irreducibility: 7, 49
Isomorphism: 25, 27, 28, 113, 170, 205, 212, 223, 292

K

Knowing how and Knowing that: 161, 254
Knowing how to do things and how things are: 161

L

Language Centric Being: 286
Language Game: 227, 228, 278
Language of Science: 31
Language of the mind: 184
Language Processing: 70
Language of Thought/ Language of the Mind: xvii, xviii, 184, 186, 201
Language Use: xii, xviii, 64, 170, 172 - 176, 179, 181, 208, 212, 217, 219, 236, 287, 292, 293
Language: ix, 46, 114, 154, 169, 170-172, 182, 183, 222, 289, 290
Latency: 96, 114, 226
Lattice structure: 5
Law of causality: 17, 29, 37
Laws of Neuroscience: 29
Level of consciousness: 13
Level of intentionality: 272
Life world: 285, 286
Linguistic Activities: xi, 169, 170
Linguistic Behaviour: 181, 197, 198, 209, 211, 215, 221
Linguistic being: 285, 287
Linguistic Categories: 221, 293
Linguistic community: 154, 180, 182, 200, 208
Linguistic Entities: 114
Linguistic Field: 223
Linguistic Representation: xiii, xvii, xviii, 71, 113, 115, 116, 172 - 174, 184, 194, 202, 209, 212, 221 - 224, 227, 292
Linguistic Rules: 178, 197
Literal Meaning: 217, 218
Lived Experience: 142, 144
Local Supervenience: 128
Logical Connection: 33
Logical Form: 279
Normal Function: 36

M

Manifestation: xiv, 58, 75, 96, 104, 113, 114, 212, 226, 270
Materialism/ Materialistic: 1, 8, 14, 15, 18, 33, 38, 39, 92, 93, 271
Meaning: xii, 17, 138, 172, 179, 194, 195, 219, 287
Mental Causation; xiii, 6, 54, 119, 256, 262
Mental Field: 223
Mental life: 3, 23, 28, 42, 44, 45, 54, 62, 63, 101, 173, 181, 211, 237, 243
Mental Representation: xiii, xvii, 115, 127, 131, 173, 176, 184, 185, 189, 192, 201, 203, 223
Mentalese: xviii
Metaphor: 74, 141, 159
Metaphysical Dependency: 240
Metaphysical foundation: 14
Metaphysics: xiv, 11, 12, 91

Metaphysics of Mind: 294
Methodological Solipsism: 129
Methodological Unity: 1
Micro - Macro: xiv, 4 - 7, 35, 45, 113, 189, 200, 207, 225, 227, 243, 244, 248, 250, 260, 261, 267, 269, 272, 273, 286, 289
Mind-Body problem: 49, 237, 246, 272, 273, 274, 289
Mind-to-World: 11, 111, 115, 119, 177, 291, 293
Mood: 61
Multiple-Draft-Model: xvi, 64, 69, 72, 251
Mystery of Consciousness: 63, 274, 276

N

Naïve Dualism/ Naïve Mentalism & Naïve Physicalism: 238, 257, 289
Narrow Content: 128, 129
Naturalism: xv, 30, 34, 39, 43
Naturalistic Methodology: 29
Network: 25, 66, 82, 112, 160-163, 173, 221, 252-254, 271
Neurobiology: 92, 278
Neurophysiological: xiii, xv, 1, 3, 4, 6, 7, 9, 23, 29, 42, 45, 47, 65, 71, 82, 84, 91, 94, 96, 97, 99, 103, 127, 135, 156, 173, 189, 210, 239, 247, 254, 264, 269, 289, 290
Neuroscience: 28, 42, 265
Neuro-syntactical: xvii, xviii
Noema; 144, 145, 149, 287
Noematic Content: 145
Noesis: 144
Normal Explanation: 37, 38
Normal Function: 36
Normative Features/ character: 28, 29
No-theory of Meaning: 202
Noumena (lism): 278, 280

O

Objectivity: 7, 56, 75, 259, 273, 293
Objective Phenomenology: 275
Ontological Asymmetry: 208
Ontological level: 97, 98, 142
Ontological Reduction: 7, 258
Ontology of Subjectivity: 261, 274, 291
Ontology: xiii, xiv, 7, 8, 28, 55, 63, 73, 95, 96-98, 100, 101, 103, 127, 164, 169, 225, 253, 253, 257, 259, 261, 270, 290, 291
Organic Chemistry: 37
Optimality: 137, 139
Optimal Condition: 133
Optimizing Strategy: 152
Overflow: 59

P

Paradigm: xii
Paradox: 289
Paradoxical Asymmetry: 42, 121
Perlocutionary Act: 216
Personal Level: 65-67
Perspectival: 110
Phenomenal Experience: 22
Phenomenal Properties: 22
Phenomenal Similarity; 80 - 82
Phenomenality; xiii, xv, 75, 77, 82, 94, 97, 98, 102, 109, 116, 122, 138
Phenomenological Description: 64, 282

Phenomenological Experience: 21
Phenomenological fallacy: 21
Phenomenological Method: 74, 143, 149, 150, 248, 282
Phenomenological Stance: 88
Physical explanation: 68
Physical Properties: 22
Physicalism: 34
Physical Sciences: 30
Physicochemical Properties: 22
Physics: 10, 30, 32, 37, 138, 181,
Physicalistic Methodology: 42
Physiology (ical): 4, 27, 245, 257,
Pleasure and Unpleasure: 61
Potency: 58
Pre-Scientific: 258, 259, 285, 259,
Primary Qualities: 10
Principle of Neurophysiological Sufficiency: 2, 3
Prior Intention: 117, 118, 176
Privacy: 100
Private Sense Experience: 85
Probability: 34
Probabilistic Automata: 26
Productivity of Language: 187
Proper Function: 35-37, 212, 213
Proper Laws: 32
Pro-scientific Worldview: 33
Proper Linguistic Behaviour: 212-215
Property Dualism: 9, 39, 40
Propositional Attitude: xviii, 24, 131, 135, 136, 185, 186, 188, 200-204, 206, 207, 208, 209
Propositional Content: 111, 113, 224
Propositional Representation: 77, 115
Psycho-chemical Materialism: 18, 19
Psychological Explanation: 266
Psychological information processing: 269
Psychological Mode: 111, 113, 173, 220, 224, 280, 293
Psychological Properties: 32
Psychology: 27, 31, 32, 42, 33, 138, 155, 237
Psychophysics: 133, 134

Q

Qua-language: 131-133, 135, 136, 138, 151, 153-155, 185, 188, 189
Qualia: xv, xvi, 54, 55, 76, 78, 79, 80 - 89, 94, 98, 100 - 102
Qualitative Space: 80
Quasi Qualia: 79, 82, 83
Quining Qualia: 55, 83

R

Rational Agent: 200
Rational Choice: 200
Rationality: 133, 137, 140, 192
Real intentionality: 260
Relational Proper Function: 36
Realism: 259
Realistic Naturalism: 276
Reality: xi, 259, 272, 279
Realization: xvii, 3, 103, 114, 125, 171, 175, 193, 196, 261, 271, 283, 284
Realized in: xiv, 1, 5, 261, 271
Reductionism: xi, xii, 6, 31, 32, 42, 103, 210, 211, 238, 249, 258
Reflexivity: 63, 77, 143, 245, 263, 264, 265, 281, 282, 285
Representation: 114
Representational Content: 113

Representational Intention: 172, 175, 176
Res Cogitans and Res Extensa: 92, 236

S

Scientific Explanation: 34, 43, 276
Sea of Language: 227
Searlean Dualism: 239, 290
Searlean Metaphysics: xv
Searlean Subjectivity: 288
Secondary Qualities: 10
Seeing as: 122, 134
Self: 48, 71, 73, 241, 283, 284
Self-Consciousness: 222, 264, 265
Self-Referential (ity): xvi, 116, 118, 122, 123, 174, 178, 180, 293
Self-Reflexivity: 263 - 264
Semantic Content: 41, 153, 154, 184, 204, 210, 269
Semantic Evaluation: 110, 125, 126, 129
Semantic Properties: 127, 201, 204
Semantic Representation: 170, 190-193, 223
Semantic Rules: 219
Semantic Understanding: 269
Semantics: xvii, xviii, 41, 74, 154, 205, 206
Sensitive (sensitivity): 13
Sensitivity: 104, 193
Simulation: 26, 27
Sinn: 287
Social life: 43, 46
Social Meaning: 178
Social Naturalism: 283
Social Sciences: 30, 42
Solipsistic Individuation: 129
Special Sciences: 32, 33, 42, 43
Species Specific: xi, 45, 75, 252
Speech Act: xii, 113, 177, 220, 287
Stabilizing Function: 213, 214
Stimulus-Responses: 19
Stabilizing Function: 213, 214
Strategic Independence: 199
Stream of Consciousness: 71, 142, 145
Structure of Consciousness: 56, 109, 142, 143, 169, 261, 221, 280
Structure of Intention: 175,
Subjective Attitude: 261, 272,
Subjective Experiences: 7, 10, 11, 258
Subjective feeling: 57
Subjective Ontology: 261, 262
Subjectivity: xiii, xvi, 6-8, 28, 38, 46, 48, 49, 83, 94, 99 - 102, 109, 181, 237, 238, 255, 265, 261, 262, 272 - 274, 276, 281-284, 289-293
Sub-Personal Level: xvi, 64-66, 91, 155, 250, 251, 253
Substances: 8
Sub-Systems: 3, 44, 64, 69, 70, 72, 92, 156, 251, 259
Super-Introspection: 283
Surface Structure: 182
Symmetric Relationship: 32
Syntactic Representation: 127, 130
Syntactic Understanding: 268
Syntax: 26, 41, 127, 135, 153, 154, 184, 185, 188, 189, 190, 202, 205, 224
Synthesis (zing): 11, 17

Systemic feature: 5

T

Third Person Point of View: 7, 56, 75, 84, 86, 141, 210, 212, 288
Thought Experiment: 267, 269, 271
Token Identity: 25
Token State: 127, 128, 131, 185, 186
Token Physicalism: 32
Top-down and Bottom up: 277
Transcendental Consciousness: 142, 147, 286
Transcendental Phenomenology: 141, 142
Transcendental Subjectivity: 281, 286, 289
Transcendental: xiii, xviii, 142, 150, 288, 289
Transducer: 131, 253
Transformation: 10, 115, 127, 184, 185, 224, 292
Truth: 287

U

Understanding: 11, 34, 55, 159, 163, 218, 219, 268
Unconscious: 72, 73, 95-99, 114, 157, 178, 249, 253, 290
Unity of Consciousness: 264, 284
Unity of Law: 33
Unity of Science: 32

V

Vertical Unity: 57,
Virtual Machine: 73, 74
Visual Experience: 115, 116
Volition: 13

W

We-Intentionality: 293
Willing: 13,
World-to-Being: 100
World-to-Mind: 119, 177, 220, 224, 293

✧✧✧